Corporate Governance and Value Creation in Japan

Ryohei Yanagi

Corporate Governance and Value Creation in Japan

Prescriptions for Boosting ROE

 Springer

Ryohei Yanagi
Eisai
Bunkyō, Tokyo
Japan

ISBN 978-981-10-8502-4   ISBN 978-981-10-8503-1   (eBook)
https://doi.org/10.1007/978-981-10-8503-1

Library of Congress Control Number: 2018934875

Printed on acid-free paper

This Springer imprint is published by the registered company Springer Nature Singapore Pte Ltd.
part of Springer Nature
The registered company address is: 152 Beach Road, #21-01/04 Gateway East, Singapore 189721,
Singapore

Preface

Corporate governance (CG) reform has progressed rapidly in Japan after it was passed by the Diet in June 2015, and it is adequate from an institutional standpoint. However, harsh assessments by overseas investors indicate that considerable work remains. Competitiveness-boosting structural reforms launched in 2012 are "the third arrow"—i.e., the strategy for growth—of Abenomics, which seeks sustainable growth and improved corporate value via the Stewardship Code of June 2014 (SC), the "Competitiveness and Incentives for Sustainable Growth: Building Favorable Relationships between Companies and Investors" Project by METI (*the Ito Review*) of August 2014, and the Corporate Governance Code of February 2015 (CGC), which emulates the UK's Kay Review and two Codes. Consequently, 2015 justifiably is called the "First year of governance reform in Japan."

Although these initiatives promote dialog between corporations and investors to create and maximize corporate value, it is difficult to overcome entrenched governance practices spearheaded by banks (e.g., cross-holdings of large stockholders). Furthermore, a traditional lockstep mentality prevents Japan from improving long-term corporate value. Launching Japan's three initiatives generated other problems. Misinterpretations of CG reforms—the significance of ROE 8% guidance in the Ito Review, for example—raised some concern. CGC and SC seem not to have been well communicated to their intended audiences. Thus, CG reforms to create corporate value remain stalled even though studies show clear correlations between CG and financial performance.

How do capital market participants view these reforms? What do both overseas and Japanese investors expect from Japanese companies? Why is the value of cash held by Japanese companies discounted by almost half, thereby incurring the situation where cash is greater than market capitalization or book value per share is larger than stock price? What can be done to improve and maximize corporate value? This book provides both empirical research utilizing regression analysis as quantitative evidence and a global investor survey as qualitative evidence like a "pincer approach" to clarify the status quo and current issues of Japanese companies.

In this book, I also try to propose possible solutions to unlock corporate value by focusing on "Equity Spread," defined as ROE over cost of capital. There are mainly three financial strategies (ROE management, dividend policy, and investment criteria) for improving CG reforms in a bid to maximize corporate value. This book analyzes problems presented by CG and their causes mainly from results of my 2014–2015 global investor survey, and therefore, it explains the Ito Review's actual intent theoretically and corrects corporate misinterpretations logically.

Japanese managers generally tout nonfinancial information such as ESG (Environment, Social, Governance) or CSR (Corporate Social Responsibility), whereas global investors normally seek capital efficiency represented by ROE. The book in its last part concludes that companies and investors are in the same boat and should forge long-term, mutually beneficial relationships. To that end, it proposes a symbiotic model of non-financial (ESG) and financial value (ROE) with strategies to unlock Japanese corporate value on a long-term and sustainable basis. Overall, this book enhances the financial literacy of corporations and investors, and it aids in improving corporate value in Japan via bolstering ROE in an "enlightened" way.

Although I have used empirical research and a global investor survey as consistent research design and as compelling evidence for the assertions in this book, many collaborators contributed overtly and covertly to this effort. Without their engagement, this book would not be the same. I especially acknowledge Kunio Ito, a Professor at Hitotsubashi University and the Chairperson of the Ito Review, who encouraged me and articulated the importance of "ROESG," which is an integration of ROE and ESG. Takashi Shimizu, a Professor at Waseda University Graduate School of Accountancy and the President of the Institute of Management Accountants (IMA) Tokyo Chapter, frequently guided and advised me with inspiring comments. In addition, prominent key opinion leaders such as Richard Howitt, CEO of International Integrated Reporting Council (IIRC); Kerrie Waring, Executive Director of International Corporate Governance Network (ICGN); Jeffrey Thomson, CEO of Institute of Management Accountants (IMA); Jamie Allen, Secretary General of Asian Corporate Governance Association (ACGA), together with many global investors kindly and strongly recommended that my research and assertions be published in English as soon as possible. Last but not least, my special thanks to the members of "the team Yanagi", who proofread and helped polish my drafts. As native speakers of English, Daniel Dolan, a Professor at Waseda University Graduate School of Accountancy, and Neil Faust, a Director in the Finance Unit at Eisai, contributed significantly to proofreading efforts. I also deeply acknowledge Kaoru Yamamoto, a freelance translator and a teaching associate at Toyo University, who always contributed to this project by carefully checking, editing, and improving all my rough drafts as a first examiner while encouraging and assisting me to keep up with the intended schedule and complete all the logistics. To all these partners, I would like to extend my sincerest gratitude.

Bunkyō, Tokyo, Japan   Ryohei Yanagi

Contents

About the Author

Ryohei Yanagi is Chief Financial Officer of Eisai Co., Ltd., one of the largest pharmaceutical companies in Japan. He is also Visiting Professor at Toyo University and Visiting Professor at Waseda University Graduate School of Accountancy, where he teaches corporate governance, corporate finance, and investor relations. Professor Yanagi was granted "The Best Teaching Award 2017" by President of Waseda University. He earned his Ph.D. from Kyoto University. During the last 15 years, Dr. Yanagi has conducted approximately 3000 meetings in the aggregate with global investors (about 200 meetings per annum) throughout his career with UBS as Executive Director and at Eisai as CFO. He was selected as the Best CFO in Japan's health-care sector in 2016 and 2017 by the Institutional Investor magazine. He was also ranked in the Top 10 CFOs by Forbes Japan for the second consecutive year. On behalf of corporate Japan, he has spoken at prominent international conferences such as ICGN/IIRC London 2016 and Tokyo 2018, RI Asia 2017 and 2018. In addition, Dr. Yanagi has served as advisor to the Tokyo Stock Exchange and the Ministry of Economy, Trade and Industry (METI), including the *Ito Review*. He is Secretary of the Institute of Management Accountants (IMA) Tokyo Chapter as a certified management accountant and, on his research agenda, has authored many books and theses, one of which titled "Integrating Nonfinancials to create value", written in English was accepted by *Strategic Finance* issued by IMA in the U.S. in 2018. His major published books in Japanese are as follows:

"ROE Management and Intangibles (ESG)", Chuo Keizai (2017).

"ROE Revolution and Financial Strategies in Japan", Chuo-Keizai (2015).

"Japanese-Style Beyond Budgeting Management", Doyukan (2011).

"Management Accounting to Enhance Corporate Value", Chuo-Keizai (2010).

"Financial Strategies to Maximize Corporate Value", Doyukan (2009).

Chapter 1
Dawn of Corporate Governance: Japan Must Change

Abstract Asian Corporate Governance Association White Paper (2008) and global investor surveys (Yanagi in The ROE revolution and financial strategy. Chuokeizai-Sha, 2015.) have revealed that foreign investors have harsh views and deep dissatisfaction with Corporate Japan in connection to its value-destruction arising out of the lack of corporate governance (CG) and capital efficiency (ROE) in comparison with the other advanced nations in the world. This situation is deeply rooted in the historical bank-dominance culture in Japan as evidenced by significant cross-shareholdings. However, in the wake of a collapse of the bubble economy and ensuing unwinding of cross-shareholdings, Japan has been transitioning from debt-governance to equity governance. Having learned from the voices of foreign investors who replaced cross-holdings, the Abe administration in Japan finally adopted the Stewardship Code (SC) in 2014 and the Corporate Governance Code (CGC) in 2015. This will be the dawn of Japan's CG improvement. This chapter serves as an introduction to this change.

Keywords Debt-governance · Equity-governance
Cross-shareholdings · Stewardship code · Corporate governance code
The Ito review

1.1 Japan's Stewardship Code, Corporate Governance Code, and the Ito Review (Three Pillars of Japan's Corporate Governance Reforms)

In the wake of Prime Minister Shinzo Abe's economic reforms (or "Abenomics") belatedly and finally launched in 2012, the corporate governance revamp in Japan has been making rapid progress in a bid to revitalize Japan's fragile economy. Abenomics consists of three arrows: monetary policy, fiscal policy and growth strategy. Within the third arrow of growth strategy lies corporate governance reforms with an eye to enhancing shareholder value which could lead to pension return improvement in Japan's aging society and national wealth, as well as employment and consumer spending.

In connection with corporate governance reforms in Japan, there are three pillars in turn for the purposes of seeking sustainable growth and improved corporate value. They are the Stewardship Code of June 2014 (SC), the Ito Review of August 2014, and the Corporate Governance Code of February 2015 (CGC), which emulates the UK's Kay Review and two Codes. In this context, the year 2014 justifiably is called the "Dawn of corporate governance in Japan."

First in this Chapter we should summarize these three competitive initiatives with the following key learning points excerpted from Japan's Stewardship Code (Financial Services Agency (FSA), June 2014), the Corporate Governance Code (FSA and Tokyo Stock Exchange, February 2015) and the Ito Review (Ministry of Economy, Trade and Industry, June 2014).

1.1.1   Japan's Stewardship Code: Principles for Responsible Institutional Investors to Promote Sustainable Growth of Companies Through Investment and Dialogue

The Principles of the Code

In order to promote sustainable growth of the investee company and enhance the medium- and long-term investment return of clients and beneficiaries

1. Institutional investors should have a clear policy on how they fulfill their stewardship responsibilities, and publicly disclose it.
2. Institutional investors should have a clear policy on how they manage conflicts of interest in fulfilling their stewardship responsibilities and publicly disclose it.
3. Institutional investors should monitor investee companies so that they can appropriately fulfill their stewardship responsibilities with an orientation towards the sustainable growth of the companies.
4. Institutional investors should seek to arrive at an understanding in common with investee companies and work to solve problems through constructive engagement with investee companies.
5. Institutional investors should have a clear policy on voting and disclosure of voting activity. The policy on voting should not be comprised only of a mechanical checklist; it should be designed to contribute to the sustainable growth of investee companies.
6. Institutional investors in principle should report periodically on how they fulfill their stewardship responsibilities, including their voting responsibilities, to their clients and beneficiaries.
7. To contribute positively to the sustainable growth of investee companies, institutional investors should have in-depth knowledge of the investee companies and their business environment and skills and resources needed to appropriately engage with the companies and make proper judgments in fulfilling their stewardship activities.

1.1.2 Japan's Corporate Governance Code: Seeking Sustainable Corporate Growth and Increased Corporate Value Over the Mid- to Long-Term

General Principles
  Securing the Rights and Equal Treatment of Shareholders

1. Companies should take appropriate measures to fully secure shareholder rights and develop an environment in which shareholders can exercise their rights appropriately and effectively.
   In addition, companies should secure effective equal treatment of shareholders. Given their particular sensitivities, adequate consideration should be given to the issues and concerns of minority shareholders and foreign shareholders for the effective exercise of shareholder rights and effective equal treatment of shareholders.

   Appropriate Cooperation with Stakeholders Other Than Shareholders

2. Companies should fully recognize that their sustainable growth and the creation of mid- to long-term corporate value are brought as a result of the provision of resources and contributions made by a range of stakeholders, including employees, customers, business partners, creditors and local communities. As such, companies should endeavor to appropriately cooperate with these stakeholders. The board and the management should exercise their leadership in establishing a corporate culture where the rights and positions of stakeholders are respected and sound business ethics are ensured.

   Ensuring Appropriate Information Disclosure and Transparency

3. Companies should appropriately make information disclosure in compliance with the relevant laws and regulations, but should also strive to actively provide information beyond that required by law. This includes both financial information, such as financial standing and operating results, and non-financial information, such as business strategies and business issues, risk, and governance.
   The board should recognize that disclosed information will serve as the basis for constructive dialogue with shareholders, and therefore ensure that such information, particularly non-financial information, is accurate, clear and useful.

   Responsibilities of the Board

4. Given its fiduciary responsibility and accountability to shareholders, in order to promote sustainable corporate growth and the increase of corporate value over the mid- to long-term and enhance earnings power and capital efficiency, the board should appropriately fulfill its roles and responsibilities, including:

(1) Setting the broad direction of corporate strategy;
(2) Establishing an environment where appropriate risk-taking by the senior management is supported; and

(3) Carrying out effective oversight of directors and the management (executive corporate officers) from an independent and objective standpoint.

Such roles and responsibilities should be equally and appropriately fulfilled regardless of the form of corporate organization—i.e., Company with corporate auditors called Kansayaku Board (where a part of these roles and responsibilities are performed by kansayaku and the kansayaku board), Company with Three Committees (Nomination, Audit and Remuneration), or Company with Supervisory Committee.
   Dialogue with Shareholders

5. In order to contribute to sustainable growth and the increase of corporate value over the mid- to long-term, companies should engage in constructive dialogue with shareholders even outside the general shareholder meeting.
   During such dialogue, senior management and directors, including outside directors, should listen to the views of shareholders and pay due attention to their interests and concerns, clearly explain business policies to shareholders in an understandable manner so as to gain their support, and work for developing a balanced understanding of the positions of shareholders and other stakeholders and acting accordingly.

1.1.3   The Ito Review: Competitiveness and Incentives for Sustainable Growth Building Favorable Relationships Between Companies and Investors (Final Report)

Towards a Capital Efficiency Revolution in which ROE Exceeds the Cost of Capital (Quotation as for ROE).
   As a pillar of any capitalist economy, a stock company can generate corporate value and sustainable growth only if it is achieving a ROE in excess of its cost of capital over the mid/long-term. The capital markets will naturally eliminate companies that fail to do so. A key tenet of capitalism is to maximize capital efficiency while carefully considering labor's share of income. Although the actual cost of capital differs between companies, the first step in receiving recognition from global investors is for a company to commit to achieving a minimum ROE of 8%. Needless to say, this 8% ROE is a minimum level and companies should seek to generate higher ROEs.

1.2 The Perspective of Global Investors and Japan's Corporate Value

A critical but straightforward opinion of representative overseas investors based on corporate governance theory can be observed in the following quotation from the Asian Corporate Governance Association's (ACGA)[1] White Paper in May 2008.

Most corporate managers explain that the reason for accumulating excess cash is either to prepare for the unknown risks and for the slight possibility of corporate acquisition in the future.

However, this is obvious in most cases, and such an explanation is merely an excuse for holding excess cash or for corporate managers to protect their status. in another word, the "entrenchment". This is the true purpose of the explanation, and this is not based on adequately persuasive strategies from the investors' perspectives; the actual "strategy" for entrenchment implemented by the company is acting as a "saving box."

Cash holdings do not yield benefit for shareholders and even lead to an imbalance in the capital market.

In general, in Japan, listed companies are operated by managers as if they are the owners, not shareholders. Only some vested-interest groups are treated properly, and the best interest of general shareholders is often ignored.

This reflects several anachronistic ideas in Japan: closed operations without transparency in shareholders' general meetings, poison pill tactics, cross-shareholdings, and allocation of new shares to a third party at the behest of managers.

ACGA (2008) had a huge impact on the ensuing three major governance reforms associated with the Abenomics era; the Stewardship Code published in February 2014 (SC) by the Financial Services Agency (FSA), the final report of the Ito Review in August 2014 by the Ministry of Economy, Trade and Industry (METI), and the Corporate Governance Code published in March 2015 (CG) by the FSA and Tokyo Stock Exchange (TSE).

The purpose of this book in a way is to explore corporate value from the perspective of long-term overseas investors, not short-term investors focusing on, for example, long-short oriented hedge funds. As well as ACGA (2008), global investors' opinions elicited through the survey conducted by the author are pertinent in this respect. For example:

It is sometime said that Japanese corporations are not managed for the purposes of maximizing shareholders' benefits; instead, the focus is on protecting corporations. In general, the quality of capital policy and capital efficiency is poor.

---

[1] ACGA (Asian Corporate Governance Association), the headquarters of which is located in Hong Kong, is an NPO that promotes improving corporate governance of Asian corporations and is an opinion leader of corporate governance. The ACGA white paper is signed by ten prominent, long-term oriented investors: Aberdeen Asset Management (Singapore), Alliance Trust Asset Management (Hong Kong), British Columbia Investment Management Corporation (Canada), California Public Employees' Retirement System (U.S.), California State Teachers' Retirement System (U.S.), F&C Asset Management (UK), Hermes Fund Managers (UK), PGGM (Netherlands), Railway Pension Investments (UK), and Universities Superannuation Scheme (UK.).

Managers of Japanese corporations are accountable not only in terms of dividends, but also management strategies and governance. In general, there are too many managers and Investor Relations (IR) officers who do not understand the concept of principal-agent relationship, capital cost, or shareholders' returns.

In most cases, Japanese managers do not always understand the purpose or meaning behind listing (going public) and managing the public companies.

The tendency of inadequate return on equity (ROE) and lack of explanation for dividend policy seems to be caused principally by lacking capabilities among management. Logical observation is required in order that Japanese managers learn and understand how to create and sustain value in corporations.

These severe comments are provided from respondents to a global investor survey[2] conducted between December 2011 to January 2012 (115 valid responses comprised of 57 Japanese companies and 58 overseas companies) (Kondo and Yanagi 2013).

Such an investor survey represents the principal method of data collection and research design in this book. It is generally very difficult for Japanese academicians to gauge the true intention of overseas investors; hence this is the unique feature and the rationale for the author's conducting this novel survey based upon his accumulated 3000 meetings and ensuing relationships with overseas investors during the last 15 years in his career. As seen above, overseas investors are "vocal and assertive investors" who vigorously pursue activities conducive with expectations posited by finance theory and governance theory.

Describing the background in short, Japanese corporations significantly lag behind many of their global counterparts in terms of board independence and ROE. This was the case at least before Abenomics. Overseas investors usually conduct international comparisons to optimize global investment portfolios, whereas Japanese investors are less aggressive in this respect because of inherent culture and history considerations surrounding corporate governance and capital efficiency in Japan (see Figs. 1.1 and 1.2).

However, corporate financial performance indicators including ROE[3] have gradually improved by virtue of economic policies associated with Abenomics. Ultra-monetary easing and an alleged policy of letting the yen fall in value on foreign exchange markets are pertinent in this regard. Moreover, the three major corporate governance reforms in the third arrow have been favorably accepted by overseas investors.[4]

---

[2] The research design employed in this book is based on global investor surveys supported by UBS Securities. The author could successfully obtain valid responses from more than 100 companies around the world every year. The total amount of Japanese stock investment of respondents is basically about 100 trillion yen (estimated amount at the end of March 2015 by UBS Securities). As a tendency, overseas investors are more severe and vocal than Japanese investors.

[3] According to The Life Insurance Association of Japan (2015), on average, ROE of Japanese companies reached 8.5% in FY2013. However, compared with ROE on average of U.S. companies (14.7% in FY2013), the gap to fill is still large (Yanagi 2015).

[4] A symbolic about-face or dramatic makeover example of the impact of introducing corporate governance is as follows: After FANUC Corporation's stock prices rose sharply, in an article interviewing the CEO of FANUC corporation in Nikkei newspaper on March 13, 2015. CEO Yoshiharu

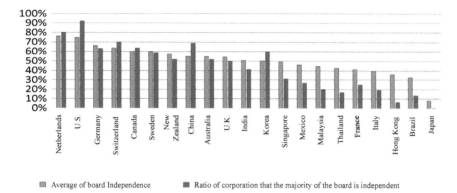

Fig. 1.1 International comparison with board independence. *Note* Parent group comprise the companies that are subject of the survey by ISS in 2012–2013 and is also held by more than half of customers. For example, in the case of Singapore, stick chart on right side indicates about 30%, which means 30% of the board has more than half of independent directors. The graph on the left side indicates the composition ratio of the board in average, which means 50% of Singapore corporates' board is composed by independent director, in other words, 5 of 10 directors are independent director. *Source* Institutional Shareholder Services Inc. (ISS)

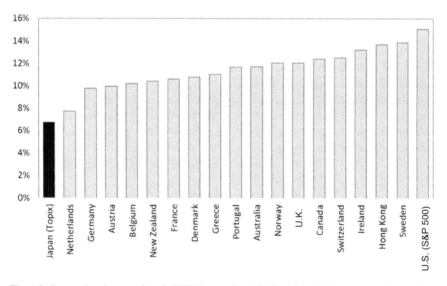

Fig. 1.2 International comparison in ROE (in past decade). *Note* Calculating average value excluding aberrant value, that is based on ROE in average of primary index by each country (capitalization weighted index) on the result of 4Q (2004–2013) by Bloomberg. *Source* Moving the mountain study group (2014)

Inaba said, "We will think highly of dialogue with investors, and we are intending to promote shareholders' return." The share price hike of FANUC may be attributable to the fact that was disclosed at the beginning of February: Third Point LLC, a prominent shareholder activist, acquired FANUC

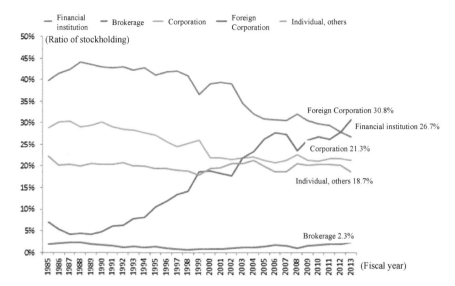

Fig. 1.3 Changes in major shareholders ownership of listed Japanese companies. *Source* Yanagi (2015)

A Nikkei newspaper article published on April 11th 2015 titled "Nikkei Average index is 2.3 times in 2.5 years, outstanding performance around the world market. Temporarily 20,000 yen now" reported that "The average Nikkei index price on the stock market on 10th April exceeded 20,000 yen for the first time in fifteen years (since April 2000 c.f. the Internet technology bubble time). Japanese stock drew attention because of extra investment due to more favorable global macroeconomic conditions. Since the onset of Abenomics, overseas investors balance vis-à-vis buying of Japanese stock is 18 trillion yen in two and a half years. The level of stock price is more than double and thus outstanding in the world."

Furthermore, the "Ratio of shareholdings by overseas investors is more than ever"; on June 6th, 2015, the Nikkei newspaper reported that the ratio of shareholdings by overseas investors vis-à-vis 225 companies which comprise the Nikkei stock price had increased to 35.3% ownership as of the end of 2014.

Looking at all Japanese companies, overseas investors owned about 30% of issued stock (Fig. 1.3). The trading share of buy-selling in TSE by overseas investors is more than 60% (Table 1.1).

Therefore, overseas investors account for more than half of Japanese stock flows, they have decisive pricing power, and they own the rights to vote as independent parties at the Annual General Meeting of shareholders (AGM). Accordingly, the

---

stock, and request of share buyback was reported. However, rather than the stock acquisition and request by Third Point LLC, it is pointed out that root cause of the FANUC's change was "Corporate Governance Code." On April 28, 2015, the Nikkei stated the decision made by FANUC resulting from the dialogue: largely, shareholder returns aimed to double the dividend payout ratio and introduction of an outside director. With that, FANUC stock prices are rising sharply again.

Table 1.1 TSE trading share by entity category in FY2014 (market share of trading volume by entity)

Investor by Category	Sell-buy share (%)
Overseas investor	61
Individual investor	26
Trust bank	4
Others	6

Source Yanagi (2015)

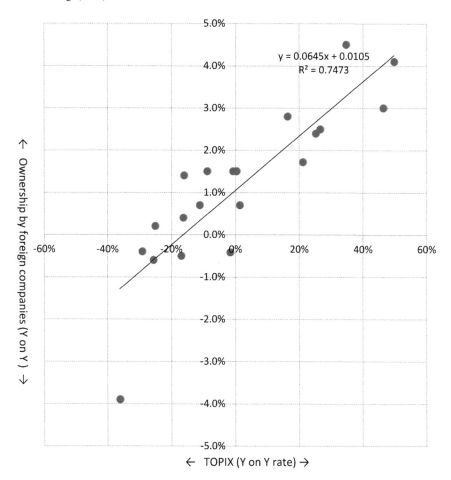

Fig. 1.4 Ratio of correlation of TOPIX return and changes in stockholdings by foreign institutional investors (1995–2014). *Source* Yanagi (2015)

correlation is strong between the ratio of equity holdings by overseas investors and return of TOPIX (Fig. 1.4).

In the global capital market, the ownership structure of Japanese listed companies has rapidly changed after the collapse of the economic bubble in the 1990s. This happened in the context of genuine funds and pensions steadily developing and looming large against traditional Japanese cross-held shareholders while having experienced upheavals and generated economic bubbles that finally burst, thus leading to financial crisis. As a result, due to the plight of banks and other financial institutions, the cross-shareholdings by the financial sector owning Japanese stocks once in excess of half have finally and drastically decreased. The revolution from bank-led governance to shareholder-oriented governance rapidly accelerated since then.

The ratio of cross-shareholdings decreased to 15.9%[5] at the end of FY (fiscal year) 2014 from 51% at the end of FY1998. The equity acquirers after the institutional release of cross-shareholdings were overseas investors who consider fiducial duty, governance, and corporate finance theories for the purposes of optimizing decision making and maximizing value.

Stable and entrenched shareholders with vested interests still exist under the surface even now, excepting cross-shareholdings, but the ratio of floating stock appears close to 80% and genuine shareholders who behave in accordance with financial and market theories are increasing.

A gap exists between the global standards required by overseas investors and the situation in Japanese companies because of cultural and systemic divergences between Japan and international contexts. Companies do not always have to accept all the requests of investors as if what they say is law, but companies have to fulfill their accountability as a fiduciary duty at least.

In that context, the principle "Comply or Explain" has to be adopted especially in Japan where there is a deeply rooted yet unique history and culture of capitalism.

Japanese companies should not be afraid to accept overseas investors' opinions. That is because they can be synchronized based on common goals of enhancing sustainability of corporate value creation. It is a win-win situation.

Overseas investors will often show companies what the Japanese did not realize in the past and, in doing so, possibly act as a good textbook for corporate finance in some cases. Hence, Japanese companies then have to simply and proactively conduct constructive dialogue with long-term investors and where needed fulfill accountability as to their unique management strategies in accordance with financial theory.

In this book, which introduces overseas investors' true intention–the main points of which are hidden and unknown in general—I elaborate on corporate value and demonstrate financial strategies. As noted, fundamentally, *corporate value* should be a common language between investors and companies defined in terms of "market capitalization on a long-term basis" including non-financial value.

---

[5]Data of the flash report in FY2013 by Nomura Securities Co. Ltd. Cross-shareholding ratio, in a broad sense, is the total ratio of shareholdings by listed companies (excluding life insurance companies), that is, mutually holding stock of other companies including property and casualty insurers.

References

Asian Corporate Governance Association (ACGA). (2008). White Paper on Corporate Governance in Japan.

Financial Services Agency. (2014). Principles for responsible institutional investors ≪Japan's Stewardship Code≫ -To promote sustainable growth of companies through investment and dialogue.

Financial Services Agency, Tokyo Stock Exchange, Inc. (2015). Japan's Corporate Governance Code [Final Proposal] Seeking Sustainable Corporate Growth and Increased Corporate Value over the Mid-to Long-Term.

Kondo, K., Yanagi, R. (2013). *Financial, IR & SR strategies for improvement of Corporate value.* Chuokeizai-Sha.

Life Insurance Association of Japan. (2015). *Survey results on approaches toward enhancing equity values FY2014.* Life Insurance Association of Japan.

Ministry of Economy, Trade and Industry. (2014). *Ito review of competitiveness and incentives for sustainable growth—Building favorable relationships between companies and investors—*Final Report.

Moving the mountain study group. (2014). *Reform Japan, the LLDC (least less developed country) of ROE.* Nikkei Publishing Inc.

Yanagi, R. (2015). *The ROE revolution and financial strategy.* Chuokeizai-Sha.

Chapter 2
Cash Valuation Assessment of Japanese Corporations: When 100 Yen Is Valued at 50 Yen

Abstract This chapter presents the book's initial proposal for promoting constructive dialogue. It unwraps the entrenched hypothesis of cash value discounting in
a manner different from previous studies. It identifies the ideal solution sought by
the corporate governance (CG) reforms and the Ito Review. It makes a key correlation between value creation (capital efficiency) and corporate governance. The
chapter begins by considering why foreign investors discount 100 yen on the books
of Japanese companies to 50 yen. That cash held by Japanese companies exceeds
their market capitalization shows the market's (especially foreign investors') concerns about agency cost and value-destructive investments of Japanese companies.
Previous empirical research (Ditmmar and Mahrt-Smith 2007) attributes the discounting of cash held by US companies to poor corporate governance. Jensen's free
cash flow hypothesis (Jensen in Am Econ Rev 57:283–306, 1986) argues that companies holding excess cash routinely invest in low-yield, value-destroying projects.
Although existing empirical research is centered upon US firms, this chapter introduces the author's latest empirical research applied to Japanese companies, proving
50% discount of cash value using 2005–2016 Tokyo Exchange data. In addition, I
offer qualitative research from a global investor survey alongside quantitative evidence for Japan. The chapter concludes with suggestions for improving cash value
from survey results that show that only improving corporate governance and capital
efficiency will motivate investors to value 100 yen as 100 yen or more.

Keywords Value of cash · Corporate governance discount
Agency cost · Cross-shareholdings

2.1 Why Is 100 Yen Valued as 50 Yen?: Discounting the Value of Cash Held by Japanese Companies

Global investors often value Japanese companies' cash at 50%. In other words, 100
yen is valued as 50 yen.

Moreover, many Japanese listed companies hold excessively huge cash reserves
relative to market capitalization.

© Springer Nature Singapore Pte Ltd. 2018

R. Yanagi, *Corporate Governance and Value Creation in Japan*,
https://doi.org/10.1007/978-981-10-8503-1_2

Overseas investors often note, "Japan is a country of mystery." Why is this?

The stock market in FY2013–2014 received a boost through Abenomics. However, as of the end of March 2015, approximately 82 trillion yen (cash and cash equivalents) was accumulated on the balance sheets of the companies listed on the First Section of the Tokyo Stock Exchange (3463 companies excluding the finance sector). Moreover, the total amount would be 166 trillion yen if investment account securities (including cross shareholdings) were included.

These figures have been validated by 3rd party financial accounting auditing institutions. However, would these figures be corroborated if a managerial accounting approach had been used instead? In addition, how do financial theories affect this consideration? A useful way of approaching these issues is by thinking in terms of the link, 'Managerial accounting or financial theories ⇒ market evaluation (market capitalization)'.

As of the end of March 2015, stock prices were higher as a result of Abenomics. Despite that, 148 companies or 4% of listed companies (excluding financial businesses) existed where cash on the balance sheet was larger than market capitalization, and 379 companies (11%) existed where the outstanding cash and investment securities balance was larger than market capitalization. Therefore, simply put, in more than 10% of listed companies "cash holdings plus investment securities" exceeded "market capitalization." There were also 115 companies (3%) where even "cash holdings plus portfolio securities minus interest-bearing debts" were larger than market capitalization.

Table 2.1 shows the Price to Book-value Ratio (PBR). PBR = Stock Price ÷ Book Value of Equity per share under GAAP (Generally Accepted Accounting Principles) = Market capitalization ÷ Equity Book-value on accounting. At the end of March 2015, even after rising stock prices thanks to Abenomics, the PBR of companies whose cash exceeds market capitalization was 0.76 times, and the PBR of the companies whose cash plus securities exceed market capitalization was 0.68 times (on average).

This situation is obviously unusual. This is because net asset (equity book value) is the breakup value in financial theories. A situation where market capitalization is below the breakup value is apparently abnormal because many companies whose net assets are below their market capitalization are alerted by the stock market to "delist and break up companies immediately to return the capital."

In fact, on the date before the stock prices rose in the end of September 2012 under Abenomics, 530 (16%) of the 3392 listed companies (excluding financial businesses) described their cash holdings as larger than market capitalization and 974 companies (29%) described cash and outstanding balance of securities as exceeding market capitalization.

In other words, in the cases of approximately 30% of listed companies in Japan, significant value destruction to financial assets was already factored in by the market, consciously or unconsciously.

Are overseas investors' criticisms justified vis-à-vis the excessive cash holdings of Japanese companies relative to companies in other countries? This can be explored via Figs. 2.1, 2.2 and 2.3 shown below.

Table 2.1 Relationship between cash holdings and market capitalization (end of September 2012 compared to end of March 2015)

Term	End of September 2012	End of March 2015	
Closing price of the Nikkei stock average index	8870.16 yen	1,9206.99 yen	PBR 1.9 times (Average)
Universe	Listed Companies (3392 companies excluding Financial companies)	Listed Companies (33,463 companies excluding Financial companies)	
Cash ≥ Market Cap	530 companies (16%)	148 companies (4%)	PBR 0.76 times (Average)
Cash + Portfo-lio ≥ Market Cap	974 companies (29%)	379 companies (11%)	PBR 0.68 times (Average)

Source Author based on Bloomberg

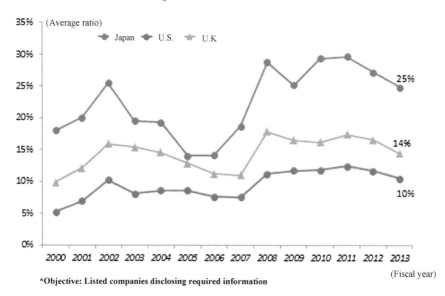

Objective: Listed companies disclosing required information

Fig. 2.1 Cash/Market capitalization index. International Comparison of average ratio (%) of cash holdings to market capitalization (chronological order). *Source* Yanagi (2015)

Figure 2.1 indicates that cash holdings of Japanese companies are double that of U.S. and Europe listed companies. Overseas investors analyze companies based on international comparison; it is understandable that the overseas investors' analysis or evaluation is unfavorable because of excess cash holdings by Japanese companies.

High stock price, affected by Abenomics, is seen to have improved the value of cash holdings as of the end of March 2015; however, the trend over the past

composition ratio

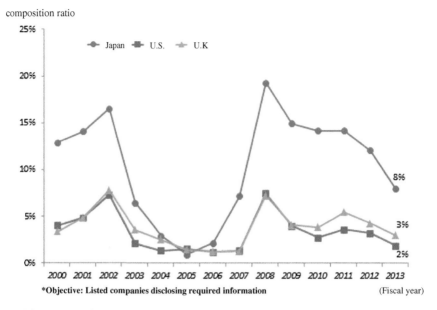

Fig. 2.2 The ratio of number of the companies with Cash/Market Capitalization 1.0 time or more. International Comparison of Ratio of the number of companies where cash exceeds market capitalization out of all listed companies (chronological order). *Source* Yanagi (2015)

decade shows that Japanese companies' ratio of cash holdings greater than market capitalization was double that of American and European companies (Fig. 2.2).

Overseas companies are conscious of optimal capital structure. Looking at Fig. 2.3, a high mountain (peak point of bell shape curve) centered around net cash plus minus zero point. It appears that many overseas companies seek equilibrium (whereas cash plus securities minus interest-bearing debt equals to zero) for optimal capital structure with awareness of cost of capital. On the contrary, for Japanese companies, a large mountain (peak point of the graph at the long tail) appears on the right side of the Figure because the number of Japanese companies with net cash, "cash plus securities minus interest-bearing debt" larger than 50% of the market capitalization is significant (Fig. 2.3).

Thus, many listed companies in Japan have been regarded by the market as "Holding too much cash."

In financial theory, when purchasing and in turn breaking down the company whose amount of cash holdings exceed market capitalization, the buyer could recoup 100% of the investment proceeds immediately and also still obtain a large amount of cash (profit) as instant capital gain. Is this a normal situation? There is a lot of room for arbitrage.

Composition ratio

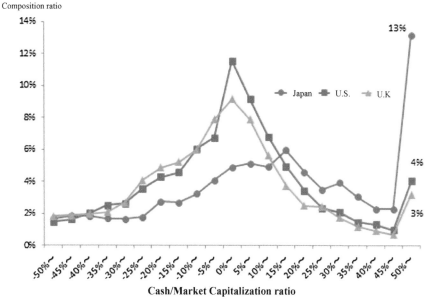

Cash/Market Capitalization ratio

*Objective: Listed companies disclosing required information

Fig. 2.3 Composition of the ratio of Net financial assets vs market cap(below −50% ~ above +50%) (FY2013). International Comparison by composition of the number of companies by the ratio of "cash plus securities held minus debt (- : Net Debt Company, +: Net Cash Company)" to market capitalization (FY2013). *Source* Yanagi (2015)

This extraordinary situation actually is observed in many Japanese companies.

Such discount of the value of cash is probably relevant to internationally low PBR (Kondo and Yanagi 2013; Yanagi 2015). On average, the PBR of Japanese companies was hovering around 1.0 before Abenomics; in other words, it is basically below the breakup value. In addition, circa 40% of companies' PBR is still below 1.0 even after Abenomics.

From the perspective of capital markets, by how much is the cash value of Japanese companies discounted? In addition, why have these negative valuations occurred? Moreover, what is the solution?

In this Chapter, a qualitative approach is taken to explore this solution, which also provides support for existing empirical studies, which have dealt with this issue. In addition, at the end of this Sect. 2.3, newly conducted empirical research showing the marginal value of Japanese cash holdings will be introduced (Yanagi and Uesaki 2017).

2.2   Background of Cash Discount Previous Academic Research Results: 100 Yen of Japanese Company Is Worth Only 55 Yen

Equity spread is a management accounting index adopted by the Institute of Management Accountants (IMA) as a key performance indicator (KPI) for shareholder value creation; along with EVA (Stewart 1991) it is defined in the chapter of "Shareholder value accounting" in Statements on Management Accounting (SMA).

Although the book describes equity spread as a percentage, the amount in absolute value could be used like EVA.

In Japan, ES is adopted and used as the standard of selection of "Corporate Value Improvement Awards" by Tokyo Stock Exchange (TSE), these awards were established in 2012—a year before the Ito Review (TSE 2012).

How much is the market discount of the value of cash held by Japanese companies and what is the reason behind why this occurs?

Opler et al. (1999) indicated that companies with limited access to capital markets tend to exhibit high ratios of cash holding to total assets based on a sample of U.S. companies from 1971 to 1994.

That could resonate with the Japanese context; companies that have high financing costs or small cash flow to their investment needs tend to secure cash for continuous investment with the feeling of "appropriate risk management."

We have to investigate the factors in discounting the value of cash held by Japanese companies.

First, according to the free cash flow hypothesis by Jensen (1986), cash-rich companies tend to invest in low-profit yielding projects (below the capital cost and value destroying projects). Cash-rich companies tend to waste money. Moreover, it also implies that companies with weak corporate governance systems do not efficiently utilize cash holdings. Such companies hold excess cash for the sake of management entrenchment. It is called the "agency cost problem".

Similar to Jensen (1986), Harford (1999) indicated in a mergers and acquisitions context (M&A) that cash-rich companies tend to pursue value-destroying investments with overpayment. This could explain why overseas investors often lament, "Cash-rich Japanese companies buy companies at high prices."

Do Japanese companies hold too much cash? Answers to this question vary depending on whether a corporate or investor perspective is taken.

Results from a questionnaire[1] by the Life Insurance Association of Japan (2015), for both Japanese companies and investors, are interesting.

As Fig. 2.4 indicates, most Japanese companies consider the level of holding cash as proper and unproblematic. On the other hand, as Fig. 2.5 indicates, Japanese

---

[1]Questionnaire by Life Insurance Association of Japan: [Questionnaire for Japanese companies] Survey targets: 1074 listed companies. Implementation period: FY2014 October 10–November 10. Number of companies: 589, rate of response: 54.8%. [Questionnaire for Japanese institutional investors] Survey targets: 159 companies (Institutional investors). Implementation period: FY2014 October 10–November 10. Number of companies: 86, rate of response: 54.1%.

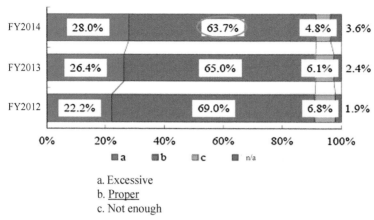

a. Excessive
b. Proper
c. Not enough

(Respondents: FY2014: 589, FY2013: 575, FY2012: 571)

Fig. 2.4 Do you think the level of cash holdings by Japanese companies is proper? Japanese companies judge the level of cash holdings as optimal by themselves. *Source* The Life Insurance Association of Japan (2015)

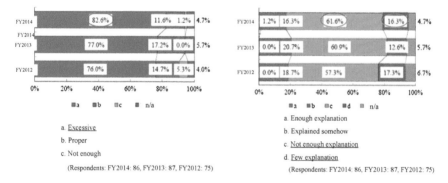

a. Excessive
b. Proper
c. Not enough

(Respondents: FY2014: 86, FY2013: 87, FY2012: 75)

a. Enough explanation
b. Explained somehow
c. Not enough explanation
d. Few explanation

(Respondents: FY2014: 86, FY2013: 87, FY2012: 75)

Fig. 2.5 *Left*: Perception on the level of cash holdings [by Investor]; *Right*: Rationale for the level of cash holdings [by Investor]. Japanese investors value the level of cash holdings by Japanese companies as excessive level. *Source* The Life Insurance Association of Japan (2015)

investors consider that Japanese companies are holding too much cash without sufficient justification.

The recognition gap as well as the lack of communication possibly leads to cash discounting of Japanese companies.

On the other hand, the relationship between corporate governance and market value of cash holdings might be a function of discounting.

A certain Japanese CEO: Our cash is 300 billion yen.
Overseas Investor: No. No. No. It is not YOUR cash but OUR cash.

This anecdote is an excerpt from a real conversation I heard while sharing a table during an IR meeting between a Japanese company and overseas investors when I was employed by UBS Securities as a Senior IR Advisor back in 2007.

At that time the company had no debts with equity to total asset ratio of 90%, and total of cash and investment securities held was 300 billion yen. Accumulated cash was not invested at all with no additional dividend hike or share buyback—Never invest, never return but just keep cash; this was based on the belief that "The higher the cash holding is, the greater the management is." As a result, the PBR of the company at issue was below 1.0 with share price being traded well below equity book value per share.

The comment by the overseas investor in question above was sarcasm to the inefficient Japanese management without financial literacy, and the principle of corporate governance theoretically emphasizes that the owner of cash reserves should not be management, but unambiguously the shareholders.

Pinkowitz et al. (2006) analyze the impact of protection of the best interest of investors, which is an important aspect of corporate governance, in 35 major countries: They indicate that countries with weak investor protection tend to lead to lower valuation of cash holdings and higher valuation of dividend payout, reflecting agency cost.

As a note, according to a ranking of countries in terms of their corporate governance (released by GMI on September 2010), Japan is ranked very low, 36 out of 39 countries.[2]

Research focused on U.S. companies by Dittmer and Mahrt-Smith (2007) indicates that the value of cash held by U.S. companies with weak corporate governance is just 0.42–0.88 per dollar; by contrast, the present value of cash held by well governed companies is 1.27–1.62 per dollar. Therefore, it can be concluded that inefficient utilization of cash holdings is factored in through market valuation.

Even for U.S. companies, one dollar of bad-governance companies is valuated only at 42 cents.

In terms of Japanese companies, Suwabe (2006) conducted empirical research that is conceptually similar to the study by Dittmar and Mahrt-Smith (2007). As a result of the study, the market value of cash on average after June 2006 is 0.858, which is below the equity book-value which should be 1.0. Moreover, it is also describing the large-gap of the value of cash on the market by companies. In fact, the companies whose corporate governance could function efficiently, in other words, with higher ratio of foreign institutional holdings as proxy thereof as for shareholder composition, has a higher market valuation of cash holdings and the estimated cash value is greater by 23.1% on average per a standard deviation. On the contrary, if

---

[2]GMI used to be an independent rating agency for corporate governance, but it is currently affiliated with MSCI. The governance ranking is as follows: 1st rank is the U.K at 7.6 points, 2nd is Canada at 7.36 points, 3rd is Ireland at 7.21 points, and 4th is the U.S. at 7.16 points. Compared with the top 4—all of whom have above 7 points—Japan has only 3.3 points, less than half the points of the top 4. The criteria for ranking includes considering shareholder rights, ratio of outside directors, independency, independency and diversity of all boards, separation of chairman and CEO, independency of rewarding, designation, and audits.

the standard deviation of corporate governance proxy declines by 1, it means a cash value discounting of 23.1%.

Moving on to the empirical analysis for the market value of Japanese companies' cash holdings by Yamaguchi and Baba (2012) it proves that during valuation, 1 yen on the balance sheet of Japanese companies is actually being discounted to 0.55–0.74 yen on the average. The causes of the discounting are implied as excess cash holdings being wealth transfer from shareholders to banks or being agency cost (the problem whereby the corporate manager as agent does not act in the best interests of shareholders, the principal without fiduciary duty being fulfilled). It is astonishing data that 100 yen held by Japanese companies is valued at only 55 yen.

Though simply comparing to the Dittmar and Mahrt-Smith analysis (2007) is not always appropriate given the different research conditions, if the comparison is allowed with the analysis by Dittmar and Mahrt-Smith, the average of Japanese companies' cash valuation is the same level of the average of bad-governance U.S. companies (Yanagi 2015). That means the cash held by Japanese companies would be valued as almost half.

To be more precise, in the next section, the author's latest empirical evidence findings using the Dittmar model are introduced in detail.

2.3 Latest Empirical Research on the Marginal Value of Japanese Companies' Cash—Evidence and Reconfirmation of the 50% Discount

ROE above the cost of equity (expected rate of return by investor or their opportunity cost), that is, maintaining positive equity spread in the long term, is essential for creating shareholders' value as mentioned earlier, but the perceived standard level of ROE or expected ratio that should be achieved is completely different between companies and investors. A severe dichotomy exists.

According to The Life Insurance Association of Japan (2015), the perception gap is visible in the data.

Yanagi and Uesaki (2017) conducted empirical research on the marginal value of cash with respect to Japanese companies by applying the multi-regression model of Dittmar and Mahrt-Smith (2007).

The preceding qualitative analysis based on a global investor survey (Yanagi 2015) suggested that the cash held by Japanese companies is valued at only 50%. This is mainly attributable to investors' concern about investment decisions and the agency cost of Japanese entities. It seems that a series of corporate governance reforms by recent Abenomics have been improving the situation year by year.

Nevertheless, still corporate valuation of many companies with excess cash is discounted. As of March 2017, TSE 1st section companies have 93 trillion yen cash and 170 trillion yen cash and securities whereby cash and securities held by around 7% of companies that exceeded their market cap. This paper assesses the value of cash by applying the methodology adopted by Dittmar and Mahrt-Smith (2007) to Japanese companies. As a result, it is found that cash and securities are valued at only 36–37% of face value and that those held by good corporate governance entities are highly evaluated and worth 67–78% of face value.

In addition, the level of corporate governance is also significantly impacting the quantity of cash holdings. With that, it is implied that by improving corporate governance via engagement with investors, Japanese companies could regain the confidence of investor constituencies and reinvigorate the Japanese equity market and its investment return.

2.3.1 Research Design and Sample

2.3.1.1 Corporate Governance Rating Scales

As a scale for measuring corporate governance, this research uses evaluations based on "Information Disclosure related to Corporate Governance" in selecting good disclosure companies, as published by the Securities Analysts Association of Japan. Selections were first made in 1995, with fiscal 2016 being the 22nd time, and are carried out by corporate analysts responsible for each industry type on both the selling and buying sides. The evaluation for each 12-month period ending on June 30 of each year is generally announced in October. The current evaluation system has been in place since fiscal 2005, with the evaluation standard comprised of five items,[3] including items based on "Information Disclosure related to Corporate Governance," in addition to a comprehensive evaluation. Evaluation targets are selected as standards based in principle on market capitalization values listed in the First Section of the Tokyo Stock Exchange, and although there are some fluctuations depending on the year, since fiscal 2005 onwards evaluations of 148–285 companies in 10–16 industries have been carried out.[4] In fiscal 2016, the number of companies subject to evaluation was 242 companies in 15 industries, and the market value ratio for the First Section of the Tokyo Stock Exchange was approximately 60%.

Substantially quantifying whether corporate governance is functioning effectively is a difficult task. However, it is not some uniform, external criteria to show corporate attitudes toward corporate governance through revealing reports in the form of

---

[3]Other items include "management's approach to IR, functions of IR divisions, and basic stance for IR," "disclosure of information at briefings and interviews and through explanatory documents," "fairness of disclosure," "disclosure of corporate governance-related information," and "voluntary disclosure of information that conforms to the conditions of each industry." Allocated points for "Information Disclosure related to Corporate Governance" in the comprehensive evaluation (max score: 100 points) has been rising year by year. In fiscal 2005, the score was 9.3 points (simple average across industries subject to evaluation), but in fiscal 2016 it rose to 16.5 points, indicating that the importance of this evaluation is increasing.

[4]In addition, simultaneous evaluations are also being carried out for emerging equity markets such as JASDAQ and MOTHERS in Japan.

information disclosures, nor is it to see whether a company's corporate governance is actually meaningful based on evaluations by analysts in contact with the company each day. Rather, this evaluation has been adopted because it is believed to be able to provide substantial albeit perhaps limited insight.

In this paper, the original value of this evaluation is standardized by point in time and industry type, and scored to show an average of 0 and a standard deviation of 1 (below, CG1).

In corporate governance, there are many points on which shareholding composition has an influence. Nishizaki and Kurasawa (2002) found that major shareholders (overseas investors and institutional investors) influenced corporate value through monitoring activities and reported on the role of large shareholders in governance. Uno and Kamiyama (2009) also pointed out the same points from the viewpoint of the investment horizon. Therefore, as a second substitute index of corporate governance, this paper also examines the shareholding ratio of foreign-owned stock (below, CG2).

2.3.1.2   Analysis Model Setting

To examine the effect of corporate governance on the value of cash held, this paper follows the method of Faulkender and Wang (2006) and Dittmar and Mahrt-Smith (2007) to estimate by a regression equation of Eq. (2.1) below. In this method, changes in shareholder value according to changes in cash in a certain period are measured, and then it is verified as to whether or not the degree of change varies depending on whether corporate governance is good or bad.

$$
\begin{aligned}
r_{i,t} = {} & \gamma_0 + \gamma_1 \frac{\Delta C_{i,t}}{M_{i,t-1}} + \gamma_2 \frac{\Delta E_{i,t}}{M_{i,t-1}} + \gamma_3 \frac{\Delta N A_{i,t}}{M_{i,t-1}} + \gamma_4 \frac{\Delta R D_{i,t}}{M_{i,t-1}} + \gamma_5 \frac{\Delta I_{i,t}}{M_{i,t-1}} + \gamma_6 \frac{\Delta Div_{i,t}}{M_{i,t-1}} \\
& + \gamma_7 \frac{C_{i,t-1}}{M_{i,t-1}} + \gamma_8 L_{i,t} + \gamma_9 \frac{N F_{i,t}}{M_{i,t-1}} + \gamma_{10} \frac{C_{i,t-1}}{M_{i,t-1}} \cdot \frac{\Delta C_{i,t}}{M_{i,t-1}} + \gamma_{11} L_{i,t} \\
& \cdot \frac{\Delta C_{i,t}}{M_{i,t-1}} + \gamma_{12} \cdot Gov_{i,t} \cdot \frac{\Delta C_{i,t}}{M_{i,t-1}} + \sum_{sector} \gamma^{sector} \cdot \delta_{i,t}^{sector} \\
& + \sum_{year} \gamma^{year} \cdot \delta_{i,t}^{year} + \epsilon_{i,t}
\end{aligned}
\tag{2.1}
$$

Here $r_{i,t}$ is logarithmic returns (including dividends) on the past 12 months to time of calculation, $M_{i,t-1}$ is market capitalization one year before calculation, $C_{i,t}$ is cash—"cash" as above or "cash (gross)" as in 2, $N A_{i,t}$ is net assets minus debt from total assets, $E_{i,t}$ is net income, $R D_{i,t}$ is R&D expenditures, $I_{i,t}$ is payment interest, $Div_{i,t}$ is the total dividends, $N F_{i,t}$ is net finances or the total amount of debt repayments minus repayment and amount of shares issued minus redemption or amortization, $L_{i,t}$ is leverage or the value obtained by dividing the debt by the sum of the debt and total market capitalization. Using the value at the latest closing date that can be acquired at the time of calculation, Δ represents the amount of change from the previous period. $Gov_{i,t}$ represents either of the two aforementioned corporate governance scales (CG1 or CG2).[5] $\delta_{i,t}^{sector}$ is the industry-type dummy[6] and $\delta_{i,t}^{year}$ the year dummy variable. Subscript i indicates a company, while t indicates a point in time. Financial data is acquired from Nomura Research Institute analysis data and services.

The left side of Eq. (2.1) is the stock return for the corresponding period and captures the change in the stock value at the same time as the change in cash, although Dittmar and Mahrt-Smith (2007) and many other previous studies use the excess return on benchmark portfolio described by Fama and French (1993). In this paper, industry-type dummy variables and year dummy variables are included in the regression model, but this is because when carrying out the corporate governance evaluations in each industry and limiting analysis samples to relatively large companies, the adjustment of risks considered to affect stock return as described in Dittmar and Mahrt-Smith (2007) is also implemented practically in the same analysis.[7]

In addition, this document also followed Kalcheva and Lins (2007) in verifying the following equation to examine the relationship between the amount of cash held by a company and its corporate governance.

$$
\begin{aligned}
\frac{C_{i,t}}{NA_{i,t}} = {} & \beta_0 + \beta_1 \ln\left(TA_{i,t}\right) + \beta_2 \frac{D_{i,t}}{TA_{i,t}} + \beta_3 \frac{Capex_{i,t}}{TA_{i,t}} + \beta_4 \frac{NWC_{i,t}}{NA_{i,t}} \\
& + \beta_5 \frac{CF_{i,t}}{NA_{i,t}} + \beta_6 Sgr1y_{i,t} + \beta_7 \delta\left(Div\right)_{i,t} + \beta_8 Tobin_{i,t} + \beta_9 Gov_{i,t} \\
& + \sum_{sector} \gamma^{sector} \cdot \delta_{i,t}^{sector} + \sum_{year} \gamma^{year} \cdot \delta_{i,t}^{year} \\
& + \in_{i,t}
\end{aligned}
\tag{2.2}
$$

Here $TA_{i,t}$ is total assets, $D_{i,t}$ is debt, $Capex_{i,t}$ is capital investment or the amount obtained by subtracting the sum of tangible fixed assets and current depreciation expenses from tangible fixed assets for the current term, $NWC_{i,t}$ is net working capital or the amount after subtracting the sum of current liabilities and short-term borrowings from the total of current assets and cash deposits, $CF_{i,t}$ is operating cash

---

[5]Depending on whether corporate governance is good or bad, in the analysis model the Gov variable is included in the intersection term with the change in the amount of cash held, so as to measure the degree of change in shareholder value according to the change in the cash. Where corporate governance directly affects shareholder value change, it is also necessary to include the Gov variable directly in the explanatory variable of Eq. (2.1). When doing so, it is necessary to additionally consider what kind of route the influence takes. In this paper, as discussed in the model of Eq. (2.2), the degree of corporate governance indirectly establishes a relationship with shareholder value through influence on the level of cash held.

[6]Companies are evaluated and selected for excellent disclosure practices in each industry type, although the types of industries within the scope of the evaluation may differ from year to year.

[7]Even if explicitly introducing PBR (stock price net asset multiplier) as an alternative indicator of value and logarithmic market capitalization as an alternative indicator of size in explaining variables of the regression model of Eq. (2.1), the qualitative result remains unchanged.

flow,[8] $Sgr1y_{i,t}$ is revenue growth rate or the value obtained by dividing sales for the current quarter by the previous year sales minus 1, $\delta(Div)_{i,t}$ is 1 if flagged for as dividend-paying in the most recent book-closing period and a 0 dummy variable if not, and $Tobin_{i,t}$ is the value arrived at by dividing the amount obtained after adding the difference between the market capitalization amount and the book value of net assets using Tobin's Q ratio by the total asset value.

Two definitions of "cash equivalents" are used. The first is "cash," meaning the value of cash and deposits in financial statements, or cash in the narrower sense. The second meaning is "cash (gross)," meaning the value obtained by adding short-term securities and investment securities to cash and deposits, or cash in the broader sense. In earlier research, analysis commonly focuses on "cash (gross)," but in this paper both definitions are used to verify and confirm the difference in results. Furthermore, this paper also analyzed "cash (net)" by adding short-term securities and investment securities to cash and deposits and then subtracting interest-bearing debt. The results, however, did not change.

Analysis focused on companies listed in the First Section of the Tokyo Stock Exchange (excluding finance), whose data was available. Emerging market stocks were therefore not included in the sample. The data sampled was that of the end of June of each year from 2005 to 2016. The analysis period and time frame was set based on the criterion date for selection for excellent disclosures being the end of June of each year and the fact that evaluation items were different pre-2005. This meant a total of 1851 companies sorted by year excluding abnormal values above and below 1% for each variable from the sample. Table 2.2 shows the analysis sample statistics.

CG1 has an average value of 0.02 and a standard deviation of 0.94. Due to the effect of excluding samples where financial data was unavailable after standardizing only companies that were given a score, the average could not precisely be 0 and the standard deviation could not precisely be 1. The average value of CG2 was 27.5, and while this signified that the average foreign-owned share ratio was 27.5%, the maximum value was 78.0% and the minimum 0.8%, indicating a relative wide gap and distorted distribution. The correlation coefficient between the two surrogate corporate governance indices used in this study was a low 0.09. As Chatterji et al. (2014) have also pointed out, indicators such as governance do not converge because their viewpoints are different, demonstrating the need for a more three-dimensional approach using multiple scales.

The average value of returns over the last 12 months was 5.82%. During the analysis period, on average, the Japanese stock market experienced a moderate rise. The average market capitalization of samples was approximately ¥1.1 trillion, with a focus on relatively large companies.

Looking at "cash," the average value of C/M was 0.177, and in the analysis sample there were cash deposits of 17.7% of market capitalization on average. The average of "cash (gross)" with securities added was 0.385, and about 40% of market capi-

---

[8]If data cannot be obtained: Operating income + Depreciation expenses − Payment interest rates − Dividends

Table 2.2 Analysis sample statistics descriptive statistics

		Average value	Standard deviation	Maximum value	25% Score	Median	75% Score	Minimum value	A number of sample
CG1	CG1	0.02	0.94	3.47	0.60	0.01	−0.55	−5.38	1851
CG2	CG2	27.52	12.90	78.00	35.29	26.40	17.75	0.81	1851
Return in past 12 months, %	r	5.82	31.43	289.44	22.80	2.40	−15.01	−69.35	1851
Market capitalization (billion yen)	M	1122	1983	28,158	1128	527	258	24	1851
Cash[a]	C/M	0.1771	0.1283	0.9351	0.2344	0.1479	0.0856	0.0133	1851
Change of cash[a]	ΔC/M	0.0086	0.0481	0.2334	0.0317	0.0056	−0.0137	−0.1762	1851
Cash(gross)[a]	C(g)/M	0.3852	0.2600	1.7921	0.4745	0.3278	0.2095	0.0432	1851
Change of cash (gross)[a]	ΔC(g)/M	0.0190	0.0720	0.4012	0.0527	0.0140	−0.0179	−0.2652	1851
Change of net profit[a]	ΔE/M	0.0024	0.0461	0.2747	0.0158	0.0040	−0.0089	−0.2841	1851
Change of net asset[a]	ΔNA/M	0.0395	0.0760	0.3504	0.0725	0.0358	0.0030	−0.3206	1851
Change of R&D expense[a]	ΔRD/M	0.0007	0.0045	0.0193	0.0016	0.0000	−0.0003	−0.0260	1851
Change of interest expense[a]	ΔI/M	−0.0003	0.0018	0.0091	0.0003	−0.0001	−0.0007	−0.0106	1851

(continued)

Table 2.2 (continued)

		Average value	Standard deviation	Maximum value	25% Score	Median	75% Score	Minimum value	A number of sample
Change of dividend[a]	ΔDiv/M	0.0011	0.0037	0.0182	0.0025	0.0007	-0.0000	-0.0183	1851
Leverage	L	0.4656	0.2112	0.8949	0.6352	0.4811	0.2938	0.0328	1851
Net finance[a]	ΔNF/M	-0.0033	0.0762	0.4142	0.0188	-0.0041	-0.0365	-0.2936	1851
Total asset (million yen, natural logarithm)	Ln(TA)	13.762	1.198	17.682	14.586	13.632	12.889	10.845	
Debts[b]	D/TA	0.509	0.179	0.908	0.649	0.528	0.375	0.032	1851
Capital investment[b]	Capex/TA	-0.033	0.034	0.079	-0.011	-0.030	-0.053	-0.142	1851
Working capital[c]	NWC/NA	0.170	0.260	0.790	0.340	0.200	0.015	-0.578	1851
Cash flow[c]	CF/NA	0.174	0.091	0.502	0.227	0.166	0.111	-0.112	1851
Sales growth[c]	Sgr1y	0.038	0.093	0.398	0.088	0.037	-0.008	-0.274	1851
Dividend paying flag	d(Div)	0.994	0.077	1.000	1.000	1.000	1.000	0.000	1851
Tobin's Q	Tobin	1.295	0.477	4.044	1.389	1.135	1.011	0.764	1851

Note [a]Ratio to market capitalization to previous year, [b]ratio to total asset, [c]ratio to net asset.
Source Yanagi and Uesaki (2017) Chart 6

Table 2.3 Correlation table

		1	2	3	4	5	6	7	8	9	10	11
1	CG1	1.00										
2	CG2	0.09	1.00									
3	Return in past 12 months, %	0.05	0.10	1.00								
4	Market capitalization (billion yen)	−0.06	0.21	0.13	1.00							
5	Cash[a]	−0.14	−0.01	0.15	−0.09	1.00						
6	Change of cash[a]	−0.00	−0.00	0.12	−0.00	0.32	1.00					
7	Cash (gross)[a]	−0.15	−0.10	0.17	−0.08	0.64	0.17	1.00				
8	Change of cash (gross)[a]	−0.02	0.03	0.31	0.03	0.26	0.59	0.39	1.00			
9	Change of net profit[a]	0.03	0.03	0.28	0.04	0.07	0.06	0.07	0.13	1.00		
10	Change of net asset[a]	0.01	0.09	0.47	0.08	0.14	0.11	0.24	0.44	0.44	1.00	
11	Change of R&D expense[a]	−0.01	0.07	0.04	0.05	−0.05	−0.05	−0.03	−0.02	−0.00	0.13	1.00

(continued)

Table 2.3 (continued)

	1	2	3	4	5	6	7	8	9	10	11
12	Change of interest expense[a]	0.03	0.07	−0.04	0.02	−0.00	0.07	0.00	0.01	−0.06	−0.04	0.07
13	Change of dividend[a]	0.12	0.14	0.23	0.13	−0.02	0.07	−0.03	0.12	0.34	0.31	0.18
14	Leverage	−0.01	−0.24	−0.23	−0.02	0.24	−0.00	0.36	−0.01	−0.07	−0.04	−0.05
15	Net finance[a]	−0.01	0.03	−0.10	0.05	−0.02	0.22	−0.04	0.23	−0.28	−0.08	0.01
16	Total asset (million yen, natural logarithm)	−0.03	0.22	0.02	0.63	0.02	−0.00	0.13	0.04	0.02	0.09	0.03
17	Debts[b]	0.08	−0.17	−0.05	0.05	0.14	0.03	0.20	0.03	−0.01	0.01	−0.03
18	Capital investment[b]	−0.02	0.14	0.15	−0.07	0.05	0.00	0.09	0.06	0.05	0.32	0.12
19	Working capital[c]	0.07	0.22	−0.03	−0.03	−0.07	−0.06	0.03	−0.04	−0.02	−0.00	0.03
20	Cash flow[c]	0.10	−0.04	0.04	0.14	−0.06	0.18	−0.16	0.13	0.16	0.04	0.01
21	Sales growth	0.05	0.12	0.27	0.07	−0.02	0.09	−0.02	0.10	0.27	0.31	0.27
22	Dividend paying flag	−0.02	0.07	0.03	0.03	−0.16	−0.02	−0.07	−0.02	0.10	0.03	0.05
23	Tobin's Q	0.05	0.28	0.31	0.07	−0.21	0.03	−0.34	0.03	0.07	0.06	0.05

(continued)

Table 2.3 (continued)

		12	13	14	15	16	17	18	19	20	21	22	23
1	CG1												
2	CG2												
3	Return in past 12 months, %												
4	Market capitalization (billion yen)												
5	Cash[a]												
6	Change of cash[a]												
7	Cash (gross)[a]												
8	Change of cash (gross)[a]												
9	Change of net profit[a]												
10	Change of net asset[a]												
11	Change of R&D expense[a]												
12	Change of interest expense[a]	1.00											
13	Change of dividend[a]	0.03	1.00										
14	Leverage	−0.15	−0.15	1.00									
15	Net finance[a]	0.25	−0.12	0.06	1.00								

(continued)

Table 2.3 (continued)

	12	13	14	15	16	17	18	19	20	21	22	23
16 Total asset (million yen, natural logarithm)	−0.07	0.05	0.48	0.08	1.00							
17 Debts[b]	−0.15	−0.05	0.87	0.06	0.47	1.00						
18 Capital investment[b]	0.20	0.12	−0.14	0.20	−0.13	−0.07	1.00					
19 Working capital[c]	0.13	−0.00	−0.18	0.04	−0.14	−0.27	0.03	1.00				
20 Cash flow[c]	−0.19	0.12	0.15	−0.27	0.21	0.33	−0.30	−0.37	1.00			
21 Sales growth	0.19	0.38	−0.16	0.01	−0.01	−0.03	0.24	−0.02	0.08	1.00		
22 Dividend paying flag	0.05	0.10	−0.07	−0.07	0.00	−0.10	0.07	0.04	−0.04	0.02	1.00	
23 Tobin's Q	0.07	0.16	−0.67	−0.03	−0.28	−0.38	0.20	0.01	0.12	0.27	0.02	1.00

Note [a]Ratio to market capitalization to previous year, [b]ratio to total asset, [c]ratio to net asset.
Source Yanagi and Uesaki (2017) Chart 6

talization was cash in the broader sense. The maximum value in the analysis sample was 1.79, and in the sample of 70 it exceeded 1.0, while cash and deposits exceeding market capitalization and securities are also accounted for on the balance sheet. In addition, the average value of "change in cash" and "change in cash (gross)" were both positive, and on average, companies were seen to have accumulated internally a part of their profits in the form of cash during the analysis period.

2.3.2 Empirical Results and Analysis

2.3.2.1 Corporate Governance and Cash Value

Examine the influence of corporate governance on cash value. The regression analysis results of Eq. (2.1) are shown in Table 2.4. "Cash" and "cash (gross)" are cash value and CG1 and CG2 are corporate governance scales, with four results in all. If the γ_{12} coefficient is positive, the change in stock value (in this case stock return) due to the marginal increase in cash held is larger the higher the corporate governance scale is.

First, when looking at the influence on "cash," no statistical significance was seen in the γ_{12} coefficient in CG1, while in CG2 a positive significance level of 10% was observed. For cash in the narrower sense, in CG2, the higher the ratio of foreign-owned shares the relatively higher the evaluation.

On the other hand, the results for "cash (gross)" showed the γ_{12} coefficient to be significantly positive regardless of whether CG1 or CG2 was used. This indicates, therefore, that the cash of companies with excellent corporate governance is worth more than that of companies with poor corporate governance. Furthermore, when compared to the "cash" results, the "cash (gross)" results suggest that investors may think this value is more influenced by whether a company's governance is good or bad. In the company's balance sheet, "cash (gross)" is on average more than twice as large as "cash" and, therefore, suggests that we seriously ask what the purpose of holding investment securities and the like really is.

Next, using the coefficients obtained in Table 2.4 and the sample statistical values shown in Tables 2.2 and 2.3, we can see in Table 2.5 how the marginal value of ¥100 cash held by a company differs depending on the level of corporate governance. Here, we show the values for an average company. As mentioned above, in all cases the better the company's corporate governance, the higher the value of cash held, while in most cases this was also statistically significant. "Cash" is estimated to be approximately ¥44 to ¥48 in companies with average corporate governance,[9] whereas

---

[9]In the left side of the analytical model of Eq. (2.1), there are four terms relating to $\frac{\Delta C_{i,t}}{M_{i,t-1}}$ cash change: $\gamma_1 \frac{\Delta C_{i,t}}{M_{i,t-1}}$, $\gamma_{10} \frac{C_{i,t-1}}{M_{i,t-1}} \cdot \frac{\Delta C_{i,t}}{M_{i,t-1}}$, $\gamma_{11} L_{i,t} \cdot \frac{\Delta C_{i,t}}{M_{i,t-1}}$, $\gamma_{12} \cdot Gov_{i,t} \cdot \frac{\Delta C_{i,t}}{M_{i,t-1}}$. In the $\gamma_1 + \gamma_{10} \frac{C_{i,t-1}}{M_{i,t-1}} + \gamma_{11} L_{i,t} + \gamma_{12} \cdot Gov_{i,t}$ coefficients enclosed by cash change, each γ is estimated based on the regression shown in Table 2.4, while for the other variables, the marginal value of owned cash is estimated by using the average value in the sample statistics showed in Tables 2.2 and 2.3. Where

Table 2.4 Cash value estimate results

Target of measure CG	(1)		(2)		(3)		(4)	
	Cash		Cash		Cash (gross)		Cash (gross)	
	CG1		CG2		CG1		CG2	
	Coefficient	p-value (%)	Coefficient	p-value (%)	Coefficient	p-value (%)	Coefficient	p-value (%)
$\gamma 1$	59.7	3.7	14.5	69.7	30.9	12.0	−16.9	52.5
$\gamma 2$	101.9	0.0	102.4	0.0	106.5	0.0	106.1	0.0
$\gamma 3$	28.5	0.1	28.0	0.1	16.2	6.0	15.9	6.3
$\gamma 4$	−42.3	68.9	−30.6	77.2	−20.2	84.8	−19.8	85.0
$\gamma 5$	−437.4	11.3	−444.6	10.7	−532.7	5.3	−511.5	6.3
$\gamma 6$	399.0	0.5	393.6	0.6	396.6	0.5	401.5	0.5
$\gamma 7$	22.4	0.0	22.6	0.0	13.2	0.0	13.1	0.0
$\gamma 8$	−29.6	0.0	−29.2	0.0	−32.1	0.0	−31.8	0.0
$\gamma 9$	−10.7	11.0	−11.0	9.7	−12.9	6.1	−12.6	6.6
$\gamma 10$	−14.7	82.1	−16.7	79.5	−20.7	36.7	−29.8	18.9
$\gamma 11$	−27.5	58.7	−10.2	84.3	25.2	48.3	44.6	22.3
$\gamma 12$	4.1	70.9	1.5	5.5	16.7	2.4	1.6	0.3
δsec	Yes		Yes		Yes		Yes	
δyear	Yes		Yes		Yes		Yes	
adj-R2 [%]	58.0		58.0		58.4		58.5	

Source Yanagi and Uesaki (2017) Chart 7

in companies with good corporate governance (here, + 2 standard deviation) it is considered to be about ¥52 to ¥86. Meanwhile, "cash (gross)" in companies with average corporate governance was estimated to be approximately ¥36 to ¥37 for every ¥100, while for companies with good corporate governance the estimate was approximately ¥67 to ¥78. When comparing "cash" and "cash (gross)," the latter was lower in its evaluation with the result consistent with investor's voice as shown in ensuing Sect. 2.4.1, Fig. 2.6 through 2.10 (the result of global investor survey).

In earlier research, the valuation of cash held by companies is said to be somewhat different depending on certain company characteristics. For example, Faulkender and Wang (2006) examined US companies from 1971 to 2001 and reported that the more cash holdings and the higher the leverage, the lower the cash value was, with easier access to the capital market posited as the reason for this. In this analysis, however, we did not get a result where cash value depended significantly on leverage and the

---

"cash" is the measurement target CG1 is used as a scale of corporate governance, the calculation is $(59.67 - 14.66 \times (0.1771 - 0.0086) - 27.54 \times 0.466 + 4.12 \times \text{Gov})$. Based on that, estimate values can be calculated as Gov = 0.02 in companies with average governance, and Gov = 0.02 ± 2 × 0.94 in companies with good (poor) governance.

Table 2.5 Marginal values of ¥100 owned by an average company

Target of measure CG		Cash CG1	Cash CG2	Cash (gross) CG1	Cash (gross) CG2
CG	Good (+2σ)	52.3	86.0	67.1	77.8
	Average	44.5	47.8	35.5	36.8
	Bad (−2σ)	36.7	9.5	3.9	−4.2

Source Yanagi and Uesaki (2017) Chart 8

Table 2.6 Corporate governance and other company characteristics, and amount of cash held

Target of measure CG	(1)		(2)		(3)		(4)	
	Cash		Cash		Cash (gross)		Cash (gross)	
	CG1		CG2		CG1		CG2	
	Coefficient	p-value (%)	Coefficient	p-value (%)	Coefficient	p-value (%)	Coefficient	p-value (%)
β1	−0.043	0.0	−0.048	0.0	−0.023	0.0	−0.025	0.0
β2	0.115	0.0	0.127	0.0	0.198	0.0	0.191	0.0
β3	0.161	15.9	0.126	26.9	0.594	0.1	0.571	0.2
β4	−0.213	0.0	−0.236	0.0	−0.242	0.0	−0.267	0.0
β5	0.117	0.8	0.087	4.5	−0.038	59.3	−0.077	28.2
β6	−0.065	9.2	−0.071	6.4	−0.088	16.6	−0.099	12.0
β7	−0.290	0.0	−0.298	0.0	−0.232	0.0	−0.233	0.0
β8	0.080	0.0	0.067	0.0	0.084	0.0	0.075	0.0
β9	−0.015	0.0	0.002	0.0	−0.025	0.0	0.001	7.2
δsec	Yes		Yes		Yes		Yes	
δyear	Yes		Yes		Yes		Yes	
adj-R2 [%]	38.2		38.4		25.1		24.3	

Source Yanagi and Uesaki (2017) Chart 9

amount of cash already held.[10] In Japan since the 2000s, where the importance of leverage compression was emphasized in the context of low interest rates, it is also possible that market assessment in regard to leverage changed at the time due to ease of access to external funds and changes in expectations for growth.

Compared with previous studies for companies in the US and other countries, Japanese companies generally have low valuations of cash value. This suggests that corporate governance in Japan is relatively weak and that even if there are good investment opportunities they are not effectively utilized and there is strong demand for payouts in the form of dividends or similar. In particular, a stricter assessment of companies with poor governance regarding "cash (gross)" would reflect investor concerns over traditional "cross-shareholdings." Among them, the higher the level of

---

[10]The γ_{10} and γ_{11} coefficients were not significantly different from 0.

corporate governance, the higher the value of cash rose significantly. This is evidence that investor expectations can be recovered and that corporate value can be raised by effectively implementing good corporate governance.

2.3.2.2 Corporate Governance and Amount of Cash Held

Next, Table 2.6 shows the results of the regression analysis of Eq. (2.2) for the amount of cash owned by companies and corporate governance and other company characteristics. Regarding "cash," the lower this value was in CG1 and the higher it was in CG2, the more the holding amount was. Furthermore, the smaller the company size, the higher the debt, the less working capital was, and the larger Tobin's Q ratio was where dividends were unpaid, the higher the amount of cash was. Regarding "cash (gross)," the findings were almost identical, although in CG2 there was no significant influence, while on the other hand the larger the capital investment the higher the amount of cash was.

Given the agency costs resulting from the asymmetry of information between investors and management, lower corporate governance levels means a higher cash amount. While CG1 is consistent with this hypothesis, CG2 results were either insignificant or suggested the opposite to be true. CG1 is a score provided by analysts, so it is possible that it is evaluated by adding the cash amount as one element of corporate governance. On the other hand, CG2 is a score based on investors' equity, which may be different, though indirectly so, in that it can control the use of held cash.

In any case, corporate governance, like other company characteristics, has proved to be a significant influence on both the amount itself and the quality of cash held, or value of cash.

Thus, previous empirical research explains how far the market discount goes in conjunction with the value of cash held by Japanese companies.

Considering Japanese corporate governance status in reference to the result of empirical research, the hypothesis could be set up as follows: "Conservatively speaking, the market valuation of cash holdings by Japanese companies is estimated to be about 50% of the accounting face value."

This hypothesis shows correlation to the situations where cash holdings exceeds market capitalization and the average PBR is below 1.0. In other words, it could be investors' concern for corporate governance and decision-making process tendencies among Japanese companies.

2.4 85% of Overseas Investors Discount the Value of Cash Held by Japanese Companies

As shown in the previous sections, there are many past studies in connection with corporate cash holdings, most of which are empirical and quantitatively-oriented. These analyses confirm that the market value of cash held by companies with weak governance is discounted to approximately the 50% level, and implies that this is a function of poor corporate governance and concerns regarding investment criteria (investing return below capital cost as opportunity cost).

Above all, Yanagi and Uesaki (2017) proved that the marginal value of Japanese companies' cash of 100 yen is worth circa 50 yen through multi-regression analyses by applying Dittmar's model to Japanese companies.

However, to explore the validity of these findings in the Japanese context, new analyses from a qualitative perspective should be provided.

For this purpose, the author conducted a global investor survey focused on major institutional investors to analyze the intention of "market participants," because cash valuation is assumed to be in the following flow order: "managerial accounting (financial theory) rather than financial accounting $\Rightarrow$ Market value (Market capitalization)" and that is; cash value $\Rightarrow$ Market value (market capitalization) $\Rightarrow$ intention of market participants (Yanagi 2015). That is why we have to grasp the opinions of market participants, the investors.

Importantly, access to overseas investors is highly limited and they do not widely disseminate their real strategies. Hence there are few large-scale global investor surveys currently available in conjunction with Japan's corporate governance or value of cash held by Japanese companies.

The survey was conducted with the close cooperation of the Japanese stock Sales Team from UBS Securities that covers investors in Japan, U.S., Europe and Asia. Though the response rate was low and the absolute number of respondents was limited, major global institutional investors tend to manage many funds and the amount of Japanese investment by respondents at issue is estimated to be in the region of 10 trillion yen [11] for capital market composition.

The global investor survey targeted 200 core clients of UBS. The overriding ethos of the questionnaire was simplicity, taking only a short time to complete in recognition of the typical workload of the sample population and, in more general terms, the inverse relationship between survey length and response rate.

---

[11] Estimated calculation by UBS Securities. The author conducted surveys; the targets of the surveys are all major customers of UBS Securities, which is composed of 200 UBS core companies and major global institutional investors. Though the rate of response is just about 50%, the total amount of Japanese stock investment by respondents is approximately 100 trillion yen (estimated calculation at the end of March 2015 by UBS Securities: assuming the Nikkei price on average 20 million yen based on the market price). Respondents belong to world's largest buy side institutional investors from the UBS core 200 companies (pension and asset management). They are executives who have authority above administrative positions, CIOs (investing respondents), fund managers, and analysts. They actually deal with Japanese stock investment and are known by the author or UBS securities sales.

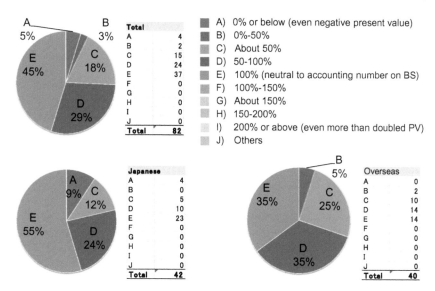

	Total	
A		4
B		2
C		15
D		24
E		37
F		0
G		0
H		0
I		0
J		0
Total		**82**

A)	0% or below (even negative present value)
B)	0%-50%
C)	About 50%
D)	50-100%
E)	100% (neutral to accounting number on BS)
F)	100%-150%
G)	About 150%
H)	150-200%
I)	200% or above (even more than doubled PV)
J)	Others

	Japanese	
A		4
B		0
C		5
D		10
E		23
F		0
G		0
H		0
I		0
J		0
Total		**42**

	Overseas	
A		0
B		2
C		10
D		14
E		14
F		0
G		0
H		0
I		0
J		0
Total		**40**

Fig. 2.6 Q1. What percentage of cash (defined as cash and cash equivalent) on BS of Japanese companies do you (or should we) value (premium/discount) in your valuation in general? *Source* Yanagi (2014)

To make a difference, the survey includes many striking opinions from prominent overseas investors—for example, ACGA members who have invested in Asian stock markets on a long-term basis and thus emphasize corporate governance as key opinion leaders.

2.4.1 Global Investor Survey Results

In order to understand investors' voices, the author conducted a global investor survey on Japan's cash holdings in 2012 (Yanagi 2015). As for the question on valuation of cash held by Japanese companies, 82 valid responses were received (41% response rate), consisting of 42 Japanese companies and 40 overseas companies (Fig. 2.6 through 2.10[12]).

More than half of investors responded that cash held by Japanese companies is below half of book-value.

Q1 asked the percentage of value of cash held by Japanese companies. Nearly half of respondents answered that they value the cash held by Japanese companies

---

[12](Implementing term) Three months (October 1, 2012–December 31, 2012)

(Conductors of survey) Author and UBS Securities Japanese stock sales team

(Targets of survey) 200 UBS core (200 global major institutional investors)

(Valid responses) 41% (Japanese institutional investors: 42, overseas investors: 40, total: 82).

as 100% in accordance with face value. It is a relief to find that many investors are valuing 100% of cash.

However, the stark reality we have to face is that the ratio of the respondents above is just 45%, below the half-way points. In other words, the result indicates that more than half of investors actually discount the value of cash somehow or think that the value of cash held by Japanese companies should be discounted.

Looking at the breakdown of the result of respondent ratio for value of cash (defined as cash and cash equivalent), 55% of Japanese investors answered that they value cash as 100, and 45% discount the value. On the other hand, only 35% of overseas investors value cash as 100, and as many as 65% discount the cash positions. The outcome is, as expected, that the value discount by overseas investors is severe (Fig. 2.6).

Note that no respondents answered that the cash should be valued with a premium. The results are not surprising, considering that Japanese companies' corporate governance was ranked lower in international ranking, and could be in line with Dittmar and Mahrt-Smith (2007). Moreover, the results correspond to the empirical research of Japanese companies by Yanagi and Uesaki (2017). In conclusion, the result of qualitative empirical research is consistent with the global investor survey as the qualitative study in this section.

The respondents of Q1 who answered that they value the cash as 100 explained the reasoning as such;

"I principally apply the cash amount of balance sheet duly audited by independent accountants," because this is a convincing reason.

On the other hand, respondents who support the value discounting explained as below; the most common reason is concern with value destructive investment (overpayment or return of investment is below the cost of equity), which is leading to a low ROE, and the anxiety over corporate governance or entrenchment (agency cost) is the second most common reaction (Fig. 2.7).

Furthermore, valuation by investors would be even worse when factoring-in the outstanding balance of investment securities held, including that of cross-shareholdings.

The ratio of investors who value cash and securities as 100 at face value decreased to 23%, which is half compared to the ratio of Q1, and 77% of respondents are discounting the value. When it comes to the comparison of Japanese investors with overseas investors, 35% of Japanese investors value it as 100 but with 65% discounting, whereas 15% of overseas investors value it as 100 and 85% are discounting. We obtained similar results for valuation of cash only assumption; overseas investors' valuations reflect the undeniable reality, which is harsh. It should be noted that 85% of overseas investors discount the value of cash and securities held by Japanese companies (Fig. 2.8).

Once again, no one voted for the valuation with a premium.

The result of Q2 would coincide with the empirical research by Yanagi and Uesaki (2017) and Yamaguchi and Baba (2012).

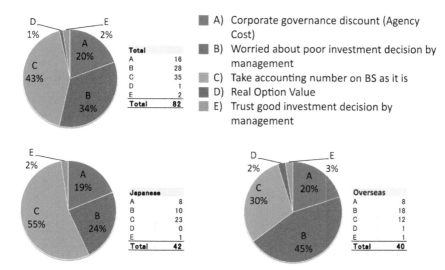

A) Corporate governance discount (Agency Cost)
B) Worried about poor investment decision by management
C) Take accounting number on BS as it is
D) Real Option Value
E) Trust good investment decision by management

Fig. 2.7 Q2. What is the main reason why you selected to the answer Q1? *Source* Yanagi (2014)

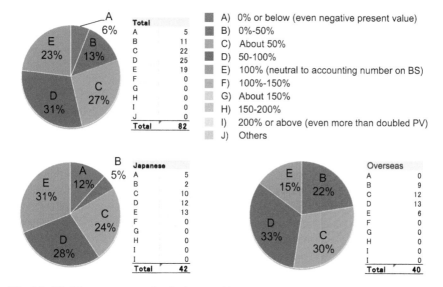

A) 0% or below (even negative present value)
B) 0%-50%
C) About 50%
D) 50-100%
E) 100% (neutral to accounting number on BS)
F) 100%-150%
G) About 150%
H) 150-200%
I) 200% or above (even more than doubled PV)
J) Others

Fig. 2.8 Q3. What percentage of cash plus securities (defined as cash and cash equivalents + long-term investment securities including cross-shareholdings) on the BS of Japanese companies do you (or should we) value (premium/discount) in your valuation in general? *Source* Yanagi (2014)

Same as Question 2, 23% of investors who granted 100% as face value basically cite the reason as "principally applying the amount of balance sheet on the audited financial statements."

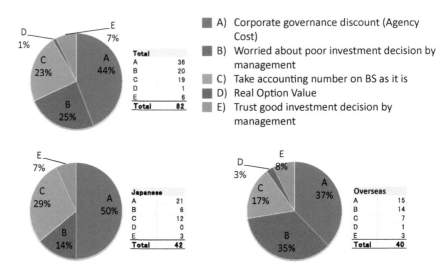

Fig. 2.9 Q4. What is the main reason why you selected the answer to Q3? *Source* Yanagi (2014)

On the other hand, the top two reasons to cause discounting are exchanged: "the concern of corporate governance (agency cost)" is at the top and "worries about poor investment decision by the management (low ROE)" is second (Fig. 2.9).

Dissatisfaction by overseas investors with respect to Japanese traditional cross-shareholdings makes rating of corporate governance worse [ACGA (2008)], and it serves as the background to such severe criticism of value destruction by investment securities held.

Taking a look at the silver lining or brighter aspects, as we can see, more than 60% of major global institutional investors intend to increase their investment in the Japan equity market if corporate governance in Japan would be improved including financial literacy vis-à-vis shareholder value creation (Fig. 2.10). The results of Q5 suggests that improving corporate governance would hence lead to capital inflow with superior stock market performance, thereby enhancing corporate valuation and positively contribute to growth strategies in Japan and maximize gross national product (GNP) via increased investment and employment. This is the intention of corporate governance reforms under Abenomics.

2.4.2 Major Comments by Overseas Investors Concerning the Value of Cash Held by Japanese Companies

In connection with the survey on Japan's cash holdings in 2012, qualitative feedback is also obtained (Yanagi 2015). Since most survey respondents could only commit enough time to answering questions due to busy schedules, only a few narrative

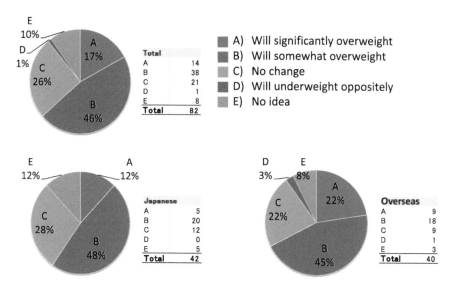

Total	
A	14
B	38
C	21
D	1
E	8
Total	**82**

- A) Will significantly overweight
- B) Will somewhat overweight
- C) No change
- D) Will underweight oppositely
- E) No idea

Japanese	
A	5
B	20
C	12
D	0
E	5
Total	**42**

Overseas	
A	9
B	18
C	9
D	1
E	3
Total	**40**

Fig. 2.10 Q5. Hence should Japanese investees significantly improve corporate governance in the future, do you intend to enhance your valuation of cash holdings thereof and try to overweight Japan Equity more? *Source* Yanagi (2014)

comments were obtained available from a subset of these Japanese and overseas opinion leaders. [13]

With that said, the limited number of opinions albeit under anonymity had significant implications as qualitative evidence proving the rationale behind the cash value discount. Major comments as such are introduced below;

Asset Management affiliated with Japanese Bank A

Our company strongly agrees with the value discounting of cash held by Japanese companies due to agency cost. Investors have to be actively involved to improve corporate value and ultimately contribute to justifying the premium valuation through engagement activities.

Asset Management affiliated with Japanese Bank B

It is ideal to improve cash value by promoting the understanding by management of capital efficiency and shareholders value and enhance ROE based on self-motivated actions; however, we consider it as just an ideal and the possibility of realizing this ideal is too low. Fundamentally, we believe that only enhanced outside pressure would lead to a change in the current situation, that is why we expect systematic support

---

[13]Comments by the head of department of each institution. The author obtained permission to quote them under the condition of anonymity. The total amount of Japanese stock investment by the 14 companies that submitted comments (Japan: 6, U.K.: 3, Europe: 2, U.S.: 3) is 10 trillion yen (estimated by UBS Securities).

for prohibition against excessive antitakeover measures, enforcement of regulation against cross-shareholdings and so on.

Asset Management affiliated with Japanese Life Insurance Company C

Improvement of corporate governance is the crucial starting point. Such improvements would increase financial literacy and serve to decrease excessive cash holdings (and cash equivalent) and improve capital efficiency. Finally, this leads to enhancement in corporate valuation.

Asset Management affiliated with Japanese Insurance Company D

In the case of Japanese companies, some cases of holding excessive cash are caused accidentally through low financial literacy rather than intentional control. It means that institutional investors' efforts would be required to improve the situation. The engagement hopefully bears the fruit of ultimately achieving premium valuation of investee companies and we believe it.

The listed companies obligated to create active shareholders return also have to also improve capital efficiency and decrease agency costs. In addition, the Japanese saying would ring a bell; "Money comes and goes," in line with the Japanese saying. In fact, excessive deleverage with the cash-hoard mentality by the corporate sector decreased the effective demand in the macroeconomy since the bubble economy's collapse, and this has become a major reason for continuous deflation in Japan.

Asset Management affiliated with Japanese Insurance Company E

In general, the corporate valuation of cash-rich companies with a low ROE tend to be discounted due to the discounting value of cash. We cannot stop worrying that "such companies must be wasting cash on invalid investments or acquisitions" and many companies could be categorized as such. Actually, cash-rich investee companies are negatively affected in our investment decision mainly from the perspective of qualitative evaluation, and it virtually equals to our discounting the value of cash held by these companies. The root cause of discounting is nothing else but corporate governance.

Japanese Independent Asset Management F

We consider the value of cash held by Japanese companies to be 50% of its face value, but 50% discount is based on rough valuation. The 50% valuation is kind of a compromised decision; 100% valuation is not appropriate, because it's not a realistic idea in most cases that cash-rich companies would return all cash holding to shareholders, or invest for maintaining or improving ROIC (Return on Invested Capital) or M&A. On the contrary, zero valuation also would not be a realistic idea to be considered. That's why we cannot value 100% but as 50%.

In my experience, 50% is actually appropriate in the end; when observing the case where the stock price of cash-rich companies, the level of valuation mostly settles down in a justifiable range when cash of these companies valued with 50% discount.

Major Pension Fund G in U.K.

We would like to emphasize that capability of management for improving corporate governance and capital efficiency is strongly required to obtaining trust of Japanese stock investors. The management could engage in business to improve capital efficiency through revamping of corporate governance system, such as introduction of independent directors and enhancement of transparency in business.

Independent Asset Management H in U.K.

Most companies in the Japanese market are undervalued by the EV/EBITDA index; Such stock is not attractive to investors because of ambiguous cash spending. Excess cash should be returned to shareholders as dividends or share buyback. If shareholders return is not the first choice, increasing the wages of employees with high productivity could be considered an effective option. A wage hike may lead to the economic revitalization.

The structure is strange; individual level savings are decreasing and, by contrast, corporate savings are increasing, and the bank purchases government bonds. Dramatic changes in the Japanese economy potentially depend on the way cash is used by the corporate sector.

Independent Asset Management I in U.K.

Our funds would increase the amount of investment in Japan, if there would be a significant increase in the number of Japanese companies who met our investment criteria through improvements in corporate governance. Companies' optimal cash holding levels depend on the volatility of income and expenses, working capital and capital budgets.

Though a certain level of cash holdings is reasonable to avoid running out of cash that is cash drain, many Japanese companies are holding excessive cash, and it causes capital inefficiency and low ROE.

Excessive retained earnings have to be repatriated to shareholders who in turn will reinvest the proceeds in other growth opportunities.

Independent Asset Management J in Europe

Balance sheet management would not be a priority in many Japanese companies. It seems that the way of thinking about cash in a broad sense is inadequate and the idea, "leverage is evil," is deeply rooted without any exception. On the surface, the number of companies have been increased that set improving EVA [Stewart (1991)] or ROE as a corporate goal, but the perspective of streamlining balance sheet (efficiency) is fundamentally lacking. Such lack of consciousness of capital efficiency is apparently caused by the lack of consciousness of capital cost by management.

Moreover, M&A cases by companies with limited organic growth opportunities has been frequently reported, especially in cross-border M&A cases. However, there were many cases in which companies paid an overvalued price for the project (blindly

*following investment bankers suggestion). If the companies have excess cash to poten-
tially overpay for cross-border acquisition, it might be better for them to merge with
domestic peers in Japan to seek lessening of competition in the market.*

*The payment for the control premium on the acquirer side is reasonable to some
extent considering the advantage of being a major shareholder in the case of M&A.
However, it is hardly acceptable to tout the elusive "synergy effect" as a reason of
premium in case of Japanese companies M&A. Therefore, the reason why investor
often require the discount as an agency cost on value of cash held by Japanese
companies.*

*Indeed, financial assets held by many Japanese companies are valued at a signif-
icant discount, needless to say about the cross-shareholdings. The root causes of the
problem is not only affected by companies but also social structure of Japan.*

*If companies could show a sincere desire to deal with corporate governance issues,
valuations by Japanese and overseas investors would naturally improve, reduction
of cash value discount and boost in the stock price.*

Independent Asset Management K in Europe

*I think that cross-shareholding destroys corporate value of Japanese listed compa-
nies. We believe that good corporate governance would contribute to appropriate
capital allocation and capital efficiency.*
*Though investment and risk are two sides of the same coin, "return above cost of
equity" is crucial. If it is not, retained earnings have to be repatriated to shareholders.
That is the fiducial duty of corporate management.*

Independent Asset Management L in U.S.

*Our valuation of cash is based on the potential deployment of that cash in, primarily,
investment cases such as M&A. Since most Japanese companies do not actually spend
it for such activities (despite their frequently-stated intentions to exercise M&A),
we cannot value the cash with a premium. If a company seems to exercise value
destruction through M&A with overpayment in our judgement, we would discount
the cash value beforehand, or we would more likely to divest the stock. This is even
worse outcome for companies there, as it means that they get no consideration of
value creation by potential investment cases at all.*

Major public pension M in U.S.

*Considering excessive cash holdings on the balance sheet, lack of consciousness
vis-à-vis cost of equity and inferior corporate governance might lower the corporate
value of Japanese companies low.*

Independent Asset Management N in U.S.

*Low ROE, lack of corporate governance system, lack of conscious of capital effi-
ciency; these are the results caused by insufficient knowledge of capital structure on
Japanese corporate management side.*

Even today, Mr. James B. Rosenwald from Dalton Investment LLC said as below in Nikkei newspaper on September 12th 2017: "We value the cash held by Japanese companies as 'half," because corporate governance is the missing piece in Japan."

In addition, Mr. Kwok Chern-Yeh, Head of Japan from Aberdeen Asset Management said on September 2017, "In general, we regard Japan's cash 100 yen as 50 yen due to corporate governance discount from a certain valuation angle."

In this way, before and after Abenomics, perspective from overseas investor remains intact.

These specific narrative comments by major global institutional investors (including caustic comments, but these are the true intention of the investor[14]) shows the result of the global survey in this chapter; the factor hereof causes discounted valuation by the market in conjunction with the cash held by Japanese companies. This is convincing and supporting evidence in line with the global investor survey.

Moreover, the facts provided by these comments corroborates with the empirical research in this domain including Yanagi and Uesaki (2017) as introduced in Sect. 3.

2.5 How Can Japanese Companies Obtain the Market Valuation of 100 Yen as 100 Yen?

In this chapter, the cash value of Japanese companies is the main topic on the assumption that market participants' opinions directly affect stock valuation owing to the causal link: the "managerial accounting (Financial theories) rather than financial accounting (audited financial statement) $\Rightarrow$ Valuation $\Rightarrow$ Market value (aggregation of decision-making by all the market participants)". Hence, in a bid to grasp the opinion of market participants, the author conducted a global investor survey targeted at major global institutional investors and received specific comments from opinion leaders. These qualitative comments corroborate the existing quantitative research in this domain.

The results could be summarized as follows[15];

Cash holdings by Japanese companies tends to be discounted to circa 50% of face value due to the fact that global investors are significantly concerned with the inadequate corporate governance (agency cost) and the inefficient investment decision (overpayment) of Japanese investees.

---

[14] Though the survey in the book is rare and difficult to collect, it will often change as time passes. That is why it is important to consider chronological analysis. Moreover, the survey is conducted under the bust period of Japanese stock, which does not affect Abenomics, and the comments by investors regarding stock prices would be reflected on the situation as some of them expressed their dissatisfaction. Their stance has relatively eased after Abenomics, but the dissatisfaction or discounting valuation has not dissipated fully. The core of the investors' opinions for improving the current situation would not change dramatically.

[15] ACGA requests the improvement of corporate governance and ROE in Japanese companies, as described in ACGA (2008).

Regarding corporate governance, just superficially introducing an "outside director" is insufficient to solve the real issue. Analyzing the comments from global investors, substantially extending corporate governance is important in order that company management pursuant of optimizing corporate value proceeds with operations based on proper financial literacy (including consciousness of capital cost) to improve capital efficiency.

In short, "corporate governance" and "capital efficiency" are keywords for improvement of cash valuation. These could coincide with the intentions of three governance reforms under Abenomics: The Stewardship Code, the Corporate Governance Code, and the Ito Review.

The global investor survey shows that overseas investors value 100 yen of Japanese cash as 100 yen at par if the companies ameliorate corporate governance and capital efficiency. Needless to say, corporate value (market capitalization on a long-term basis) is also enhanced ipso facto.

Concretely speaking, constructive dialogue between investors and Japanese companies is essential to deploying high quality financial strategies and to fulfilling accountability as a fiduciary duty. In other words, we have to cordially bend our ear to investors' voices as evidenced by the global investor survey and take measures to realize an ideal dialogue.

However, overseas investors do not only demand simple shareholder returns but appropriate investment to ensure growth in order to generate future shareholder value. For example, according to the Nikkei newspaper on April 28, 2015, Chairman Larry Fink from BlackRock Inc., which is one of the largest asset management players, issued a warning letter as for short-termism.

> We don't intend to just disagree with share buyback or increased dividend. However, we are concerned that increasing repatriation in the short-term prevents companies from research and development as investment for growing. If R&D sets behind the short-term returning, that is not a favorable situation.

On the other hand, Warren Buffet, the famous U.S. investor implies that companies should be repatriating cash to shareholders rather than retaining the earnings unless otherwise corporate management is highly confident in having investment cases which will surely create value for shareholders.

> Allowing retained earnings is only the case; when companies could enhance the value of cash, for example, 1 dollar would be valued as above par of 1 dollar in the future by using its retained earnings.

Moreover, ACGA that represents overseas investors is asserting (ACGA 2008) below;

> Japanese companies are a kind of "saving box" formed as companies (saving box business model). The purpose of cash holdings by management is obviously protecting their own status. The cash holdings do not lead to the best interest of shareholders but to even twist of the capital market.

To be more precise, Japanese companies need to enhance corporate value on a long-term basis rather than short-termism (short-sighted management). In other words, investment for creating corporate value should be the priority rather than a dividend for myopic shareholders, and investing has to be considered whether or not the project truly creates value (prudent investment decisions would be required). Ending up with excess cash without or beyond investment opportunities, companies then have to repatriate cash to shareholders.

It should be noted that both holding too much cash (overcapitalization) and too little cash (undercapitalization) is not an appropriate situation. Companies have to pursue optimal ROE management, shareholder return, capital structure, and a justifiable level of cash holdings along with investment for future growth.

In this book, starting with Chap. 3, the author will introduce and elaborate on the critical points as mentioned above and propose concrete financial strategies to enhance corporate value, focusing upon capital efficiency (ROE), equity spread, value-creative investment criteria, optimal dividend policy as well as Investor Relations by way of capitalizing on global investors' voices. In addition, Chap. 5 in conclusion will show the author's value proposition that is "Synchronization of non-financial capital (intangibles) and equity spread (ROE)".

References

Asian Corporate Governance Association (ACGA). (2008). *White paper on corporate governance in Japan*.

Chatterji, A., Durand, R., Levine, D., & Touboul, S. (2014). *Do rating of firms converge? Implications for strategy research*. IRLE Working Paper 107(14).

Dittmar, A., & Mahrt-Smith, J. (2007). Corporate governance and the value of holdings. *Journal of Financial Economics, 83,* 599–634.

Fama, E., & French, K. (1993). Common risk factors in the returns on stocks and bonds. *Journal of Financial Economics, 33,* 3–56.

Faulkender, M., & R. Wang (2006). Corporate financial policy and the value of cash. *Journal of Finance, 61*(4), 1957–1990.

Harford, J. (1999). Corporate cash reserves and acquisitions. *Journal of Finance, 54*(6), 1969–1997.

Jensen, M. C. (1986). Agency cost for free cash flow. Corporate finance, and the take-overs. *American Economic Review, 57*(2), 283–306.

Kalcheva, L., & Lins, K. (2007). International evidence on cash holdings and expected managerial agency problem. *Review of Financial Studies, 20,* 1087–1112.

Kondo, K., & Yanagi, R. (2013). *Financial, IR & SR strategies for improvement of Corporate value*. Chuokeizai-Sha.

Life Insurance Association of Japan. (2015). *Survey results on approaches toward enhancing equity values FY2014*. Life Insurance Association of Japan.

Nishizaki, K., & Kurasawa, M. (2002). *Constitution of stock holding and corporate value—Study of corporate governance*. Bank of Japan Financial Market Department Working Paper Series 2002 (4).

Opler, T., Pinkowitz, L., Stulz, R., & Williamson, R. (1999). The determinants and implications of corporate cash holdings. *Journal of Financial Economics, 52*(1), 3–46.

Pinkowitz, L., Stulz, R., & Williamson, R. (2006). Does the contribution of corporate cash holdings and dividends to firm value depend on governance? A cross-country analysis. *Journal of Finance, 61*(6), 2725–2751.

Stewart, G. Bennet. (1991). *The quest for value*. HarperBusiness.

Suwabe, T. (2006). Dividend policy for improving shareholders value. *SAAJ Journal, 2006*(7), 34–47.

Tokyo Stock Exchange. (2012). *Corporate value improvement award*.

Uno, J., & Kamiyama, N. (2009). *Shareholders holding structure and liquidity cost: Affection of investing horizon*. Waseda University Institute of Finance Studies, Working Paper W1F 9 (2).

Yamaguchi, K., & Baba, D. (2012). Valuation of market to holding cash of Japanese companies. *Management and Finance Studies, 2*(1,2), 108–122.

Yanagi, R. (2014). Managerial Accounting and cash value of Japanese companies. *Melco Managerial Accounting, 7*(1), 3–14.

Yanagi, R. (2015). *The ROE revolution and financial strategy*. Chuokeizai-Sha.

Yanagi, R., & Uesaki, I. (2017). Relevance of corporate governance and holding cash value on Japanese company. *Investor Relations, 11*, 22–40.

Chapter 3
Abenomics Requires Enhancement of Corporate Value via ROE

Abstract This chapter presents the underpinnings of the book's message. It addresses the issues of Return on Equity (ROE) in general and answers; What is ROE? Why is the ROE of Japanese firms the world's second lowest? What is the benefit for investors and corporations of improving ROE? The chapter also correlates total shareholder return (TSR) and ROE, which investors regard as an alternate index of returns. FACTCAST points out that during the past five years the 5.6% ROE of Japanese firms is second lowest in the world behind Greece. Defining ROE as margins × leverage × turnover, DuPont attributes Japan's low ROE to margins that are half those of US firms even though leverage and turnover resemble those in other countries. The book's survey results show that improved ROE is a priority for investors: the 2014 pre-CG (corporate governance) reform survey indicates 62% of foreign investors and 48% of Japanese investors believe ROE is a crucial subject for dialogue with corporations. Post-CG reforms, 42% of foreign and 39% of Japanese investors hope the CG reforms will improve ROE. Over three decades, the TSR of Japanese corporations has averaged 6% and ROE 5%, whereas both averaged 12% in the US and Europe. This chapter closes by articulating the benefits of improved ROE for investors and Japanese companies and shows they can be synchronized to enhance corporate value.

Keywords ROE · PBR · PER · TSR · DuPont equation

3.1 What Is ROE?

"The low Return on Equity (ROE) for Japanese companies reflects the poor management capability of Japanese management: (Yanagi 2015a)." This statement from a senior analyst belonging to a large global fund, headquartered in New York City, reflects the deep frustration with the ROE of Japanese companies felt by overseas investors.

What is ROE (Return on Equity)?

ROE means the rate of return on equity that is calculated by the following formula:

$$ROE = Net\ income/Equity\ (book\ value)$$

The ROE formula is the period's "profit" (net profit) figure in the profit and loss statement (PL) divided by the "equity (net assets)" figure in the balance sheet (BS). Together they express capital efficiency. In practice, from the equity investor perspective, it is easy to understand what kind of assets companies want to invest in by looking at the extent that final returns are being created for shareholders. Investors know that long-term investment returns converge with long-term ROE, and because there are also disclosures in the financial statements of listed companies, the index makes for easy comparisons of chronological dates, competitors, and other industries; meaning that, in general, when it comes to "capital efficiency," ROE is often used as the representative indicator. Investors regard ROE as their top propriety.

For the ROE denominator (equity) to be precise, I would like to share the following description. In fact, ASBJ (Accounting Standard Board of Japan) announced new financial standards for this aspect of net assets in December 2005, which included a combination of three equities:

- "Shareholders' equity," which is sum total of capital, capital stock, capital surplus, retained earnings, and Treasury shares.
- "Net capital" (Financial Services Agency and Tokyo Stock Exchange determinations), which includes shareholders' equity plus the valuation difference on available-for-sale securities, deferred gains or losses on hedges, revaluation differences of land, and foreign currency transaction adjustments.
- "Net assets" include net capital plus equity warrants and minority interests.

In short, there exist three kinds of capital (shareholders' equity, net capital, and net assets) and three types of ROEs (rate of return on equity, rate of net capital gains, and the rate of net asset gains). FSA and TSE determined that ROE is the return on equity for maintaining the calculated historical ROE sequence.

In this book I will focus on ROE as mostly shareholders' equity, except some parts of the formula are based on net capital due to the fact that the purpose of this book is to share the idea of corporate value from the overseas investors' perspective. I should note that ROE = ROSE (return on shareholders' equity).

Please consider the following conversation between Japanese management and an overseas shareholder:

CEO of a Japanese company touted. "Our cash position is 300 billion yen."
Overseas investor refuted. "No. No. No. It is not your cash, but our cash."

This anecdote implies the lack of corporate governance in most Japanese companies (Refer to Chap. 1).

Back to basics of corporate governance, ROE represents the return of shareholders against the capital that shareholders have entrusted to corporate officers. Corporate management is the "agent," while shareholders is the "principal" here. Capital efficiency (ROE) is a productivity of wealth creation vis-a-vis shareholders' capital (not CEO's money) and a proxy of corporate governance. However, ROE is not only for shareholders, but also for all the stakeholders as the Ito Review (METI 2014), which is officially called "Competitiveness and Incentives for Sustainable Growth–Building Favorable Relationships between Companies and Investors Project (Final Report)" says below:

> While achieving a higher ROE is the responsibility of company management, they should try to decompose ROE into accessible operational metrics that support a high motivational level for the workers at their company. Raising ROE, while maintaining a highly-motivated workforce is an appropriate and positive approach for Japanese companies, which can be called "Japanese-style ROE management."

> Japan must effectively leverage its resources such as "financial capital" which is raised both domestically and overseas, "human capital" which supports management and company operations, "intellectual capital" which is the source of innovation, "social/relationship capital" which stems from supply chains and social norms, and "natural capital" such as the environment. In other words, increasing capital efficiency in the broadest sense is crucial from the perspective of Japan's economic survival (the Ito Review).

In fact, the Japanese government has begun requiring the improvement of capital efficiency (i.e., ROE), along with advocating a corporate governance revolution, as one of its growth strategies (the three resolutions of Abenomics).

Below is a quotation from the Ito Review. The author has played an important role in the sectional committee for corporate values and has drafted this Review where relevant to ROE and the cost of capital efficiency. The Review emphasizes the importance of "capital efficiency" and ROE as a proxy for value creation. Consider the following text from the Ito Review.

> As a pillar of any capitalist economy, a stock company can generate corporate value and sustainable growth only if it is achieving a ROE in excess of its cost of capital over the mid/long-term. The capital markets will naturally eliminate companies that fail to do so. A key tenet of capitalism is to maximize capital efficiency while carefully considering labor's share of income. Although the actual cost of capital differs between companies, the first step in receiving recognition from global investors is for a company to commit to achieving a minimum ROE of 8%. Needless to say, this 8% ROE is a minimum level and companies should seek to generate higher ROEs.

The following description represent the same responses as the Ito Review toward improving ROE, which is one of the three major governance resolutions of Abenomics: ["Japan's Stewardship Code (Principles for Responsible Institutional Investors)"—to promote sustainable growth of companies through investments and dialogue (The Financial Services Agency 2014); and "Japan's Corporate Governance Code (Seeking Sustainable Corporate Growth and Increased Corporate Value over the Mid- to Long-Term)" (The Financial Services Agency, Tokyo Stock Exchange 2015)—which requires sustainable growth and capital efficiency for corporate value, and the improvement of ROE.].

In summary, the Ito Review recommends an ROE of at least 8%, and advocates neither shareholder fundamentalism nor short-termism. The Review also holds that "Japanese-style ROE management" and "capital efficiency regarding non-financial assets," in unity with field personnel, are important and a win-win for all stakeholders; and places strong emphasis on ROE that is sustainable in the long term. In addition, ROE is translated as "capital efficiency," in general, from the shareholders' perspective; and, on the (opposite) corporate side, it can also be considered as "capital efficiency." Thus we have to enhance its value the same as "labor productivity" and "equipment productivity." (Chap. 7 will elaborate on the synchronization of financial capital and non-financial capital as win-win.)

3.2 Inconvenient Truth: Japan as a Low ROE Nation Primary Cause of International ROE Inferiority Is not Leverage but Margin

3.2.1 Decomposition of ROE by DuPont Analysis Method, in Which the Primary Cause of the Problem Was not Leverage but Margin

The formula, "Shareholders' profit = Total Shareholders' Return (TSR)," which equals the total of capital and income gains, tends to converge with ROE, on average, and represents the shareholders' profit ratio on accounting in the long term (Yanagi 2010). However, the ROE of Japanese companies is inferior compared to that in other countries[1]. Recent data indicates the inferiority of Japanese companies' ROE.

This disparity causes frustration by overseas investors handling globally diverse investments (Yanagi 2015a).

Figure 3.1 (universe: all listed companies in the developed countries that disclosed information in the database) shows the international comparisons of ROE using a five-year average for the 2009–2013 period.

Although Japan is ranked in third place as a large economy, its ROE indicates that its shareholders return is among the worst countries. This fact might be considered an "inconvenient truth."

Here, using the DuPont method, ROE can be broken down into three factors as outlined below:

$$
\begin{aligned}
\text{ROE} &= \frac{\text{Net profit}}{\text{Equity capital}} \\
&= \text{Margin} \left[\frac{\text{Net profit}}{\text{Sales}} = \text{Profitability} \right] \\
&\quad \times \text{Leverage} \left[\frac{\text{Total asset}}{\text{Equity capital}} = \text{Inverse of capital adequacy ratio} \right] \\
&\quad \times \text{Turnover} \left[\frac{\text{Sales}}{\text{Total asset}} = \text{Turnover rate} \right]
\end{aligned}
\tag{3.1}
$$

---

[1] The same tendency is observed in an ROA international comparison (Yanagi 2010). The remarkable changes are not observed on the rankings of international comparisons that exclude interest and tax rates.

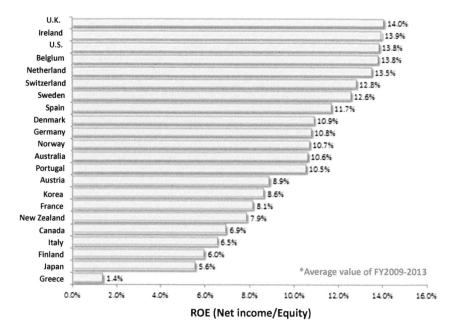

Fig. 3.1 International Comparisons of ROE (five-year average, 2009–2013). *Source* Author based on FACTSET

ROE of companies in the U.S. is unbalanced and unsustainable. There is excessive shareholder fundamentalism and short termism is rampant for both investors and companies, who artificially enhance their ROE by forcibly raising their leverages through excessive borrowing. Furthermore, the management system is limited to shareholders' equity, if it is exposed to bankruptcy risk.

This is a typical criticism of ROE from Japanese management. If it represents the truth, it is obviously a huge problem and overseas companies in the United States and other countries would not be sustainable. Hence, Japanese companies should not follow those located abroad.

Based on the same timeframe, I make an international comparison with regards to margin, leverage, and turnover.

Furthermore, I use the capital adequacy ratio (Equity ÷ Total assets) as reciprocal of leverage, which is the most frequently used ratio, in my international comparison of book leverages. Let us look at Figs. 3.2, 3.3, and 3.4.

In a ROE international comparison, the difference is mainly observed in terms of margin (Fig. 3.2) and there is no difference in regards to leverage (Fig. 3.3) and turnover (Fig. 3.4). Margin is the reason why the ROE of Japanese companies is less than half that of the major companies in the U.S. and U.K.

The ROE criticism frequently expressed by the management of Japanese companies that "ROE of companies in America is higher than that in Japan, which causes

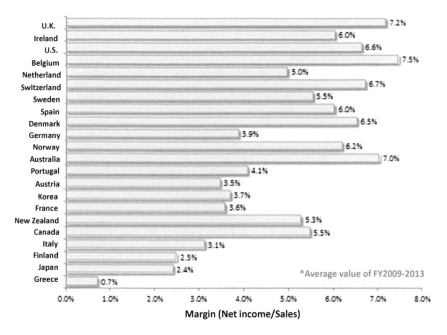

Fig. 3.2 International Comparison of Margins (five-year average, 2009–2013). *Source* Author based on FACTSET

high leverages" cannot be applied to the comparison of average values in the past five years (i.e., 2009–2013) at least.

Even the Ito Review, which proposed that "Japanese companies should aspire to a ROE above 8%," didn't mean that one "should use leverage."

There are three governance reforms in Abenomics—The Ito Review and the Japanese versions of the Stewardship Code and Corporate Governance Code require improvement of capital efficiency for sustainable growth and corporation value—and the core directive is the Japan Revitalization Strategy 2014 (the third directive in Abenomics). The theme of the Japan Revitalization Strategy is, "Get back to earnings."

This means that there should be significant improvement in the margin of Japanese companies, which is not the same as shareholder fundamentalism. Basically, no one disagrees with striving to improve corporate profitability.

Improvement of the profit ratio is the prime task for reinvigorating the Japanese economy and this has to be practical: planning a long-term management strategy, innovations, corporate tax cuts led by government, mergers and acquisitions (M&A) in the same sectors, optimization of costs, and structural reform.

That represents the high road for a growth strategy and ROE.

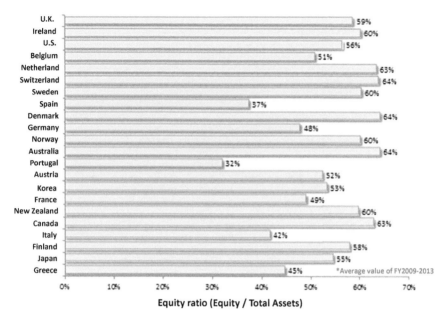

Fig. 3.3 International comparison of equity to total assets ratios (five-year average, 2009–2013). *Source* Author based on FACTSET

3.3   Leverage Matters (Life-Cycle Consideration and Optimal Capital Structure Needed for Value Maximization)

The main reason that the ROE of Japan is globally inferior is margin. It has been clarified that there are little differences in leverage and turnover. In this light, is there any problem in terms of the leverage (capital adequacy ratio) of Japanese companies?

Based on other data, verifying whether or not leverage matters focuses on a Japan–U.S. comparison of major companies in the past three years (2011–2013 data based on TOPIX500 and S&P500) (Yanagi 2015a).

Table 3.1 shows the results of a variance analysis of the ROE of major companies in the U.S. and Japan using the DuPont equation.

The average ROE of large companies in Japan improved to 8% as a result of the positive influence of Abenomics in FY2013. Regardless of the value, which was above the required level based on the Ito Review, great differences still exist. As the Ito Review proposed, the Japan–U.S. difference is mainly caused by margin and there are no large differences in the turnover ratio and leverage of the average.

While the ROE of Japan is almost half those of the U.S., the difference in leverage is very small. In other words, the average value of the capital adequacy ratio (Equity ÷ Total Assets), which represents the reciprocal of leverage, is about 40%, which is the same as that in the U.S.

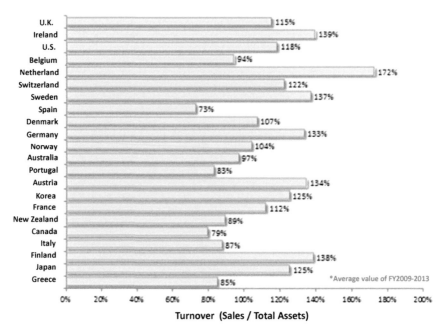

Turnover (Sales / Total Assets)

Fig. 3.4 International comparison of turnover (five-year average, 2009–2013). *Source* Author based on FACTSET

Table 3.1 ROE analysis of major companies (DuPont analysis) (three-year comparison, 2011–2013)

	Average of Japanese corporation (TOPIX500)				Average of US corporation (S&P500)			
	ROE (%)	Margin (%)	Turnover	Leverage	ROE (%)	Margin (%)	Turnover	Leverage
FY2011	5.2	4.5	0.84	4.13	18.1	11.0	0.85	3.60
FY2012	5.8	5.6	0.83	4.03	17.2	10.3	0.82	3.69
FY2013	8.2	6.9	0.88	3.76	19.8	11.7	0.83	3.59

Source Author based on Bloomberg data and Yanagi (2015c)

The truth is that the average value of the capital adequacy ratio is the same and thus it does not matter in terms of the macro economy; however, it does matter in cases based on individual companies in the micro economy (Magic of average number). As Fig. 3.5 indicates, there are contrasting distributions for the capital adequacy ratio. In the balance sheet of Japanese-listed companies, more than 80 trillion yen (82 trillion in March 2015) has piled-up in cash and that concerns overseas investors.

With reference to Fig. 3.5, although the average value of the capital adequacy ratio is approximately the same, the distribution is completely different and the large Japanese companies tend to have either insufficient capital or excessive capital. That

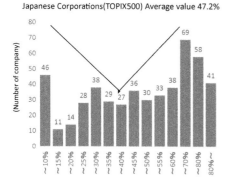

Fig. 3.5 U.S.–Japan major companies analysis of the capital adequacy ratio =Equity/Total Assets (%) (distribution of individual companies compared by 2013 data). *Source* Author based on Bloomberg data and Yanagi (2015c)

is why a V-shape appears. Regarding the Japanese capital adequacy ratio, 10% of companies indicate a value below 10% and over 30% indicate a value above 70%.

In contrast, large companies in the U.S. indicate an inverted V-shape when considering an optimal capital structure and lifestyle management. Less than 10% of U.S. companies are below 5% and more than 70% are approximately 15%.

I expect that balance sheet management, which considers an optimal capital structure, is important for Japanese companies.

From another perspective, a price book-value ratio which is market capitalization divided by equity book value (PBR) comparison between Japan and the U.S. is highly supportive in terms of corporate valuation based on ROE.

I would like to point out that PBR shows how much larger shareholder value is created over net assets in terms of the book value on accounting.

PBR can be divided by the product of PER (price earnings ratio) and ROE; PBR = PER × ROE.

The PBR of Japanese companies is relatively lower internationally and the value is less than half. PER (inverse of the stock yield) converges in the developed countries and the difference is mainly caused by ROE (Kondo and Yanagi 2013).

Figure 3.6 is a comparison chart showing the PBR of Japanese companies.

In the distribution of Japanese major companies, about 40% fall below one, even after Abenomics. In other words, according to the book value per share method of accounting, the evaluation shows that the company values are below their breakup values (equity book value).

The PBR of approximately 20% of the companies are greater than two times. In Japan, the ROE of most companies is below the cost of equity and the market reflects the impairment of their breakup values. As a result, an inverted V-shape appears on the left side of the PBR graph (value destruction).

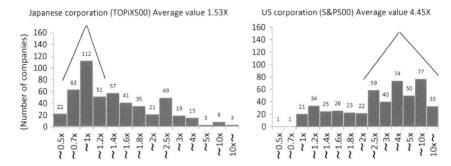

Fig. 3.6 U.S.–Japan major corporation analysis of PBR (distribution of individual companies compared by 2013 data). *Source* Author based on Bloomberg data and Yanagi (2015c)

While less than 5% of the companies in the U.S. have a PBR less than one, about 70% have a PBR greater than two, so an inverted V-shape appears on the right-hand side of the PBR graph (skewed right). (value creation)

In the U.S., companies traded below book value are much fewer than in Japan due to corporate governance (e.g., a company with a PBR falling below one is exposed to a hostile acquisition or vote-down by shareholders of its CEO). Major value creation companies therefore seek ROEs that are more than the cost of equity.

Thus, corporate governance is involved in ROE. That is why a low ROE reflected by weak corporate governance in Japan is connected with underperforming share prices and low shareholder values.

3.4 Global Investor Perceptions of ROE and Governance: Investors Expect to Improve ROE Through Governance Reforms

3.4.1 Japanese Companies and Investors, and the Gap in ROE Recognition

The Life Insurance Association of Japan (2015) conducted a survey targeting Japanese companies and investors, and its results are relevant to ROE and very interesting due to the different points of view between Japanese companies and investors.

While over 90% of Japanese investors require disclosure of ROE in terms of improving shareholder value, Japanese companies are focused on profits. Moreover, the size of profits is ranked in first place regarding disclosed KPI (key performance indicators) in mid-term management plans, while ROE is below 40% (Figs. 3.7 and 3.8).

As a matter of fact, approximately only 40% of Japanese corporations regularly set ROE targets because their first priority is the absolute value of profits.

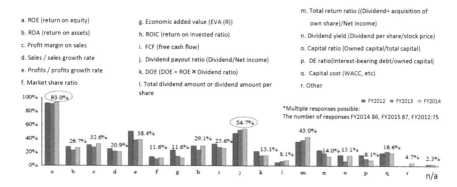

Fig. 3.7 Key Performance Indicators (KPIs) that Japanese companies should focus on (by Japanese investors). *Source* The Life Insurance Association of Japan (2015)

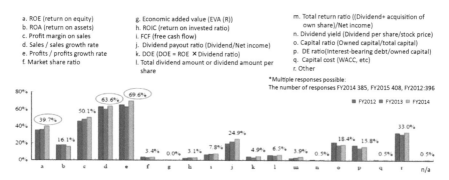

Fig. 3.8 Disclosed KPIs by Japanese companies in their mid-term management plans. *Source* The Life Insurance Association of Japan (2015)

Thus, a dichotomy exists between Japanese investors and companies. To bridge it, the Japanese Stewardship Code and Corporate Governance Code in the Abenomics strategy requires "engaging in dialog between corporation and investors." The perception of investors for these dual codes is shown in Figs. 3.7, 3.8, 3.9 and 3.10.

3.5 Global Investor Survey of Japan's Version of Its Stewardship Code

The Japanese version of the Stewardship Code (The Financial Services Agency 2014) defined institutional investors' fiduciary responsibilities and requires sustainable growth and improvement of corporate value through constructive engagement or purposeful dialogue.

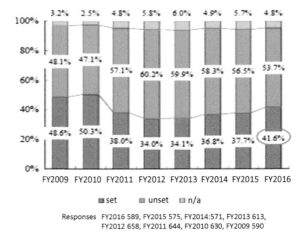

set   unset   n/a

Responses FY2016 589, FY2015 575, FY2014:571, FY2013 613,
FY2012 658, FY2011 644, FY2010 630, FY2009 590

Fig. 3.9 The ratio of Japanese companies that set proper ROE targets *Source* The Life Insurance Association of Japan (2015)

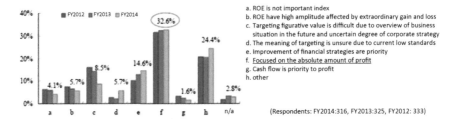

Fig. 3.10 The reasons companies do not target a specific ROE. *Source* The Life Insurance Association of Japan (2015)

I conducted a global investor survey[2] along with the Japanese version of the Stewardship Code (Yanagi 2014b), by targeting major institutional investors in Japanese stocks from Japan, the Americas, Europe, and Asia in terms of recognizing overseas investor perspectives on the Japanese version of its Stewardship Code.

The results of the survey are shown in Fig. 3.11 (Questions 1–8).

In response to Question 4, in particular, 62% of overseas investors (48% of Japanese investors) stated that the most important theme for corporation-investor engagement is ROE.

In response to Question 5, 90% of overseas investors (77% of Japanese investors) were unsatisfied that ROE was below the cost of equity. As for Question 6, the ideal shareholders' equity cost (shareholder investors' expected return = minimum ROE

---

[2]The global investor survey summary by Yanagi [2014b] is as follows: (Term) April 15–June 12, 2014; (Respondents) 110 funds had valid responses after approaching 200 core customers of UBS; (Response Rate) 55%, 50 overseas funds and 60 Japanese ones, for a total of 110 funds.

Q1. Will Japanese version of Stewardship Code be effective?

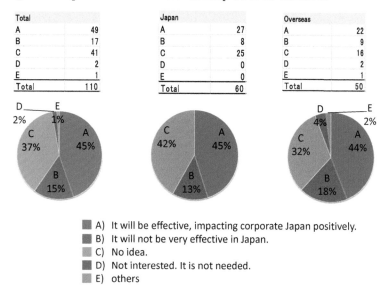

A) It will be effective, impacting corporate Japan positively.
B) It will not be very effective in Japan.
C) No idea.
D) Not interested. It is not needed.
E) others

Q2. (Let us assume it is somewhat ineffective in Japan,) Why is it ineffective in Japan?

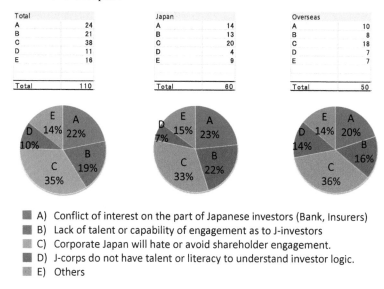

A) Conflict of interest on the part of Japanese investors (Bank, Insurers)
B) Lack of talent or capability of engagement as to J-investors
C) Corporate Japan will hate or avoid shareholder engagement.
D) J-corps do not have talent or literacy to understand investor logic.
E) Others

Fig. 3.11 Japanese Stewardship Code: Overseas investors' perception of ROE by global investor survey. *Source* Yanagi (2014b)

Q3. Will you enhance your level of engagement with Japanese corporations?

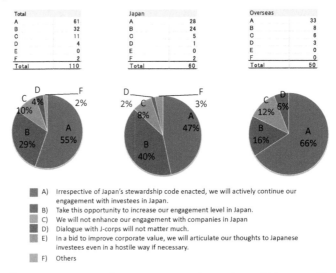

Total	
A	61
B	32
C	11
D	4
E	0
F	2
Total	110

Japan	
A	28
B	24
C	5
D	1
E	0
F	2
Total	60

Overseas	
A	33
B	8
C	6
D	3
E	0
F	0
Total	50

A) Irrespective of Japan's stewardship code enacted, we will actively continue our engagement with investees in Japan.
B) Take this opportunity to increase our engagement level in Japan.
C) We will not enhance our engagement with companies in Japan
D) Dialogue with J-corps will not matter much.
E) In a bid to improve corporate value, we will articulate our thoughts to Japanese investees even in a hostile way if necessary.
F) Others

Q4. (Let us assume you have some occasion to have dialogue with Japanese companies) What is your top priority engagement agenda in Japan? Will you enhance your level of engagement with Japanese corporations?

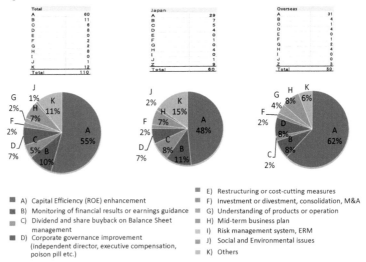

Total	
A	60
B	11
C	6
D	8
E	0
F	2
G	2
H	8
I	0
J	1
K	12
Total	110

Japan	
A	29
B	7
C	5
D	4
E	0
F	1
G	0
H	4
I	0
J	1
K	9
Total	60

Overseas	
A	31
B	4
C	1
D	4
E	0
F	1
G	2
H	4
I	0
J	0
K	3
Total	50

A) Capital Efficiency (ROE) enhancement
B) Monitoring of financial results or earnings guidance
C) Dividend and share buyback on Balance Sheet management
D) Corporate governance improvement (independent director, executive compensation, poison pill etc.)
E) Restructuring or cost-cutting measures
F) Investment or divestment, consolidation, M&A
G) Understanding of products or operation
H) Mid-term business plan
I) Risk management system, ERM
J) Social and Environmental issues
K) Others

Fig. 3.11 (continued)

Q5. Are you satisfied with Japan's ROE in general?

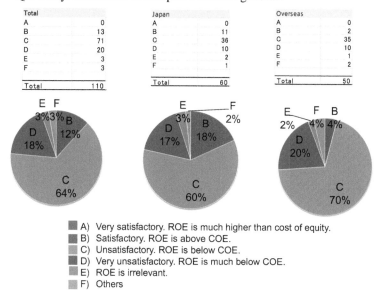

A) Very satisfactory. ROE is much higher than cost of equity.
B) Satisfactory. ROE is above COE.
C) Unsatisfactory. ROE is below COE.
D) Very unsatisfactory. ROE is much below COE.
E) ROE is irrelevant.
F) Others

Q6. In general, what is cost of equity (COE) for corporate Japan?

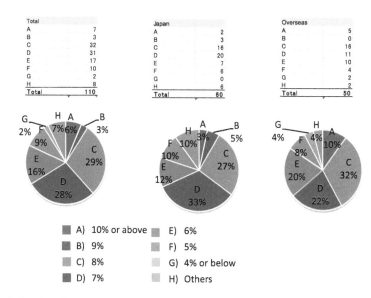

A) 10% or above   E) 6%
B) 9%   F) 5%
C) 8%   G) 4% or below
D) 7%   H) Others

Fig. 3.11 (continued)

Q7. In general what is the most important in dividend policy in Japan?

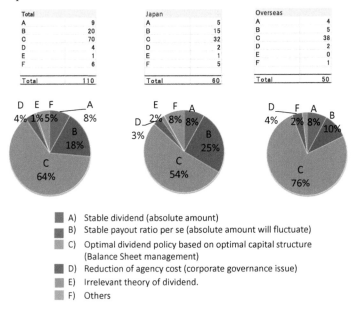

A) Stable dividend (absolute amount)
B) Stable payout ratio per se (absolute amount will fluctuate)
C) Optimal dividend policy based on optimal capital structure (Balance Sheet management)
D) Reduction of agency cost (corporate governance issue)
E) Irrelevant theory of dividend.
F) Others

Q8. Are you satisfied with Japan's corporate governance in general?

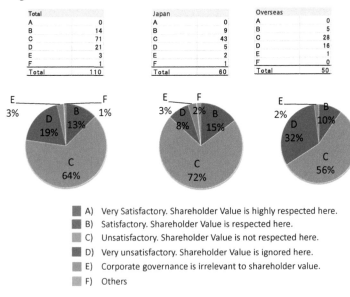

A) Very Satisfactory. Shareholder Value is highly respected here.
B) Satisfactory. Shareholder Value is respected here.
C) Unsatisfactory. Shareholder Value is not respected here.
D) Very unsatisfactory. Shareholder Value is ignored here.
E) Corporate governance is irrelevant to shareholder value.
F) Others

Fig. 3.11 (continued)

level) is above 7%, which confirms the notion that the expected level of equity costs of 8% is satisfactory (i.e., 90% of overseas investors).

In response to Question 8, only 10% of overseas investors (15% of Japanese investors) are satisfied with Japan's CG due to the fact that Japanese companies are not focused sufficiently on shareholder value.

Thus, overseas investors are unsatisfied with the ROE of Japanese companies and hope to make ROE an agenda item. Furthermore, they hope that ROE will be 8%, as a minimum. The reason for an unsatisfactory ROE is rooted in the lack of a focus on shareholder value in corporate governance.

3.5.1 Global Investor Survey About the Corporate Governance Code

The Corporate Governance Code (FSA and TSE 2015) emphasizes fiduciary responsibilities to the shareholders of listed companies and requires "engagement with shareholders" for sustainable growth and improvement of corporate value.

In this light, how do overseas investors in Japanese stock evaluate corporate governance and effort by Japanese companies?

In order to grasp the global perspective on the corporate governance code, I conducted a global investor survey (Yanagi 2015a, b, c) by targeting investors in Japan, the Americas, Europe, and Asia.[3] The results of the questionnaire survey relevant to the Corporate Governance Code are described in Fig. 3.12 (Questions 1–10) and described below.

Here, the following information should be noted;

As for ISS guideline, the proxy advisory company leader in the world, Institutional Shareholder Services Inc.(ISS) reformed their policy of proxy advisor in 2015, as follows; promoting objection voting for the selection of the management director on the basis that "the company's ROE on average in the past five terms is below 5%." According to Nikkei (May 8, 2015), Nippon Life, Resona Bank, and Mitsubishi UFJ trust bank require a ROE of 5% for Japanese companies. Actually, after the ISS reform, 16.9% of voters in Kirin HD, which recently had a 3% ROE, disagreed when voting for the director of management at their shareholders meeting in December 2014 (2.6% of voters disagreed the previous year).

In addition, with respect to Equity Spread, please refer to Yanagi (2013a). Ito Review said, "Equity Spread (ES) = ROE-CoE is the KPI for corporate value cre-

---

[3]The global investor survey summary by Yanagi (2015a, b, c) is as follows: (Term) February 1–March 6, 2015; (Respondents) 122 funds had valid responses after approaching 200 core customers of UBS; (Response Rate) 61%, 69 overseas funds and 53 Japanese ones for a total of 122 funds. The strategy by investors is highly confidential, so survey has uniqueness. However, the investors' opinions change with various situations, thus continuous surveys would be required. The author has performed periodic surveys (Yanagi 2010, 2013a, b, 2014a, b, 2015a, b, c). Yanagi (2013a) is adopted by the Ito Review (METI 2014). The trends do not change remarkably and the results of the global investor surveys have a certain robustness.

Q1. Are you satisfied with Japan's corporate governance in general?

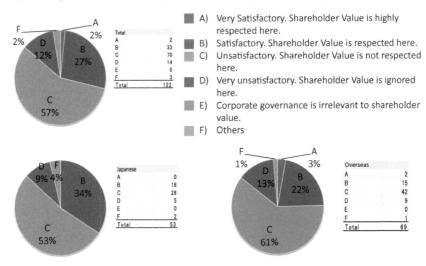

A) Very Satisfactory. Shareholder Value is highly respected here.
B) Satisfactory. Shareholder Value is respected here.
C) Unsatisfactory. Shareholder Value is not respected here.
D) Very unsatisfactory. Shareholder Value is ignored here.
E) Corporate governance is irrelevant to shareholder value.
F) Others

Total	
A	2
B	33
C	70
D	14
E	0
F	3
Total	122

Japanese	
A	0
B	18
C	28
D	5
E	0
F	2
Total	53

Overseas	
A	2
B	15
C	42
D	9
E	0
F	1
Total	69

Q2. What do you expect most in wake of Japan's Corporate Governance Code?

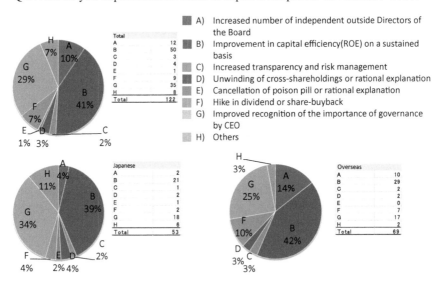

A) Increased number of independent outside Directors of the Board
B) Improvement in capital efficiency(ROE) on a sustained basis
C) Increased transparency and risk management
D) Unwinding of cross-shareholdings or rational explanation
E) Cancellation of poison pill or rational explanation
F) Hike in dividend or share-buyback
G) Improved recognition of the importance of governance by CEO
H) Others

Total	
A	12
B	50
C	3
D	4
E	1
F	9
G	35
H	8
Total	122

Japanese	
A	2
B	21
C	1
D	2
E	1
F	2
G	18
H	6
Total	53

Overseas	
A	10
B	29
C	2
D	2
E	0
F	7
G	17
H	2
Total	69

Fig. 3.12 Corporate Governance Code (Japanese Corporate Governance): overseas investors' perception of ROE by global investor survey. *Source* Yanagi (2015a, b, c)

ation." From the investor's perspective, if ES is positive, it means a value-creating corporation and if ES is negative, it means a value-destroying corporation (Yanagi 2010). Refer to Chap. 4 for details.

Q3. Will Japanese version of Corporate Governance Code be effective?

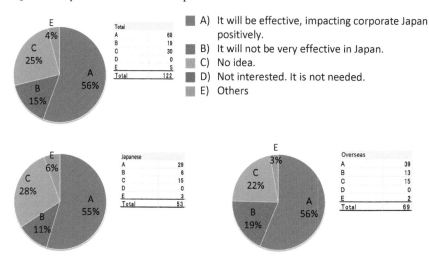

A) It will be effective, impacting corporate Japan positively.

B) It will not be very effective in Japan.

C) No idea.

D) Not interested. It is not needed.

E) Others

Q4. If CG Code not effective in Japan, what is the No.1 reason why?

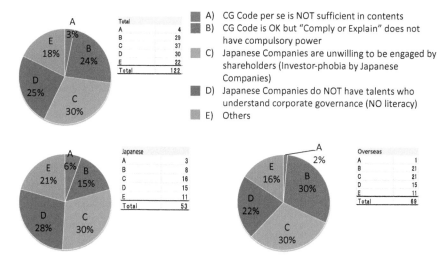

A) CG Code per se is NOT sufficient in contents

B) CG Code is OK but "Comply or Explain" does not have compulsory power

C) Japanese Companies are unwilling to be engaged by shareholders (Investor-phobia by Japanese Companies)

D) Japanese Companies do NOT have talents who understand corporate governance (NO literacy)

E) Others

Fig. 3.12 (continued)

First of all, compared to the 2014 survey, where only 10% of overseas investors were satisfied with Japanese corporate governance, the 2015 survey (Yanagi 2015a, b, c) after Abenomics governance reform was introduced showed that 25% of overseas investors (34% of Japanese investors) were satisfied with Japanese corporate governance (Question 1). I could say that there has been great progress after the reform.

Q5.Corporate Governance is related to capital efficiency (ROE)?

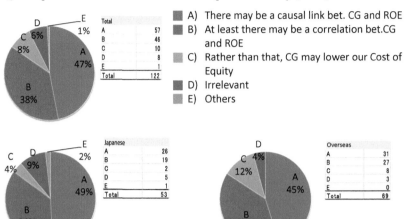

A) There may be a causal link bet. CG and ROE
B) At least there may be a correlation bet.CG and ROE
C) Rather than that, CG may lower our Cost of Equity
D) Irrelevant
E) Others

Q6.Are you satisfied with Japan's ROE in general?

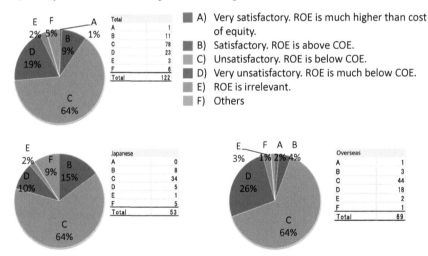

A) Very satisfactory. ROE is much higher than cost of equity.
B) Satisfactory. ROE is above COE.
C) Unsatisfactory. ROE is below COE.
D) Very unsatisfactory. ROE is much below COE.
E) ROE is irrelevant.
F) Others

Fig. 3.12 (continued)

However, as for the ROE of Japanese companies (Question 6), 90% of overseas investors (74% of Japanese investors) are still unsatisfied. The percentage has remained high compared to the previous year, although the ROE, on average, has improved to about 8% in FY2013.

In addition, in response to "What do you expect the most from CG?" (Question 2), 42% of overseas investors hope to improve ROE as a top priority (about the same

Q7.Do you agree with the statement "Japanese companies should seek at least 8% or higher ROE" in "Ito Review"?

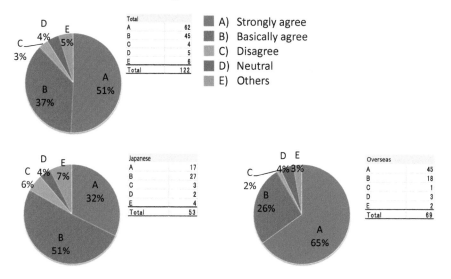

Q8.Do you agree the ISS proxy guideline "vote against the reelection of CEO if 5yrs average ROE is lower than 5%"?

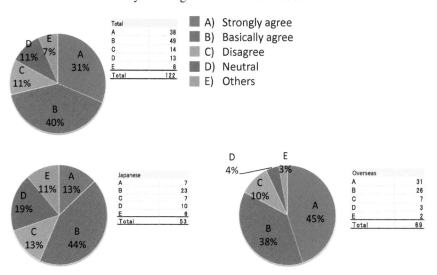

Fig. 3.12 (continued)

response as Japanese investors at 39%). The result indicates that the top priority of overseas investors is certainly an improvement of ROE in CG.

In Question 5, regarding the relationship between CG and ROE, 47% of global investors recognize the casual connection with/without practical research and 38%

Q9. In general, what is cost of equity (COE) for corporate Japan? (COE depends on each company but let assume all Japan average generally, that is beta=1 TOPIX condition)

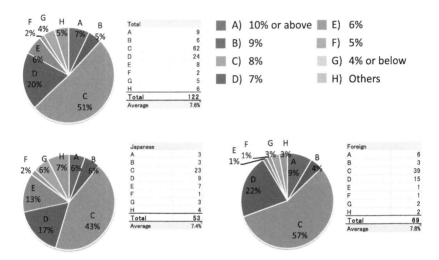

Q10. Equity Spread (= ROE minus Cost of Equity) is introduced as proxy for value creation in "Ito Review (drafted by Ryo Yanagi)". Do you support the proposal that Equity Spread must be disclosed in fiscal filing document with TSE and be openly discussed with investors in a bid to solicit more financial literacy (ROE must be higher than COE) on the part of Japanese CEOs generally?

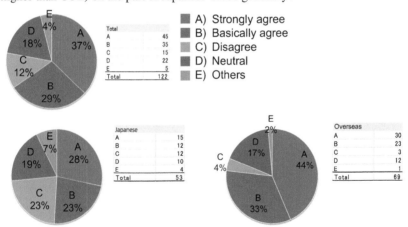

Fig. 3.12 (continued)

found some correlation. Statistically, it is clear that a majority recognizes the significant relevance between governance and ROE.

In Question 7, approximately 90% of global investors support the message, "Japanese companies should aspire toward an 8% ROE, at minimum," as I wrote in the Ito Review. Incidentally, overseas investors assertively support this notion, while Japanese investors only just support it.

In response to Question 8, although 83% of overseas investors agree with the "ISS (Institutional Shareholder Services) 5% rule" (vote against the re-election of management if the five-year average ROE falls below 5%), less than 60% of Japanese investors unassertively agree with it. This means that they have a somewhat cautious stance toward exercising their powerful voting rights. According to the ISS, about 33% of Japanese companies achieved the 5% standard in 2014.

In response to Question 9, the expected shareholders' equity cost (the expected profit rate of investors) is 7.4% for Japanese investors, on average, and 7.8% for overseas investors, on average, for a total average of 7.6%. The proposition of an 8% cost of equity was accepted by more than half of the participants and this limit was satisfactory for about 90% of the global investors and confirmed the 8% ROE goal in the Ito Review.

Finally, in Question 10, 77% of overseas investors agree with the proposal that there should be disclosure of the equity spread (ROE minus shareholders' equity cost) in financial results and announcements. However, only 51% of Japanese investors agree due to the difficulty in cost-of-equity disclosures.

The evidence shows that overseas investors expect an improvement of ROE due to the Corporate Governance Code because of the relevance between corporate governance and ROE.

Moreover, they are unsatisfied with the ROE of Japanese companies and support "ROE 8%" in the Ito Review, "ROE 5%" by ISS, and "Equity spread (ROE minus cost of equity) disclosures." In other words, ROE is the top priority for overseas investors.

3.6 Why Is ROE a Priority for Global Investors? ROE Is a Proxy of Shareholder Value

3.6.1 Total Return of Shareholders Is Attributable to ROE

In practice, the profit of shareholders is the sum of capital gains (gain on sales or potential unrealized gains) and income gains (dividends income).

In other words, shareholders have to consider the total of price increases and dividend income for generating profit. This total is called TSR (total shareholder return). It is described as an annual rate (in percent), the same as ROE.

In the short term, "noise" exists and stock prices could be misleading. However, on a long-term basis, TSR converges with ROE. This indicates that ROE determines how much of the annual return could be allocated toward business investments that are based on shareholder equity. ROE indicates the increasing (growth) rate of

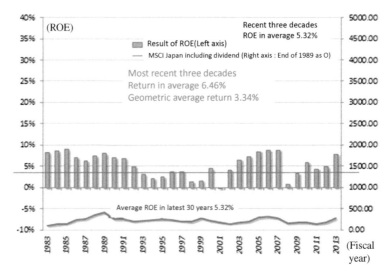

Fig. 3.13 Total return and ROE in Japan. Correlation between TSR and ROE of Japanese stock. *Calculated annual return of each areas based on MSCI of each region in end of FY1983 as 100. *Source* Author based on Bloomberg

shareholder equity that represents the shareholders' share. That is why the overseas investors' priority is ROE.

The denominator of "ROE = shareholders' equity is the book value of the shareholders' equity.

From the perspective of investors who purchase the stock priced in the capital markets, purchasing the stock by the market value is real and the book value cannot be replaced by it, thus a difference exists between the book value and market value. However, considering the long term horizon, the shareholder's equity book value and total market price have a strong correlation. In that context, TSR (return based on the market price paid by the shareholder) converges with ROE (shareholder return based on the book value).

Overseas investors who invest in global stocks reflect this fact, both consciously and unconsciously, and they mostly focus on ROE that has a strong relationship with shareholder profits.

For example, see Fig. 3.13. In the case of investors holding Japanese stock for the past 30 years, it means that an approximate 6% annual return in TSR is due to ROE, which had an annual rate of 5%, on average over the same period.

In addition, I compare the U.S. and Europe in the same way because the overseas investors can make an international comparison. Figures 3.14 and 3.15 indicate the relationship of TSR-ROE in the U.S. and Europe.

The shareholders' return, in the case of investing in U.S. stock for 30 years, is nearly 13%. That is because ROE, on average, for the same term, is 14%. Moreover, the same relationship holds in the case of Europe. The shareholders' return is 12% because the ROE, on average, for the same term is 12%.

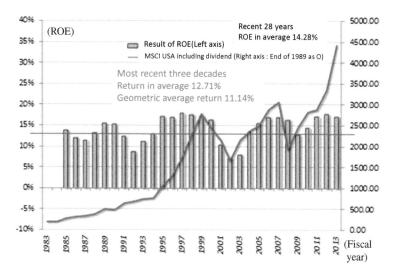

Fig. 3.14 Total Return and ROE in U.S. Correlation between TSR and ROE of U.S. stock. *Calculated annual return of each areas based on MSCI of each region in end of FY1983 as 100. *Source* Author based on Bloomberg

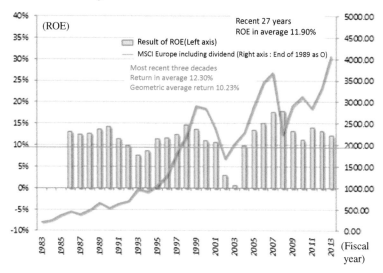

Fig. 3.15 Total Return and ROE in Europe. Correlation between TSR and ROE of European stock. *Calculated annual return of each areas based on MSCI of each region in end of FY1983 as 100. *Source* Author based on Bloomberg

As a result, I can conclude that the total return of shareholders coincides with ROE in the long term. ROE in Japan is lower than Europe and the U.S., hence TSR follows any declines, leading to overseas investor dissatisfaction. Based on this fact, these investors designate the improvement in Japan's ROE as their top priority issue.

3.7   Companies' Valuation of PBR Depends on ROE

In the stock market, the listed companies' stock is bought and sold every day and thus it is priced by the market.

Stock valuation uses various indexes. Most corporate management might aim toward the fact that the market understands the potential of their own company and, as a minimum, evaluate the value of their company on an accounting basis, which is more than the book value of the shareholders' equity (I use shareholders' equity, not net assets, in this book). Surely, the company's shareholders will want the same thing at least. In short, this is the main purpose of stock listings.

The index of shareholder valuation that reflect this desire is PBR (price book-value ratio). The PBR formula is outlined below:

$$\text{PBR} = \frac{\text{Stock Price}}{\text{Shareholder' equity book value per share}}$$
$$= \frac{\text{Market capitalization}}{\text{Shareholder's equity book value}} \text{ (times)}$$

PBR $>1 \Rightarrow$ Value creation
PBR $<1 \Rightarrow$ Value destruction

The point is to define the ratio of shareholder value vis-a-vis book values. In general, if the stock price is equal to the breakup value (book value of shareholders' equity) in the case of PBR, the ratio is one. And stock is considered a bargain when the ratio falls below one.

A ratio below one means that company's market capitalization is less than the book value of net capital of the corporation; hence, it can be interpreted that dissolving the company is possibly better than continuing to conduct business in terms of the shareholders' value.

In other words, the market does not find any future potential for the company with PBR below one. So they could be saying, "Return the capital to me by dissolving the company!" Hence, the stock listing might become meaningless.

Nevertheless, about 40% of the listed company's PBR in Japan is below one. Although PBR is basically updated every day, Japan was a country where the average PBR was about one before the introduction of Abenomics. The situation was very serious: On average, it means that nearly half of the companies were traded below their breakup values (PBR < 1).

Even after raising the stock values as a result of the effects of Abenomics, the PBR of Japanese companies on the stock exchange is still less than half of that of U.S. companies. Furthermore, nearly 40% of listed companies are traded still below book value. Why is the valuation of Japanese stock less than half that of the U.S.?

The key to answering this question is clarified by using the analysis method below and making an international comparison (refer to Table 3.2).

Table 3.2 Comparison of Advanced Countries (PBR = PER × ROE), April 2012 (May 2015 in parenthesis)

	PBR (times)	PER (times)	ROE (%)
Japan	1.0 (1.6)	15.6 (16.9)	6.4 (9.5)
U.S.	2.3 (2.9)	14.6 (18.7)	15.8 (15.5)
U.K.	1.6 (2.0)	10.2 (16.2)	15.7 (12.3)
Germany	1.4 (2.2)	11.1 (16.9)	12.6 (13.0)
Advanced countries in average	1.8 (2.3)	13.5 (18.1)	13.3 (12.7)

Source Author based on My Index

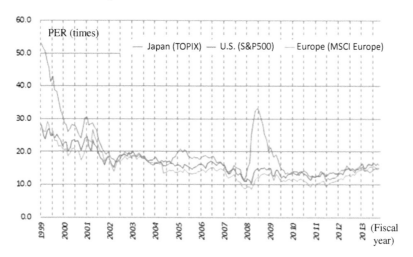

Fig. 3.16 International comparison of PER *Source* Author based on Bloomberg

PBR(Price book-value ratio = Market capitalization/Shareholder's equity)

= PER (Price earnings ratio = Market capitalization /Net profit)

× ROE (Return on equity = Net profit/Shareholders' equity)

In theory, PER converges toward the inverse of the formula[4] "equity cost(r)—perpetuity growth rate(g)," but most cases of high growth are offset by high capital costs, while low growth has low capital costs, and thus generalization is the same consequence in developed countries (Fig. 3.16).

In recent years, PER has remained stable globally at approximately 15 times.

---

[4]The premise is as follows: Stock price, P, is the total of the current value of future net profits, E (hypothesizing that they ultimately converge to 100% dividend payout ratio); capital cost, r (the expected rate of return by investors); and the permanent growth rate of net profits, g. The formula is constructed as follows: $P = E \div (r - g)$. Then divide both sides by E, $P \div E = PER = 1 \div (r - g)$. So, PER has a correlation with the inverse number of $r - g$. The following tendency

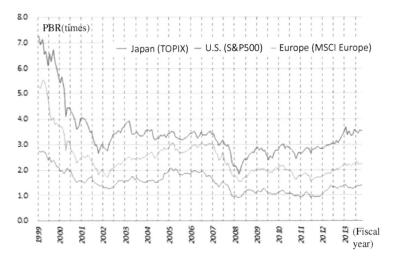

Fig. 3.17 International Comparison of PBR *Source* Author based on Bloomberg

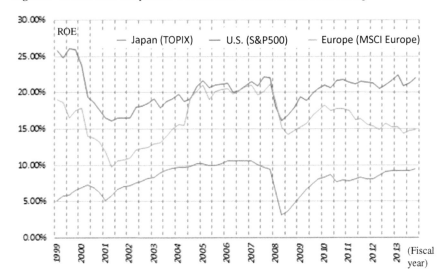

Fig. 3.18 International comparison of ROE. *Source* Author based on Bloomberg

There is not much difference in PER, as per the formula, thus the main cause of the difference in PBR is the difference in ROE (Fig. 3.18).

PBR in Japanese companies is relatively lower than other international countries and the main cause is the low value of ROE. Overseas investors that make international comparisons should be dissatisfied with the ROE of Japanese companies.

---

is observed: r is high when g is high and r is low when g is low. That is why r − g is not different in the advanced countries. Therefore, PER is not very different.

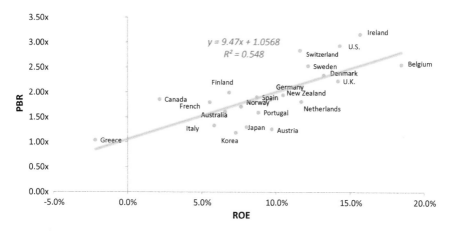

Fig. 3.19 International comparison of PBR and ROE (FY 2013). *Source* Author based on Bloomberg

While the analysis of PBR can be made from other aspects, the consequences of equity spreads will be explained in detail in Chap. 4. Equity spread, as calculated by the ROE-shareholder equity cost, is the source of value creation in line with the Residual Income Model (RIM). In other words, in the case where the equity spread is negative, PBR is lower than one because the market valuation reflects the impairment of the breakup value in the future. Here, the relationship is based on the fact that a lower ROE leads to a lower PBR.

In short, PBR and ROE have a positive correlation (Fig. 3.19). The proxy for corporate value (PBR) indicates how much more value is created over an emphasis on the book value of shareholders' equity. If the market value is consistently lower than the book value of the shareholders' equity (PBR <1), then stock listings are not meaningful (status of value destruction). As already mentioned, a low ROE of Japanese companies causes a low PBR.

Overseas investors mainly invest based on international comparisons. They are unhappy with the Japanese ROE and require an improvement of ROE, and so they sometimes make special demands as active shareholders.

3.8 High ROE Is Partly Determined by Corporate Governance

It is important to create value as a fiduciary duty, which is a matter of corporate governance. Fundamentally, governance does not have to be trivialized to the number of outside directors. The main factor is a system in which to sustainably enhance and maintain shareholder value.

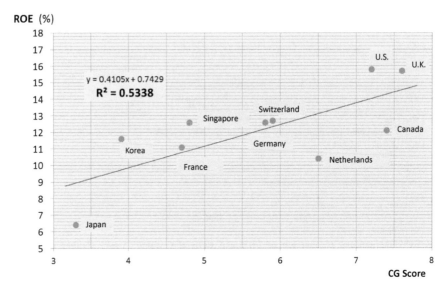

Fig. 3.20 Positive correlation between corporate governance and ROE. *Source* Author based on My Index and GMI

Professor Dittmar at the University of Michigan notes that the stock market evaluates companies with bad governance by discounting the cash holdings (Dittmar and Mahrt-Smith 2007). In other words, the cash of such corporations is discounted by about 50%. The results of my survey of overseas investors supports his statement (refer to Chap. 2).

My study shows that if corporate governance is supposed to be represented by the GMI scores, and shareholder value is proxied by ROE, their observed correlation in terms of an international comparison is obvious as shown in Fig. 3.20.

Internationally, corporate governance and ROE seem to be correlated. At least, overseas investors agree with this suggestion. Moreover, I previously mentioned (Yanagi 2015a) in the global investor survey (refer to Fig. 3.12, Question 5) that over 90% of institutional investors agree with the following statement; ROE and corporate governance are relevant and the shares of correlation and causal link are divided in half. There is an impact, since almost half of the global investors assume that ROE and governance have a causal link.

After all, ROE and governance are correlated or have a causal link, considering the fact that shareholder value-focused attitudes are directed toward improving corporate governance and ROE. In other words, governance can ensure a sustainable ROE. That is because corporate valuation is better with an improvement in governance and capital efficiency, and many overseas investors hope to overweight their portfolios with Japanese stock if Japan can improve them.

Thus, ROE is a proxy for the total return of shareholders, corporate valuation, and shareholder value, which have a positive correlation with governance in terms of investors. Moreover, it is easy to compare ROE, regardless of whether or not they represent Japanese or international companies, or the same businesses. For these reasons, overseas investors consider ROE as the most important KPI.

3.9 Japanese Companies Will Benefit from Enhancing ROE: Win-Win Situation on a Long-Term Basis

So far, we can share the idea that overseas investors require information about ROE.

However, what is the advantage for Japanese companies to enhance ROE? ROE is a proxy for shareholder value (market price/stock price in the long term) that leads to an increase in stock prices. With that said, Japanese companies will potentially benefit from ROE improvement such as corporate reputation, investor confidence, M&A, fund-raising, all leading to win-win situation. There are nine points in my view as below:

1. Companies can fulfill their fiduciary responsibility and accountability to share-holders as listed companies by the improvement of capital efficiency (ROE).
2. It is highly likely that the corporation can gain market trust and contribute toward an improvement of its corporate valuation as well as brand equity.
3. Maximizing corporate value contributes toward enhancing its status as a listed company and raising its social position by an improvement in capital efficiency.
4. Increasing total market capitalization enhances stock value as a currency in M&A, opening the option of acquisitions or possibly mergers under advantageous conditions.
5. Improvement of fundraising capability using stock, in which the relevant ability of debt finance in turn contributes toward stock value by improving capital efficiency and by expanding the selection of funding alternatives.
6. Gaining shareholder confidence leads to voting agreements for executive proposals in the meetings of shareholders. Low capital efficiency works against such proposals. ISS, which is the largest voting service advisor, provides guidelines to vote against CEOs with low-ROE.
7. Admitted broadly as companies commended by the initiatives of authorities; for example, those associated with adapting to the requirements of the JPX 400, the indexes that have focused on ROE or on corporate governance launched by the TSE. Moreover, Ito Review, Japanese Stewardship Code and Corporate Governance Code all support the improvement of capital efficiency and its important significance in engaging investors.
8. Cooperate with shareholders in win-win relationships through the alignment of interests via stock options, stock rewards, and introducing ROE-linked bonuses, so executives and employees can have incentives.
9. ROE means capital efficiency and it can be improved by regular means such as labor productivity and equipment productivity, which Japanese companies are traditionally good at, and by inventory reduction, the early collection of receivables, selling the non-performing assets, and improving margins.

These are not absolute answers, but management in listed companies have to pursue their responsibility to increase corporate value on a long term basis as agents delegated by the shareholders. Hence KPI becomes ROE. Enhancing corporate value is to be pursued through long-term ROE improvement and through engagement between companies and investors, which should be constructive, synchronized, symbiotic, and cooperative.

References

Dittmar, A., & Mahrt-Smith, J. (2007). Corporate governance and the value of holdings. *Journal of Financial Economics, 83,* 599–634.

Financial Services Agency. (2014). *Principles for responsible institutional investors «Japan's Stewardship Code»—To promote sustainable growth of companies through investment and dialogue.*

Financial Services Agency, Tokyo Stock Exchange, Inc. (2015). Japan's corporate governance code [Final proposal] seeking sustainable corporate growth and increased corporate value over the mid-to long-term.

Kondo, K., Yanagi, R. (2013). *Financial, IR & SR strategies for improvement of corporate value.* Chuokeizai-Sha.

Life Insurance Association of Japan. (2015). *Survey results on approaches toward enhancing equity values FY2014.* Life Insurance Association of Japan.

Ministry of Economy, Trade and Industry. (2014). *Ito Review of competitiveness and incentives for sustainable growth—Building favorable relationships between companies and investors—*Final report.

Yanagi, R. (2010). *Improving manual for enhancing corporate value on managerial accounting.* Chuokeizai-Sha.

Yanagi, R. (2013a). Suggestion for disclosing equity spread and engagement. *Kigyo kaikei,* 65(1), 86–93.

Yanagi, R. (2013b). Study for dividend policy and IR activities. Investor Relations, 2013(7), 58–77.

Yanagi, R. (2014a). Importance of optimal dividend policy based on optimal capital structure. *Kigyo kaikei, 66*(7), 44–51.

Yanagi, R. (2014b). Study for Japanese-version Stewardship code and capital efficiency. *Investor Relations, 8,* 48–62.

Yanagi, R. (2015a). The ROE Revolution and Financial Strategy. Chuokeizai-Sha.

Yanagi, R. (2015b). Corporate governance code and "Engagement with shareholders"—Implications of global investor survey and study for equity spread. *Investor Relations.Vol.* (9).

Yanagi, R. (2015c). Ideal relationship between companies and investors for improving ROE: Considering the Ito Review—Implications of global investor survey and study for equity spread. *SAAJ Journal, 2015*(6), 17–27.

Chapter 4
Equity Spread and Value Creation

Abstract In order to enhance corporate value via bolstering ROE on a sustained basis, the author proposes certain financial strategies in Chap. 4 through 6 as follows:

-How to Unlock the Value in Japan via Three Pillars of Financial Strategies-

Chapter 4: Equity Spread and Value Creation

Chapter 5: Value Creative Investment Criteria

Chapter 6: Optimal Dividend Policy based on Optimal Capital Structure

Equity Spread (ES) and Value Creation: ROE 8% is Japan's magic number. Chapter 3 showed that improving ROE is necessary to maximize corporate value, but why did the Ito Review specify a minimum 8% ROE when Japanese managers find 2 or 3% sufficient? This Chapter explains that 8% was chosen as a numerical target to raise Japanese managers' awareness of ROE as the first financial strategy. Using market data and survey results it verifies the adequacy of that standard and proposes the first of three strategies grounded in the premise that ROE must exceed Cost of Equity (CoE) to create corporate value as mathematically proven by the Residual Income Model (RIM). Japanese managers sometimes naively find ROE 2 or 3% sufficient because they traditionally believe operating in the black under GAAP is an absolute priority without considering CoE, mainly due to "bank-governance" described in Chap. 1. However, being in the black in financial accounting does not always create corporate value; being in the black in terms of managerial accounting does. Corporate value emerges in the Equity Spread (ES) between ROE and (CoE). That is, ES (%) = ROE − CoE. The book's survey results (2013, 2014, 2015) show that approximately 90% of global investors accept 8% as CoE or their opportunity cost. That's because 8% is an expected Cost of Equity and ROE must exceed CoE to create a positive Equity Spread as a proxy for value creation. Hence, ROE 8% or above required by the Ito Review should be theoretically and practically acceptable. That percentage is endorsed by empirical research: comparing ES and stock performance confirms that investors also focus on the correlation. In addition, long-term market data prove that positive ES is mandatory to create PBR (Price Book-value Ratio) exceeding one and its break-even-point stands at the ROE 8% level. Accordingly, this chapter advocates a positive ES as a strategy to raise consciousness of value creation among corporate managers in Japan.

© Springer Nature Singapore Pte Ltd. 2018
R. Yanagi, *Corporate Governance and Value Creation in Japan*,
https://doi.org/10.1007/978-981-10-8503-1_4

Keywords ROE 8% · Cost of equity · Residual income model · Equity spread

4.1 "Ito Review" and Equity Spread 8% Is Magic Number

Equity Spread (calculated as ROE minus Cost of Equity (investment returns expected by shareholders) is one of the KPIs for corporate value creation. In the eyes of investors, companies with positive Equity Spread are regarded as value-creating companies, and companies with negative Equity Spread are regarded as value-destructive companies (Yanagi 2010).

Cost of capital refers to the rate of return expected by the market. As there is no absolute definition, there are diverse views over the appropriate level of cost of capital. One particular survey shows that the Cost of Equity expected for Japanese equity investment by both domestic and overseas investors varies considerably, with the average for overseas investors being 7.2% and that for domestic investors being 6.3%.

According to this survey, an ROE of 8% or more would satisfy the expected cost of capital of over 90% of global investors. When engaging in dialogue with global investors, companies should be conscious that the minimum expected level of ROE is 8% (Yanagi 2013).

These are the descriptions inserted into the "Ito Review." Hence, "The guideline of 8% ROE on the Ito Review" below is partly established on the basis of the result of the global investor survey conducted by Yanagi 2013.

Although the actual cost of capital differs between companies, the first step in receiving recognition from global investors is for a company to commit to achieving a minimum ROE of 8%. This 8% ROE is a minimum level and companies should seek to generate higher ROEs.

Why should Japanese companies achieve minimum ROE of 8%? This is based on backward planning as follows: (1) We should increase returns (ROE) in excess of Cost of Equity (CoE), which is the expected return or opportunity cost of investors, for value creation; in other words, we should achieve positive Equity Spread (ES). (2) Given the fact that the global investor survey proves the hypothesis that CoE of 8% is the median value and the most frequent value of the rate of expected profit of global investors and that at a CoE taken at 8%, the expectations of approximately 90% of the global investors in Japanese stock were met. (3) Consequently, we should achieve a minimum of 8% ROE ipso facto.

The "8% ROE guideline in the Ito Review" has drawn global attention since it was first published in 2014 and greatly impacts Japanese companies.

Figure 4.1 shows the result of the global investor survey conducted by the author in 2015 and the result highlights that the support for "8% ROE in the Ito Review" is high at 88% (Overseas investor: 91%, Japanese investor: 83%).

In particular, 65% of overseas investors strongly supported this notion, whereas just 32% of Japanese investors aggressively supported it. Overseas investors assertively agree with 8% ROE as standard.

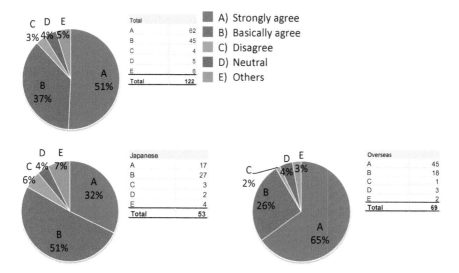

Fig. 4.1 Do you agree with the statement "Japanese companies should seek at least 8% or higher ROE" as stated in the "Ito Review"? *Source* Yanagi (2015b)

Furthermore, according to the survey "Questionnaire for listed companies (answered by 138 companies)" conducted by Nomura Investor Relations, approximately 80% of companies agree with "above 8% ROE in the Ito Review" (*IR magazine* New Year 2015 as of January 1, 2015). The result implies that both enlightened companies and investors support "8% ROE in the Ito Review."

ROE based on a long-term perspective is necessary for avoiding "short-termism".

4.2 What Is Equity Spread? The Black-Ink on Accounting Is Actually Red-Ink in Some Cases

4.2.1 What Is Equity Spread (ES)? Residual Income Model (RIM) Verifies It

Equity Spread is a management accounting index adopted by the Institute of Management Accountants (IMA) as a key performance indicator (KPI) for shareholder value creation; along with EVA (Stewart 1991) it is defined in the chapter of "Shareholder value accounting" in Statements on Management Accounting (SMA) (IMA 1997).

Although this book describes Equity Spread as a percentage, the amount in absolute value could be used like EVA.

In Japan, ES is adopted and used as the standard of selection of "Corporate Value Improvement Awards" by Tokyo Stock Exchange (TSE), which was established in 2012—a year before the Ito Review (TSE 2012).

Earlier, Japanese management did not pursue pure shareholder return because of cross-shareholdings or "debt-governance" as described in Chap. 1, and so they do not fear shareholder's voting rights under bank-led governance. In this historical context, some managers think that "With net profit on accounting in the black without any debts and ROE at 2% every year, what should be the problem?"

Traditional Japanese management are obsessed with whether financial accounting figures are in red or black only, but they are not concerned about their earnings ratio exceeding expected rate of return by investors or opportunity cost; that is, whether their ROE exceeds cost of capital or not.

On the other hand, from the risk-taking and selective investors' perspective, it is not enough for a company in which they are investing to be in the black as for nominal accounting. Instead, they seek sustainable increase in "ROE exceeding Cost of Equity (CoE)"—positive Equity Spread—as a source of value creation.

For example, as the "Ito Review" states, assuming 8% of CoE, a company with ROE 2% is, regardless of black ink in financial accounting, a red-ink company in management accounting (in terms of shareholder value accounting); that is, ROE 2% minus CoE 8% equals negative 6%, which is red ink!

The definition of Equity Spread consistent with IMA or the Ito Review is as follows:

Equity Spread (%) = ROE−CoE[1]

Generally, shareholder value (long-term market capitalization or theoretical value) can be calculated by adding market value added (MVA) to shareholders' equity book value (BV). In the residual income model (RIM) and Ohlson model (Ohlson 2001), shareholder value is calculated using the following formula:

$$\text{Shareholder value} = Book\ value + \sum_{t=1}^{\infty} \left(\frac{Net\ income - \text{CoE} \times \text{BV}_{t-1}}{(1 + \text{CoE})^t} \right)$$

SV: Shareholder value (Market capitalization), BV: Shareholders' equity book value, CoE (r): Shareholders' equity cost, t: Fiscal year

This expansion formula is as follows[2]:

$$\text{SV}_0 = \text{BV}_0 + \frac{(\text{ROE}_1 - \text{CoE})\text{BV}_0}{1 + \text{CoE}} + \frac{(\text{ROE}_2 - \text{CoE})\text{BV}_1}{(1 + \text{CoE})^2} + \frac{(\text{ROE}_3 - \text{CoE})\text{BV}_2}{(1 + \text{CoE})^3} + \ldots .$$

---

[1] Equity Spreads are indicated by ratio, but to not fall into a state of reduced equilibrium, residual profit (current profit − shareholders' equity cost amount), which is the absolute amount, is also considered. This report discusses the ratio and the amount.

[2] It is obvious from the expanded formula, but the assumptions made in the residual income model and Equity Spread are not the current short-term ROE, but a long-term ROE stream in the future and therefore not a case of short-termism. The intent of "The Ito Review's 8% ROE Guideline" is also here.

SV: Shareholder value (Market capitalization), BV: Shareholders' equity book value, CoE: Shareholders' equity cost, t: Fiscal year

Clearly, regarding shareholder value, theoretically ROE is an explanatory variable and the "unnecessary ROE theory" is a misunderstanding of the residual income model (RIM) and its factor, Equity Spread theory. In Nishikawa et al. (2016), Professor Hiroyuki Ishikawa of Osaka City University stated the following points. "Although there is an antithesis against the advocates for ROE, this criticism is naively based on an unfamiliarity with a theoretical model, the residual income model (RIM). Since there are many misunderstandings about ROE, I would like to point out the importance of ROE again. RIM is mathematically derived by substituting the clean surplus relationship, the basic principle of accounting, into the dividend discount model, which is a representative model for evaluating the intrinsic value of the stock. As is clear from the mathematical expression of the residual income model (RIM), it is not the current ROE that is important in evaluating stock value, but the time series of long-term ROE in the future. For example, ROE can be raised temporarily and mechanically by buying one's own shares, but the important thing is whether or not we can sustain the increased ROE over the long term. Unless the entity of the enterprise does not change, high ROE will return to average."

Furthermore, dividing both sides of this equation by shareholders' equity book value B_0 we get as follows[3]:

$$
\begin{aligned}
\text{PBR} &= \frac{SV_0}{BV_0} \\
&= 1 + \frac{ROE_1 - CoE}{1 + CoE} + \frac{(ROE_2 - CoE)BV_1/BV_0}{(1 + CoE)^2} \\
&\quad + \frac{(ROE_3 - CoE)BV_2/BV_0}{(1 + CoE)^3} + \ldots
\end{aligned}
$$

SV: Shareholder value (Market capitalization), BV: Shareholders' equity book value, CoE: Shareholders' equity cost, t: Fiscal year

As you can see from the residual income model (RIM), PBR tends to be affected by long-term Equity Spread (ROE—CoE). In other words, incorporating positive Equity Spread (ROE $\geq$ CoE) creates market value added (MVA), which tends to

---

[3]Professor Ishikawa also insists on the following points (Nishikawa et al. 2016): "There are some executives claiming that their shares are valued at a reasonable price on the ground that stock price net asset multiplier (PBR) is below 1. However, the idea is also wrong, and if the future expected ROE is r (CoE), then PBR exceeds 1. Conversely, if the future ROE is less than r on average, the PBR will be cut into by 1. (PBR <1) does not mean cheap, but the company is seen as a value-destroying company that can only achieve ROE below r for a long time on average from the market. Even if the ROE is high in the short term, if future company growth cannot be expected, "PBR reduced by 1" can sufficiently occur. RIM, along with the importance of ROE, also points out the importance of its benchmark, shareholders' equity cost (r)." Regarding the Equity Spread, there is a trend to criticize the comparison of ROE and shareholders' equity cost (r), which is also because of a misunderstanding of the residual income model.

make PBR more than 1 time (value creative company). Conversely, if you are aware of the negative Equity Spread (ROE $\leq$ CoE), the probability that MVA will be negative and PBR will be less than 1 time (value-destroying company) will increase. Basically, whether PBR will be more than 1 time depends on whether the Equity Spread is positive or negative. Therefore, Equity Spread is considered as a proxy variable of value creation.

Figure 4.2 shows the details of the mathematical basis of the residual income model (RIM) assuming a clean surplus relationship and steady state.[4] (Looking at this, as long as the sustainable growth rate (g) of corporate earnings does not exceed capital cost (r) ($r \geq g$) (unless it is a high-growth company), if the Equity Spread becomes negative, PBR more clearly breaks down in value to 1 time. That is, market capitalization falls below shareholders' equity book value. If the Equity Spread (ES) becomes positive, PBR tends to exceed 1 time. In addition, in the model described in Chap. 7 of this book, it is said that the book value of shareholders' equity is "related to financial capital,' while the Market Value Added (MVA) created by the positive Equity Spread is "related to non-financial capital," but non-existent without positive ES. It is thought that the ES can be synchronized with non-financials from the viewpoint of the companies that emphasize non-financial information.

4.2.2 Equity Spread and Value Creation Indicated by Empirical Data

Even with quantitative empirical data, on a time axis of 10 years, when the expected ROE is less than 8% there are still many cases where added value evaluation is sluggish at PBR 1 time or less (or thereabouts), and when the expected ROE exceeds 8%, and PBR improved more than 1 time. After all, there is a tendency for value creation to rise to the right shoulder, as can be observed and reconfirmed again and again in multiple quantitative data sources (Fig. 4.3).

In addition to the consensus of the qualitative investor survey, the evidence of these quantitative demonstration data also shows that an ROE of 8% has become a defining line in value creation, which is the reasoning for the Japanese stock market phrase, "8% is the magic number."[5]

---

[4]DDM: shareholder value is the theory that sums up the streams of dividends to be received in the future to the present value by discounting the streams of dividends to be received in the future) to the clean surplus relationship (the year-end shareholders' equity book price = beginning and closing shareholders' equity book value + current income − current term dividend) and the relationship between residual income and net income (residual income = current income − initial shareholders' equity book value × shareholders' equity cost). (Ohlson 2001; Nishikawa et al. 2016)

[5]*The Nikkei*. August 26, 2014. "*Scramble, 8% is magic number, Market valuation has changed by raising ROE* " (Ken Kawasaki, reporter) and *The Nikkei*. June 25, 2016. "ROE management for breaking down the temporary lull (part2) The management with cost of capital-consious would be required for the engagement with capital market" (Mitsuaki Hirasawa, reporter; et al.).

(Net Income NI, Equity Book Value: BV, Dividend: D, Cost of Equity: CoE, Residual Income: RI, Shareholder Value: SV, t=0: at present, t=1: one year later growth rate: g)

Residual income in one year is defined as follows:

$$RI_1 = NI_1 - BV_0 \times CoE \qquad (1)$$

(1) is expanded to define Net income

$$NI_1 = BV_0 \times CoE + RI_1 \qquad (2)$$

Equity Book Value in one year is defined as below; (clean surplus relation)

$$BV_1 = BV_0 + NI_1 - D_1 \qquad (3)$$

(3) is expanded to define dividend

$$D_1 = BV_0 + NI_1 - BV_1 \qquad (4)$$

Substitute (2) into (4) and simplify:

$$D_1 = BV_0 + BV_0 \times CoE + RI_1 - BV_1$$
$$= (1 + CoE) \times BV_0 + RI_1 - BV_1 \qquad (5)$$

Shareholder value is defined by Dividend Discount model as such;

$$SV_0 = \frac{D_1}{(1 + CoE)^1} + \frac{D_2}{(1 + CoE)^2} + \cdots \qquad (6)$$

Substitute (5) into (6) and simplify;

$$SV_0 = \frac{(1 + CoE)BV_0 + RI_1 - BV_1}{(1 + CoE)^1} + \frac{(1 + CoE)BV_1 + RI_2 - BV_2}{(1 + CoE)^2} + \cdots$$

$$= \frac{(1 + CoE) BV_0}{(1 + CoE)^1} + \frac{RI_1}{(1 + CoE)^1} - \frac{BV_1}{(1 + CoE)^1} + \frac{(1 + CoE)BV_1}{(1 + CoE)^2} + \frac{RI_2}{(1 + CoE)^2} - \frac{BV_2}{(1 + CoE)^2} + \cdots$$

$$= BV_0 + \frac{RI_1}{(1 + CoE)^1} - \frac{BV_1}{(1 + CoE)^1} + \frac{BV_1}{(1 + CoE)^1} + \frac{RI_2}{(1 + CoE)^2} - \frac{BV_2}{(1 + CoE)^2} + \cdots$$

$$= BV_0 + \frac{RI_1}{(1 + CoE)^1} + \frac{RI_2}{(1 + CoE)^2} + \cdots$$

Divide both sides by Equity Book Value now and due to $(RI_1 = NI_1 - BV_0 \times CoE)$ relation;

$$\frac{SV_0}{BV_0} = PBR = 1 + \frac{(ROE_1 - CoE)}{(1 + CoE)} + \frac{(ROE_2 - CoE) BV_1 / BV_0}{(1 + CoE)^2} + \frac{(ROE_3 - CoE) BV_2 / BV_0}{(1 + CoE)^3} + \cdots$$

Simplify the equation and assume clean surplus relation and stable state;

$$PBR = 1 + \frac{\text{Equity Spread (ROE - CoE)}}{CoE - g}$$

(The final formula assumes that residual profits grow at a fixed rate.)

Fig. 4.2 Mathematical basis of residual income model (RIM) and Equity Spread to explain PBR

In line with Equity Spread theory with RIM mathematical development as shown in Fig. 4.2, the fact that 8% is the threshold for value creation in Japan is evidenced by multiple empirical research above (Fig. 4.3).

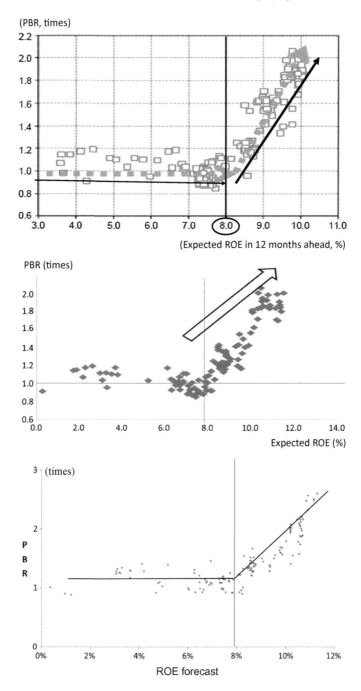

Fig. 4.3 Diagram of correlation between PBR and expected ROE—Empirical data for "8% is the magic number"

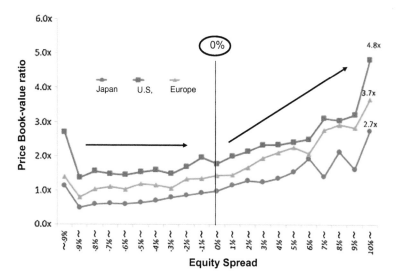

Fig. 4.4 PBR and Equity Spread (FY2013). Correlation between Equity Spread and PBR (International Comparison in FY2013)

In addition, observing international comparison (between Japan and the United States, Europe) on another data (Fig. 4.4), the relation between ES (premise 8% of CoE) and PBR, is same as the result of analysis by SMBC Nikko Securities and others in Fig. 4.3.

Price Book-value ratio (PBR) in Japan is lower than in the United States and Europe, and is obviously stagnant and flat in case of negative Equity Spread, whereas PBR is proportionately improved in case of a positive ES. In fact, positive ES is the precondition for value creation.

Furthermore, as Fig. 4.5 shows, from the perspective of the number of companies in Japan although the data is from before Abenomics, PBR of the companies that have negative Equity Spread tends to be below 1 under the premises for 8% of capital cost. In other words, market capitalization is likely to be below breakup value (equity book value); that is, the result reflects value destruction by the market.

Looking for the distribution of PBR by international comparison as of the data after Abenomics, end of September 2014, PBR of Japanese companies is mostly below 1 (Fig. 4.6), and the major cause is ROE below 8% (Fig. 4.7).

Thus, the major cause of inferiority of Japanese companies with regard to corporate valuation is negative Equity Spread (ROE tends to be below 8%).

$$PBR = \frac{\text{Market capitalization}}{\text{Shareholder equity book value}} = 1 + \frac{\text{Equity spread}}{\text{Equity capital cost} - \text{Sustainable growth ratio}}$$

The data above proved that the formula of PBR-Equity Spread relationship could be applied to the market in reality.

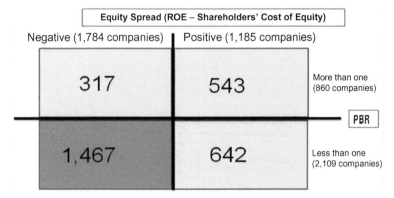

* 1,784 companies **out of 2,969 surveyed companies** (60%) were in negative Equity Spread
* 1,467 companies out of 1,784 companies in negative equity (82%) had PB less than one
* 1,467 companies out of 2,109 companies with PR less than one (70%) were in negative Equity Spread
* Surveyed 2,969 companies for which calculation was able to conduct using FY2012 financial results available in CD-ROM Kaisha Shikiho published by Toyo Keizai Shinpo (Assuming 8% level of shareholdersí cost of equity (β=1)

The Japan Company handbook (quarterly corporate report)

Fig. 4.5 The number of Companies with negative-Equity Spread and traded below shareholders' equity book value (Analysis in FY2012). *Source* "More than half Japanese companies failed to meet the expectation of shareholders (by Kaoru Hosaka)" Yomiuri Newspaper (October 11, 2012)

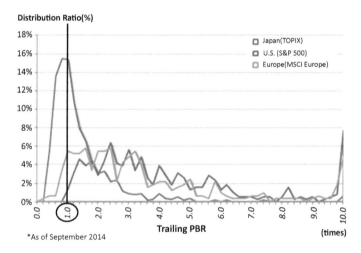

Fig. 4.6 Distribution chart PBR by International comparison. *Source* Author based on FACTSET, Bloomberg

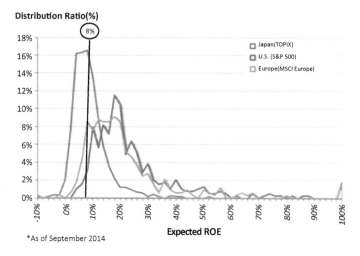

Fig. 4.7   Distribution chart ROE by International comparison. *Source* Author based on FACTSET, Bloomberg

4.3   The Perception Gap Between Japanese Companies and Investors: Dialogue on Equity Spread Could Bridge the Gulf

ROE above Cost of Equity (expected rate of return by investors or their opportunity cost), that is, maintaining positive Equity Spread (ES) in long term, is essential for creating shareholders' value as mentioned earlier, but the perceived standard level of ROE or expected ratio that should be achieved is completely different between companies and investors. In fact, a severe dichotomy exists.

According to The Life Insurance Association of Japan (2015), the perception gap is visible in the data.

As seen in Fig. 4.8 from the investors' perspective, a majority of Japanese investors consider that ROE is below the expected rate of return (ES is negative), but, on the other hand, more than half of Japanese companies consider that ROE is above capital cost by investor or equal (ES is not negative at least).

Moreover, as Fig. 4.9 shows, 40% of Japanese investors hope for 10–12% ROE in mid-long term and 60% of investors require above 8% ROE. However, in fact, 60% of Japanese companies' ROE is below 8% against the suggestion by the Ito Review and 70% is below 10% ROE (Fig. 4.9).

These data show the enormous dichotomy between company and investor.

In conclusion, though there is a gap between companies and investors, the two codes would hopefully ease and fulfill the difference for enhancing corporate value via "purposeful dialogue between company and investor" in Japan's Stewardship Code (SC) for institutional investors and "dialogue with shareholders" as the basic principle of the Corporate Governance Code (CGC) for listed companies.

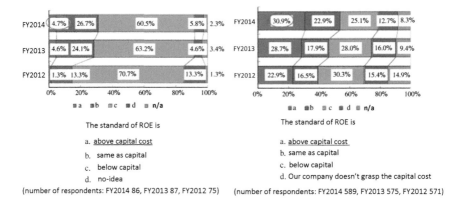

Fig. 4.8 Expected rate of return and ROE (Perspective of investor:*Left graph* and company: *Right graph*). *Source* The Life Insurance Association of Japan (2015)

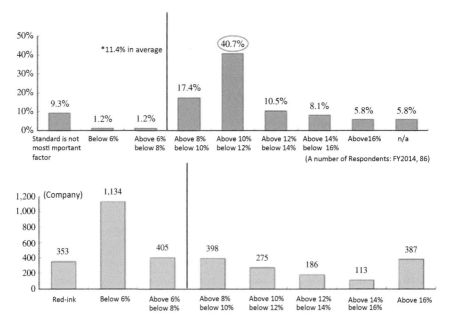

Fig. 4.9 The gap of perspective to ROE between Japanese companies: *Lower graph* and investors: *Upper graph. Source* The Life Insurance Association of Japan (2015). *Note* The universe is listed companies on the market (including red-ink companies, excluding financial business group)

The two codes promote engagement; that is constructive communication and discussion between companies and investors. In addition, "The Ito Review" also promotes Japan as an "advanced country of dialogue."

4.4   Value Proposition of Disclosure of Equity Spread and Engagement: We Have to Feel the Pain as Pain for Change

It is necessary to raise consciousness of companies through self-disclosure and constructive engagement with investors for value creation.

As mentioned earlier, Equity Spread (ES) is defined as follows:

$$\text{Equity spread } (\%) = \text{ROE} - \text{Cost of equity (CoE)}$$

Applying the formula to their own management situation of Japanese companies, it would help for CEOs to recognize whether their ROE is above Cost of Equity (CoE) commensurate with investors' expectation.

For example Japanese management might naively refute as follows: "We have no problem at all, because of black-ink numbers on our accounting book every year. We have huge cash without any debts. Though ROE is always 2%, how does it matter? The final profit on P/L is always plus. No debt. Huge cash."

However, if the following phrase is written on the Fiscal Report filed with the TSE, these Japanese managers would, for the first time in their lives, realize red ink on management accounting and ensuing value destruction and might try to deal with and rectify it:

Equity Spread is negative 6% red ink, with ROE 2% minus CoE 8% equal to minus 6%.

Japan is said to be a country of not money but shame. It is seen by many managers as shameful if they disclose red ink numbers in public. It may be a catalyst to change Japan.

According to the JIRA (2014),[6] just 10% of listed companies are "calculating and comprehending their own Cost of Equity (CoE)." CoE may vary depending upon respective companies.

If a company cannot exactly grasp its Cost of Equity, it is recommended to use "Cost of Equity = 8%," which satisfies 90% of overseas investors' expectation. Although it is a rough estimation, it could be used as a guide to lead awareness reform. We have to feel the pain as pain for change.

Because Equity Spread (ES) theoretically and empirically correlates to creation of shareholders' value, self-disclosure of ES as the agenda for "dialogue between company and investor" is suggested. The advantages of the self-disclosure and dialogue of ES are as follows:

---

[6]Fact-finding survey of Japanese companies by Japan Investor Relations Association. The term of the survey is from 30 January to 10 March 2014. Among the listed companies in Tokyo Stock Exchange, 3543 were targeted and 1029 responded (Response rate: 29%).

- ES is simpler than ROIC[7] (or EVA), which is multivariable and has several definitions without disclosure. Moreover, since ROE is openly disclosed in official financial settlements filed with regulatory agencies, it is easier to compare ROE with that of other companies and make a chronological comparison: it could be a common language.
- Compared with ROA, which is calculated using total assets as invested capital and denominator, ROE is more supported by investors due to the correlation with TSR (shareholders total return, which combines capital gain and income gain), which allows focus on shareholders' capital as invested capital.
- As ROE depends on net profit after interest deduction, cost of liability is included already. "Sustainable" long-term ROE must be a precondition with a healthy and creditworthy balance sheet, avoiding excessive leverage and bankruptcy possibility (companies must seek optimal capital structure considering financial strength).
- ES in turn is superior to ROE on a stand-alone basis as an engagement agenda, because ES promotes clear consciousness to the comparison with CoE (whether ROE is above CoE or not). It would enlighten naïve Japanese corporate managers without financial literacy and sense of capital cost who are satisfied with black-ink just on accounting books despite low ROE, which is value-destructive.

According to Yanagi (2015a, b), 66% of investors (overseas investors 77%, Japanese investors 51%) support the statement, "ES must be self-disclosed in fiscal filing document with TSE." While it seems like conservative and sympathetic Japanese investors are to some extent considering the burden for disclosing, as in total, more than half of investors support self-disclosing of ES that promotes corporate managers' awareness of "whether ROE is above CoE or not." Especially, overseas investors strongly support the suggestion to change Japan (Fig. 4.10).

If TSE encourages self-disclosing by the Fiscal Report filed with the TSE, corporate managers' decision making would be more effective, seeking capital efficiency.

Again, CoE differs for each company, ROE has a life cycle, and individual justification for long-term strategies and planning by companies is required for the sake of investors' understanding and supporting Japanese companies. We have to avoid short-termism. We should return to the basic principle, "Comply or Explain (practice the guideline or give individual explanation)."

---

[7]ROIC indicates Return on Invested Capital, calculated as follows: "Net operating profit after tax ÷ (Shareholders' capital + debt with interest)." However, the definition differs by companies.

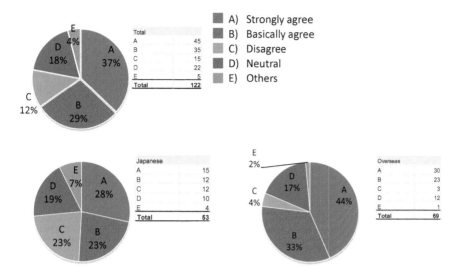

Total	
A	45
B	35
C	15
D	22
E	5
Total	122

A) Strongly agree
B) Basically agree
C) Disagree
D) Neutral
E) Others

Japanese	
A	15
B	12
C	12
D	10
E	4
Total	53

Overseas	
A	30
B	23
C	3
D	12
E	1
Total	69

Fig. 4.10 Equity Spread (ROE minus Cost of Equity) is introduced as proxy for value creation in the "Ito Review". Do you support the proposal that Equity Spread must be disclosed in fiscal filing documents with the TSE and be openly discussed with investors in a bid to solicit more financial literacy (ROE must be higher than CoE) on the part of Japanese CEOs generally? *Source* Yanagi (2015b)

4.5   Overseas Investors Views on Shareholders' Capital Cost: Evidence of 8% Backed by Empirical Research

4.5.1   Estimated Calculation of Shareholders' Equity Cost and Empirical Research

4.5.1.1   Market Data

Regarding ROE, one of the components of Equity Spread, it could be easily understood based on the result of financial statements and earnings guidance announced by the individual company. The issue is how one could set conceptual cost of shareholders' equity (CoE). There are many methods such as historical or implied estimated calculation, but it is fair to say there is no absolute answer.

For example, in accordance with CAPM style,[8] CoE is converted as follows:

---

[8]The method of calculation for cost of shareholders' equity is generally CAPM (Capital Asset Pricing Model). The basic formula is as follows: Shareholders' capital cost = Risk-free rate + β value × Market risk premium. However, the method of calculation for the three elements of CAPM in use and standards value is different by user. Generally, risk-free rate uses 10-year government bonds interest, but there is the case to use 30-year government bonds or original calculation. β value is also different, depending on how long the term of data applied and how the term of data breaks up. Market risk premium is applied 4-6% by referring to the difference between stock and investment

"Risk free rate (RFR)+risk premium (RP) in premise for β value 1(same fluctuating prices with TOPIX)."

The problem is RP, and historical RP is a moving and elusive target subject to the term of data. Estimated calculation depending on past result as cross-shareholding dominated the era of stable shareholders does not fill the expected value of future-oriented global investors.

Thus, this chapter considers "CoE estimate" by focusing on implied "future oriented," "expected value of global investors (Cost of Equity=expected rate of return of investors)."

If one conservatively considers CoE from empirical research, RP of advanced countries could be estimated as approximately 6%. According to the Fernandez and Campo (2010) survey of 2400 targeted market participants, the standards of RP in advanced countries is converged to 5–6%. In addition, in a questionnaire survey for CFOs in the United States by AFP (2011), nearly 50% of respondents of the study population answered 5–6%.

From now on, in this chapter, RP is hypothesized as 6%, and premise 2% of risk-free rate (RFR) from yield in recent Japanese 30-year bond as a going concern.

The hypothesis considered in this book is "CoE of Japanese stock is $2\% + 6\% = 8\%$.[9] (8% is average Cost of Equity of all Japanese stock and premise β value is 1)".

As evidence to support these hypotheses, Fig. 4.11 shows that risk-free rate in an advanced country is converged to 2%. Figures 4.12 and 4.13 implies that risk premium in advanced country is close to 6% given the relationship whereby reciprocal of PER (Price Earnings Ratio) tends to be converged into Cost of Equity minus perpetual growth ratio $(r - g)$ assuming clean surplus and perpetuity with growth ratio being in parallel with yield on government bond. For example, CoE 8% minus growth ratio 2% equals to RP 6% and the reciprocal of PER 16 times (as reciprocal approximation)

In addition, compelling empirical research conducted by Professor Hiroyuki Ishikawa at Osaka City University proved with statistical significance that Japan's CoE is approximately 8% as follows:

Professor Hiroyuki Ishikawa of Osaka City University has demonstrated in Nishikawa et al. (2016) shareholders' capital cost by regression analysis following the "Eton Model." Assuming that residual income grows constantly (g) and using the

---

yield of government bond in the past (actual result from post-war to August 2014 is 5.20%), current yield (anticipated stock yield of listed companies in TSE at September 2014 is about 6%). The book applied 2% of risk-free rate by 30-year government bond, conservatively 6% of risk premium, cost of Japanese stock on average as β value 1 is 8% (2% plus 6%). These percentages correspond to the result of the questionnaire; expected value for shareholders' cost of Japanese companies by investors is "8% that is the value to fill 90% of investors satisfaction."

[9]Some investors declare RFR 1%, which is based on recent 10-year government bond. In this case, it is 1% plus 6% equals 7% is CoE of Japanese stock, but satisfaction at 7% is less than half (Yanagi 2015b). Moreover, the Japanese government promises government yield for budget of 1.8% since 2001 considering interest volatility risk and 2% inflation target. As noted, many investors expect more than 10% of CoE from US companies considering RFR difference.

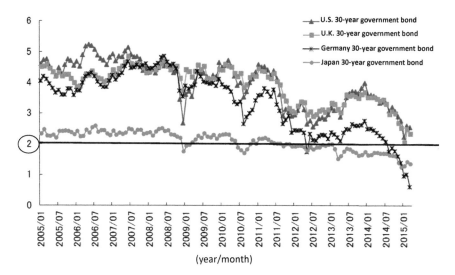

Fig. 4.11 Historical yield migration of 30-year government bond by advanced countries (adopting longest term of government bond as going concern). *Source* Author based on Bloomberg

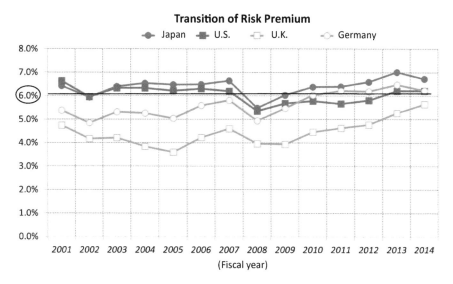

Fig. 4.12 Transition of risk premium by advanced countries (adjusting scale and kinds of business based on U.S.) by implied analysis. *Source* Author based on FACTSET

stock price as a proxy variable of shareholder value, a regression model is acquired where the ROE forecast for the first term ahead is the explained variable and current PBR is the explanatory variable (Easton et al. 2002). By estimating this model, the implied expected growth rate (g = intersection) implied by the market and the

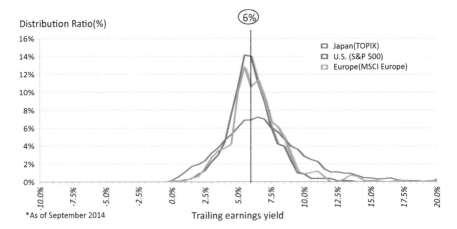

Fig. 4.13 Risk premium 6% of advanced countries implied by reciprocal of PER. *Notes* Stock earnings yield = Inverse of PER = Cost of equity (r = RFR + RP) − Permanent growth rate (g). RFR and g has offset relations each other and r − g is being converged to RP as tendency. *Source* Author based on Bloomberg

implied capital cost (r = intersection + slope) can be estimated simultaneously. US companies' r and g in 1981–1998 were 13.4 and 10.1%, respectively (Easton et al. 2002). The results of the empirical analysis conducted by Professor Ishikawa on Japanese companies are as follows (See Fig. 4.14). With respect to a total of 45,419 companies that end the fiscal year in March and satisfied the prescribed conditions in 1997–2015, using the management's forecast data for net income announced at the annual disclosure of financial results, Easton et al. (2002) carried out a similar analysis. As a result of analyzing all companies by classifying value creating companies that are more than 1 times of PBR (21,477 company years) and value-destroying companies with less than 1 times of PBR (total 23,942 company years), the latest five-year average of r and g is, Value creative enterprises were with r:8.8% and g:6.4%, value destructive companies with r:8.0% and g:0.8%. From such statistically significant empirical analysis, robustness of "shareholders' equity cost 8%" is again secured.[10]

---

[10]The fact that large-scale investor survey results continuously suggest investor's expected return of 8% as shareholders' equity cost, and demonstrative data of ROE and PBR for Japanese companies over the past 10 years is higher than the shareholders' 8%, because regression analysis following Eaton model demonstrates 8% shareholders' equity cost; there is sufficient evidence in the "Ito Review's ROE 8% Guideline." The emotional criticism that 8% is unfounded is due to such ambiguities in the evidence. (Of course, shareholders' capital cost is different for each company, and here refers to the level of Japanese companies overall.)

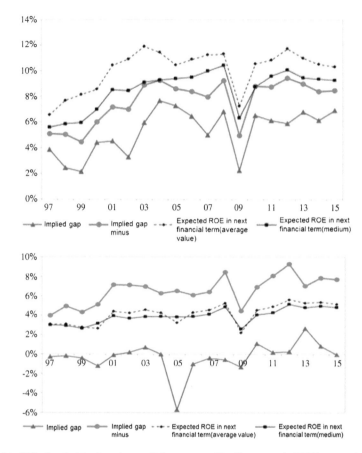

Fig. 4.14 "8% shareholders' equity cost" demonstrated by Easton et al. (2002) regression model. Value creation companies (21,477 company years): Average $r = 8.8\%$, $g = 6.4\%$ for the last five years. *Source* Nishikawa et al. (2016)

4.5.1.2 Relationship Between Equity Spread and Stock Price

Equity Spread (ES) also demonstrates its superiority in terms of stock price performance in actual markets. Empirical analysis of Yanagi et al. (2015) suggest that stock price performance is positively correlated with ES. The portfolio strategy to "long" (buy) a company with a high ES and "short" (sell) a company with a low ES was shown to outperform the benchmark with a statistically significant difference. The hypothesis that "portfolio strategy using ES yields excess return" is demonstrated in this thesis, therefore, as "ROE exceeding capital cost" is the source of value and "since ES is related to corporate value, portfolio strategies using ES generate excess returns."

In this way, ES is related to shareholder value both in the theory of the residual income model (RIM) and in the empirical data for the market, and the global investor places the most emphasis on ES, and ROE, its main component, with "8% (being) the magic number."

The superiority of the correlation with the shareholder value of the residual income model (leading to Equity Spread) has also been proved in several previous studies. Francis et al. (2000) demonstrated that residual income (RIM) is more powerful than free cash flow (FCF) and dividends, using data from US firms obtained from 1989–1993. The coefficient of determination was residual income 0.73, FCF 0.40, and dividend 0.54. This suggests that the residual income model (RIM) outperforms the discounted cash flow model (DCF) and the dividend discount model (DDM). In addition, Stark and Thomas (1998) suggest that RIM can more fully explain stock price than can accounting profits, using UK corporate data from 1990–1994. Furthermore, Fujii and Yamamoto (1999) analyzed the data of the manufacturing industry in Japan from 1983–1998, and proved that residual income is better than FCF at explaining stock price. The coefficient of determination was residual income 0.4–0.8 and FCF 0.2–0.6.

4.5.2 Estimation of Shareholders' Equity Cost by Global Investor Survey

In addition to market data and empirical research as quantitative evidence of 8% as CoE as shown above, it is important for us to grasp investor perception as qualitative evidence. Back to the starting point of "capital cost = expected rate of return by investors," what do global investors consider CoE of Japanese stock?

Here, we can see from multiple investor surveys in consecutive years that "CoE = 8%" is the rate of expected return by global investors, in connection with Japanese stock market in recent years. (Figs. 4.15, 4.16 and 4.17).

This implies robustness (reliability) of global investor surveys and validity of the "Ito Review" (Fig. 4.15).

Thus, viability of Japan's 8% of CoE in average is consistently implied by a series of global investor surveys conducted by the author.

(Addendum of this book introduces the author's latest global investor survey in 2016 and 2017 with 8% being the consensus consistently.)

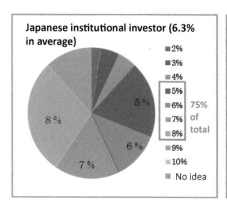
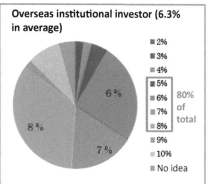

Fig. 4.15   In general, what is Cost of Equity (CoE) for corporate Japan? (The Ito Review excerpt based on the author's survey). *Note* Author conducted institutional investor survey to UBS core clients 200. Respondents are 52 of Japanese investor and 47 of overseas investor (as of April–June 2012). *Source* The Ito Review METI (2014)

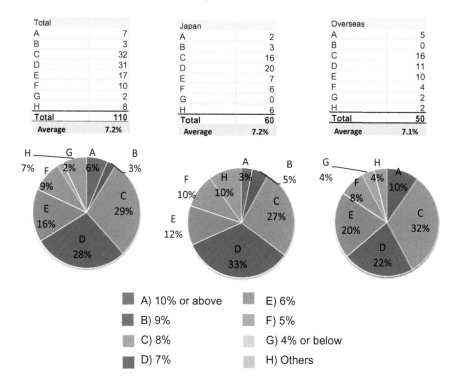

Total		Japan		Overseas	
A	7	A	2	A	5
B	3	B	3	B	0
C	32	C	16	C	16
D	31	D	20	D	11
E	17	E	7	E	10
F	10	F	6	F	4
G	2	G	0	G	2
H	8	H	6	H	2
Total	110	Total	60	Total	50
Average	7.2%	Average	7.2%	Average	7.1%

A) 10% or above   E) 6%

B) 9%   F) 5%

C) 8%   G) 4% or below

D) 7%   H) Others

Fig. 4.16   In general, what is Cost of Equity (CoE) for corporate Japan? (The author's 2014 survey). *Source* Yanagi (2014)

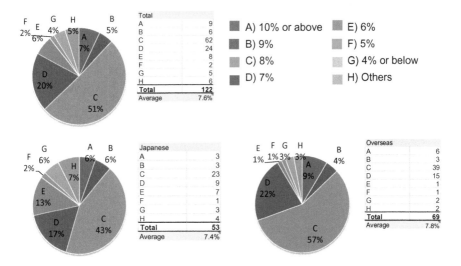

Fig. 4.17 In general, what is Cost of Equity (CoE) for corporate Japan? (The author's 2015 survey). *Source* Yanagi (2015b)

Fundamentally, creating positive Equity Spread, or increasing return that is above CoE is critically important for value creation. That is the major compelling point of the "ROE 8% guideline in the Ito Review" for which the author provided a global investor survey as evidence.

For example, if a Japanese company engages in self-disclosing of Equity Spread by Fiscal Report filed with TSE as an engagement agenda for "purposeful dialogue" and actually discusses with an overseas investor, it would lead to improved valuation for sure as proven by market data, empirical research and survey. My caveat is that Japanese companies should pursue the course in accordance with their corporate philosophy, and by explaining their own management strategies, ROE planning in the long term and how to make ROE sustainably exceed the level of CoE expected by global investors without falling into short-termism with excessive earnings adjustments.

4.6 Quantitative Analysis of Equity Spread and Performance Investment Strategy Adopting Equity Spread Wins

The discussion in the previous section shows Equity Spread and value creation theory as the expectation of global investors. This section verifies the relevance between Equity Spread (ES) and stock price performance in the actual market.

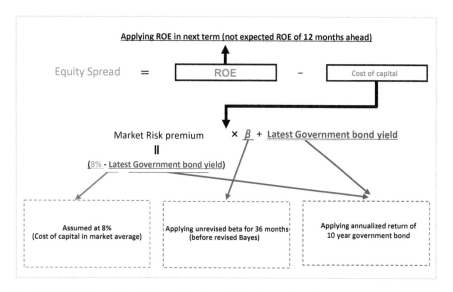

Fig. 4.18 Definition of Equity Spread for the analysis. *Source* Yanagi et al. (2015)

Theoretically, can investment strategies create additional return to the benchmark and even win ROE while using ES?

The author together with quants analysts conducted empirical research as follows:

【Hypothesis for verification】

Portfolio adopting ES creates excessive return, and because of that "ROE above CoE" would be the source of value and hence ES is related to corporate value.

【Sample】

The term of analysis is three years from April 2012 to March 2015 and universe companies for analysis as listed companies on first section of TSE as a range of investment.

【Analysis Method】

Please refer to Fig. 4.18 for the definition of ES and Fig. 4.19 for illustration of the analysis method.

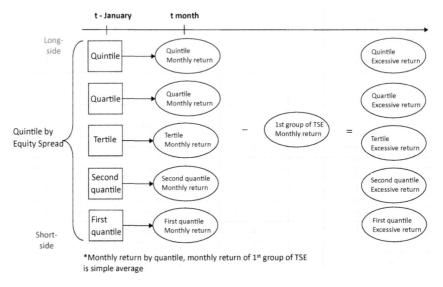

Fig. 4.19 The method of analysis—portfolio divided into five groups. *Source* Yanagi et al. (2015)

To confirm the effect of brand selection for Equity Spread,[11] analysis is conducted by quintiles and deciles[12] portfolio. Define the most attractive value for long side in both quintiles and deciles, and for short side in one quantile. The method of analysis is as follows:

1. At the end of the previous month, we sorted the data universe (listed companies on TSE) into quintiles (deciles) according to the level of ES and observed the current month return (simple average) by constructing a portfolio as these would be of equal quantile.
2. We presented monthly return of each quantile portfolio based on excess TOPIX (Average return of portfolio − TOPIX average return).
3. We rebalanced the portfolio on a monthly basis.
4. The return was spread to confirm the effect of long-short as calculated by quintiles minus first quantile (or percentiles minus first quantile).
5. The periods of observation are past one year (April 2014–March 2015) and past three years (April 2012–March 2015).

---

[11] ROE in the next term for calculating Equity Spread is defined as "anticipated after-tax profits in next term" divided by equity capital." Anticipated after-tax profits in the next term is the data quoted from Toyo Keizai, equity capital is the latest data of financial settlement (priority to consolidated data). CoE is "Market risk premium multiples βvalue + 10-year government bond." Market risk premium is anticipated considering 8% of capital cost on market average and "8% minus 10-year government bond." Moreover, βvalue is calculated based on a monthly sample for 36 months.

[12] Quintiles (deciles) analysis is a method that targets values arranged in increasing order, and a number of total sample divided by 5 (10) and creating a 5(10) group for analysis. The value is called the first quintile, median…in low order.

As in the method described, quintiles (or deciles), first quantile, and average value of spread return are calculated as for the aforementioned two terms. (Calculating average value divided by standard deviation based on perspective of the expected return per risk is important.)

With regard to the test for average value, statistical significance for the average value of spread return is confirmed. (Testing whether the return is significantly deviated from 0 (TOPIX average) or not, because return is excessive base of TOPIX average. The two-sided 5% test is conducted with significance judgment (plus-side and minus-side as 2.5%) and observing p value. [13]).

【Result of analysis】

Table 4.1 shows the result of analysis for ES and ROE performance.

In conclusion, the positive correlation between stock price performance in the past 1 year and 3 years and ES is implied by both quintiles and deciles analysis. The portfolio strategy would effectively work as long (buy) as the company with high ES and as short (sell) as the company with low ES.

On the other hand, though there is no difference in the performance between ROE and ES, improvement of model and accumulating data would be a topic for research. The cost of shareholders' equity is calculated by compendium method, but growth companies with high β value would gradually mature and even a stable company with low β table would change in terms of business operation. If considered on a long-term basis, it would be possible to infer that ES and ROE are similar because cost of shareholders' equity is converged as 8%.

This study is limited by the small sample size but the performance of ES in analysis of past one year exceeded that of ROE [14]; that is,

value of ES is above ROE. A p value below 0.05 in both quintiles and deciles is statistically significant.

Fortunately, as Abenomics has succeeded and the ROE of Japanese companies on average has begun improving since 2013, the value is normalized as allocated positive ES; the result in 1 year appears to be significant compared with the result in the past three years. In other words, it could be said that the market started to factor in ES by responding to the governance reform in this 1 year.

However, "ROE above cost of capital" is the source of value because ES is related to corporate value anyway, thus the hypothesis herein is proved; portfolio strategy using ES could exceed benchmark return and even ROE per se.

Incidentally, confirming the correlation between PBR (Price Book-value ratio) and TSR (Total shareholders return) as for Equity Spread and ROE in each by actual value in 2014 and projection of analysts in TOPIX100, the result is not much different

---

[13] The p value indicates "the probability for a given statistical model that, when the null hypothesis is true, the statistical summary (such as the sample mean difference between two compared groups) would be the same as or of greater magnitude than the actual observed results." In general, the standard value is defined as $p = 0.05$; in other words, the possibility is below 5% that "though it just coincides, it is judged as something which has meaning by mistake."

[14] Stark and Thomas (1998) proves that residual income model (Equity Spread) is superior to the profit on accounting (ROE) in terms of explaining stock price.

Table 4.1 Result of Equity Spread and ROE performance in comparison. *Last 1 year*, 2014.4–2015.3; *Last 3 year*, 2012.4–2015.3

<Quintiles of equity spread >

P1 (First quintile), P5 (Quintiles), Spread return of P5–P1

	P1(Low)				P5(High)				High-low spread return			
	Average value (%)	(p-value)	Standard deviation (%)	Average/SD	Average value (%)	(p-value)	Standard deviation (%)	Average/SD	Average value (%)	(p-value)	Standard deviation (%)	Average/SD
Last 1 year	−3.8	0.20	2.8	−1.36	5.7	0.03	2.3	2.52	9.5	0.05	4.2	2.23
Last 3 year	−1.3	0.77	7.4	−0.17	4.9	0.14	5.6	0.87	6.1	0.38	12.0	0.51

(continued)

Table 4.1 (continued)

<Quintiles of ROE in next term>

P1(First quintile), P5(Quintiles), Spread return of P5–P1

	P1 (Low)				P5 (High)				High-Low Spread Return			
	Average value (%)	(p-value)	Standard deviation (%)	Average/SD	Average value (%)	(p-value)	Standard deviation (%)	Average/SD	Average value (%)	(p-value)	Standard deviation (%)	Average/SD
Last 1 year	−5.1	0.00	1.3	−3.84	3.4	0.28	3.0	1.13	8.5	0.06	4.0	2.12
Last 3 year	−2.5	0.33	4.4	−0.57	4.7	0.12	5.0	0.93	7.2	0.16	8.7	0.83

(continued)

Table 4.1 (continued)

\<Deciles of equity spread\>

P1(First quintile), P5(Deciles), Spread return of P10–P1
(Note) Both sides measured

	P1 (Low)				P10 (High)				High-Low Spread Return			
	Average value (%)	(p-value)	Standard deviation (%)	Average/SD	Average value (%)	(p-value)	Standard deviation (%)	Average/SD	Average value (%)	(p-value)	Standard deviation (%)	Average/SD
Last 1 year	−5.9	0.13	3.6	−0.87	5.1	0.17	3.5	1.46	11.0	0.02	4.0	2.73
Last 3 year	−2.3	0.71	10.7	−0.19	7.8	0.07	7.4	1.06	10.2	0.26	15.3	0.66

(continued)

Table 4.1 (continued)

<Deciles of ROE in next term>

P1(First quintile), P5(Deciles), Spread return of P10–P1

	P1(Low)				P10(High)				High-low spread return			
	Average value (%)	(p-value)	Standard deviation (%)	Average/SD	Average value (%)	(p-value)	Standard deviation (%)	Average/SD	Average value (%)	(p-value)	Standard deviation (%)	Average/SD
Last 1 year	−5.3	0.05	2.4	−0.10	3.3	0.51	4.9	0.68	8.6	0.15	5.5	1.56
Last 3 year	−2.3	0.58	6.9	−0.21	8.3	0.06	7.3	1.13	10.6	0.14	12.1	0.87

Source Yanagi et al. (2015)

from the earlier analysis; the result that ES is superior to ROE in terms of correlation with shareholders' value is anyway confirmed (Table 4.2).

4.7 Perspective of the Company and Long-Term Investor Could Be Synchronized: Equity Spread and Non-financial Capital Are Connected Through MVA

Based on the evidence introduced in this chapter, the concept of Equity Spread (ES) should be well disseminated to corporate management to assertively engage with it, which leads to improvement of corporate value. Investors also should emphasize the relevance of ES and performance.

Having said that, it should be noted that the ES discussed here is not in short term and contracted equilibrium, but on a long-term basis and sustainable KPI for value creation, which is relevant to nonfinancial capital normally focused on by Japanese companies. Considering capital efficiency and sustainability, Yanagi (2009) defined the value relevance model between financial capital and nonfinancial capital as follows: Market Value Added (MVA) which is the portion of PBR above one time = "Organization's Value," "Customer Value," "ESG (Environment, Social, Governance)," "CSR (Company's Social Responsibility) Value."

Moreover, as a case study of integrated report as a tool for engagement, Yanagi (2015a) demonstrated the PBR model, which is a combined IIRC (International Integrated Reporting Council) framework and the model by Yanagi (2009) in FY 2014 annual report of Eisai.

Eisai's PBR model describes the value relevance of six capitals by IIRC by connecting financial capital with nonfinancial capital; "Shareholders' value = Market Capitalization in long term = Shareholders' Equity Book Value (BV) which is 'financial capital,'" +MVA (Market Value Added) which is connected with "Intellectual capital," "Human capital," "Manufacturing Capital," "Social and Relationship capital," "Natural capital."

According to Ohlson (1995), MVA is converged to the present value total of Equity Spread.

Value creation by ES, therefore, does not contradict with the value of nonfinancial capital through MVA creation in the long term.

Figure 4.20 describes mutual complement among three models: Eisai's PBR model, which states that nonfinancial capital is connected with MVA (Yanagi 2015a); intrinsic value model (Yanagi 2009); and Ohlson model that implies the relevance between MVA and Equity Spread (Ohlson 1995). These are related to each other through creating MVA.

With respect to the definition of "Capital efficiency," in a broad sense, productivity of nonfinancial capital, and not just financial capital (ROE), should be included as well.

Table 4.2 Correlation among Equity Spread, PBR of ROE and TSR

Correlation coefficient			Equity spread				ROE			
			Result of 2014	Forecast of 2015	Forecast of 2016	Forecast of 2017	Result of 2014	Forecast of 2015	Forecast of 2016	Forecast of 2017
PBR	Stock price	Value of BPS								
	End of 2014	Latest actual value of financial result	0.503	0.661	0.715	0.737	0.491	0.649	0.705	0.729
		Latest analyst expectation	0.453	0.588	0.668	0.699	0.434	0.569	0.649	0.682
	End of January	Latest actual value of financial result	0.482	0.636	0.698	0.722	0.461	0.615	0.677	0.702
		Latest analyst expectation	0.431	0.562	0.649	0.682	0.404	0.535	0.619	0.653
2014 Total return			0.146	0.289	0.426	0.432	0.089	0.23	0.355	0.357

Note All value is correlation coefficient
Source Author based on Bloomberg

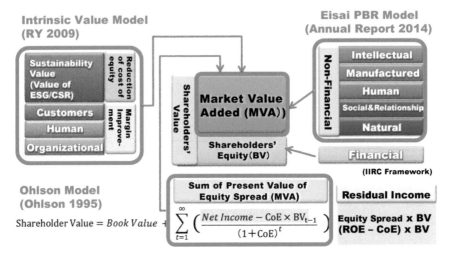

Fig. 4.20 Synchronization of Equity Spread and non-financial value through MVA. *Source* Yanagi (2015b)

The Ito Review also states, "Japan must effectively leverage the resources it has such as 'financial capital' raised both domestically and overseas; 'human capital' supporting management and operations;' 'intellectual capital' which is the source of innovation; 'social/relationship capital' stemming from supply chains and social norms; and 'natural capital' such as the environment. In other words, increasing capital efficiency in the broadest sense is crucial from the perspective of Japan's survival."

With respect to this integration of non-financial capital and Equity Spread, Chap. 5 will further elaborate on the details thereof.

References

AFP. (2011). *Current trends in estimating and applying the cost of capital—Report of survey results.*
Easton, P., Taylor, G., Shroff, P., & Sougiannis, T. (2002). Using forecasts of earnings to simultaneously estimate growth and the rate of return on equity investment. *Journal of Accounting Research, 40*(3), 657–676.
Fernandez, P., & Campo, J. (2010). Market risk premium used in 2010 by analysts and companies: A survey with 2,400 Answers. *SSRN*.
Francis, et al. (2000). Comparing the accuracy and explainability of dividend, free cash flow, and abnormal earnings equity value estimates. *Journal Accounting Research, 38,* 45–70.
Fujii, H., & Yamamoto, T. (1999). Comparative study for accounting ability for stock price by accounting information and cash flow information-attempt to apply and improve ohlson model. *Kaikei, 156*(2), 14–29.
Ide, S. (2015). Potential of ROE investing in new approach. *NLI Research Institute Report.* April 17, 2015.

IMA. (1997). Measuring and managing shareholder value creation. *Statements of Management Accounting* 1997.

Japan Investor Relations Association (JIRA). (2014). *Survey results of annual shareholder's meeting and investor relations.*

Life Insurance Association of Japan. (2015). *Survey results on approaches toward enhancing equity values FY2014.* Life Insurance Association of Japan.

Ministry of Economy, Trade and Industry. (2014). *Ito Review of competitiveness and incentives for sustainable growth—Building favorable relationships between companies and investors-*Final report.

Nishikawa, I., et al. (2016). *Financial accounting literacy for improving corporate value.* Nikkei Newspaper Publish Institute.

Ohlson, J. (1995). Earnings, book values, and dividends in equity valuation. *Contemporary Accounting Research, 11,* 661–687.

Ohlson, J. (2001). Earnings, book values, and dividends in equity valuation: An empirical perspective. *Contemporary Accounting Research, 18*(1), 107–120.

Stark, A. W., & Thomas, H. M. (1998). On the empirical relationship between market value residual income in the UK. *Management Accounting Research, 9,* 445–460.

Stewart, S. (1991). *The quest for value.* Stern Stewart & Co.

Tokyo Stock Exchange. (2012). Corporate Value Improvement Award.

Yanagi, R. (2009). *Financial strategies for maximizing corporate value.* Doyukan.

Yanagi, R. (2010). *Improving manual for enhancing corporate value on managerial accounting.* Chuokeizai-Sha.

Yanagi, R. (2013). Suggestion for disclosing Equity Spread and engagement. *Kigyo kaikei, 65*(1), 86–93.

Yanagi, R. (2014). Study for Japanese-version Stewardship code and capital efficiency. *Investor Relations, 2014*(8), 48–62.

Yanagi, R. (2015a). *The ROE revolution and financial strategy.* Chuokeizai-Sha.

Yanagi, R. (2015b). Corporate governance code and "Engagement with shareholders"—Implications of global investor survey and study for equity spread. *SAAJ Journal* (9).

Yanagi, R., Meno, H., & Yoshino, T. (2015). Study for equity spread and value creation. *Gekkan Shihon Shijyo, 2015*(7), 24–33.

Chapter 5
Value Creative Investment Criteria

Abstract In a bid to unlock corporate value in Japan, in this book, the author proposed "Three Pillars of Financial Strategies" such as Equity Spread and Value Creation, Value-Creative Investment Criteria, Optimal Dividend Policy based on Optimal
Capital Structure. If a company is to grow in the future on a sustained basis, it has
to invest in its businesses, including but not limited to R&D, human capital, factory
equipment, infrastructure for organic growth or acquire other companies, business
units, products, intangibles such as patents, in-process R&D and marketing rights for
external growth. With that said, how can a company ensure value creation and fulfill
the duty of accountability and stewardship to its stakeholders, especially shareholders? This chapter suggests, as the second financial strategy, that firms must adopt
risk-adjusted hurdle rates for individual projects to secure value-enhancing Equity
Spread (ES), which is the investment return over capital cost. A yield exceeding the
cost of capital creates corporate value in consideration of capital expenditures, M&A,
and even cross-shareholding. To foster dialogue with investors, corporate managers
must explain their process of value creation and set investment criteria considering
the cost of capital. The capital expenditures budget underwrites corporate growth,
and budgeting requires criteria for estimating corporate value creation versus cost
of capital. Yoshida et al. (2009) show that net present value (NPV) and internal rate
of return (IRR) are the criteria for comparison in the U.S., UK, Germany, and the
Netherlands, but 83% of Japanese firms adopt a simple payback period (SPP) as their
criterion. That is, Japanese companies tend to make investments without considering
the cost of capital due to the lack of consciousness of opportunity cost borne by
shareholders. Drawing from the author's experience as a CFO and a certified managerial accountant (USCMA), this chapter proposes adopting risk-adjusted hurdle
rates (for example 200 kinds of hurdle rates are illustrated) to determine NPV and
IRR in a bid to improve capital efficiency and meet fiduciary duty, the same goal
Abe's Corporate Governance Code seeks to achieve.

Keywords Value-creative investment criteria · Risk-adjusted hurdle rates
NPV · IRR · SPP · Capital cost · M&A · PI

5.1 Investment Criteria for Capital Expenditure of Japanese Companies: Too Obsessed with Simple Payback Period (SPP) Without Considering Capital Cost

"Certainly, any capital expenditure or strategic investment carries some risk, but one must consider whether the investment has a reasonable potential to increase returns above the cost of capital. In cases when management has not had an adequate opportunity to discover whether an investment will generate returns that exceed capital costs, the capital must be returned to the shareholders, in order for them to reinvest it elsewhere for value creation.

Those cross-shareholdings in Japan that aim at merely maintaining a relationship or offsetting voting without securing an economic return tend to collapse corporate value.

Though M&A (Mergers and Acquisitions) is conducted by the company as it senses that it is reaching the limits of its organic growth possibilities, such expansion via M&A especially in cross-border business can often become too expensive (especially if managers end up mindlessly following the advice of overly aggressive investment banks). Hence many Japanese companies tend to overpay. If the company has sufficient budget to make such investments, it must endeavor to merge itself into its Japanese peers in order to ease the excessively competitive environment. It is rather doubtful that any "synergy effect" will exist as they tout or that there will be something that a corporation insists upon having, even though a certain controlling premium to be paid is justifiable."

This comment is a quotation of a prominent investor in UK from a 2012 global investor survey (Yanagi 2014).

The overseas investor is concerned with these things destroying corporate value; cross-shareholdings, crossholding of stocks for self-protection by distorting voting results of Annual General Meeting of shareholders (AGM), and M&A or takeover of the investee or product at overly-high prices set by Japanese companies. Moreover, they require a return above capital cost—more than anything for investments pertaining to the budgets destined for capital expenditure by Japanese companies.

Such criteria would match the importance of the Equity Spread (ES). The consciousness of "capital cost" by management is necessary.

For improvement of corporate value, assertive investing for the future is also necessary. In other words, the budget for capital expenditure is the key to improve corporate value on corporate management accounting.

When management resources are limited, funding new investment will be too, and therefore investment criteria should be set with certain standards according to management priority for the future.

Companies have to return capital to shareholders (in the form of dividend or share buyback) in case of any excess capital they hold apart from funding necessary investment projects (i.e., a residual theory of dividend policy). In addition, if an effective project is developed in the term that is considered to be outside the budget, flexibility will be needed to avoid postponing the project (Beyond budgeting management).

In any case, the budget for capital expenditure is needed for corporate development, and any investment criteria that enhances corporate value is important. To conduct the project, it is inevitable to increase corporate value by making sure that any subsequent profit exceeds the cost of capital.

Let us think about investment criteria and the approach an investor must take.

In general, the investment project will have guidelines, for example, "it will seek black figure within three years, cleaning up any accumulated deficit within 5 years, recouping capital within 10 years (payback period)." In short, being in the black in financial accounting and calculating the payback period rendered the concept of capital cost nearly unconscious.

However, at present, earning a profit above the cost of capital is essential for value-creation management.

In the case of average Japanese companies, some investment projects are adopted as long as the black figure is indicated on an accounting statement or payback period is reasonable even if the internal rate of return (IRR) is below the minimum capital cost of 8% or even if net present value is negative. Or even if they use the NPV method, they just stick to the unified discount rate such as 8% irrespective of the risks inherent in respective projects.

The budget for capital expenditure in corporate value improvement sets the required criteria based on NPV (net present value),[1] IRR (internal rate of return)[2] and is linked to the shareholder value creation theory. However, under the investment criteria obsessed with nominal accounting or payback period in Japan arising out of "bank-dominant governance" history described in Chap. 1, the diffusion rate of NPV and IRR is not so high without considering capital cost or opportunity cost. Instead, Japanese companies usually utilize SPP (simple payback period)[3] as was previously mentioned (Table 5.1).

According to a questionnaire administered by the Life Insurance Association of Japan (2015), a gap exists between Japanese companies and Japanese investors (Fig. 5.1). While Japanese investors hope to use ROI as their criteria, a Japanese corporation focuses on SPP or sales amount and profits. Overseas investors generally focus on NPV and IRR since these are the global standards (Fig. 5.1).

---

[1] NPV(Net Present Value) is one of the criteria for investing, obtained by discounting future cash flow to the present value. It is profit measurement derived from the present values of cash inflows minus the present values (PV) of cash outflows (including initial investments). In addition, NPV can be calculated as the difference between the sums of discounted cash inflows and cash outflows. The result would be the criteria for investing.

[2] IRR (Internal rate of return) shows the discounting ratio as NPV = 0. If IRR exceeds the capital cost, invest in the project, and if IRR is below the capital cost, reject the project.

[3] SPP (Simple payback period) is one of the investment criteria; research how long the term of collecting investing amount takes. If the term is shorter than guideline, investment would be made, and if longer, it would be rejected. The SPP has an advantage of easy calculation and is understandable, but its disadvantage is that it cannot be considered as a time value of the amount and it is vague as to how the "guideline" should be set. For that reason, the limit is pointed out.

Table 5.1 International comparison of Investment criteria

	NPV (%)	IRR (%)	SPP (%)
Japan	37	22	83
U.S.	85	77	53
U.K.	47	53	69
Germany	48	42	50
Netherlands	70	56	65

NPV—Net Present Value, IRR—Internal Rate of Return, SPP—Simple Payback Period.
Sources Author, 「Accounting」 September, November 2009; Yoshida et al.
(2009), 「Accounting」 May 2010

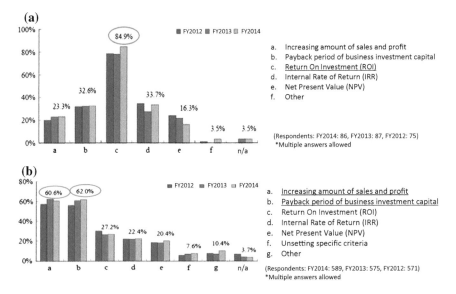

Fig. 5.1 The gap between Japanese companies and investors regarding investment criteria. **a** Index that is appropriate as investment criteria of companies (Investors), **b** Focused
index as investment criteria (Companies). *Source* The Life Insurance Association of Japan (2015)

5.2 What Investment Criteria Are Required by Investors? It Is Mandatory to Be Conscious of the Cost of Capital

Overseas investors consider "the return above the capital cost" (like an Equity Spread)
as a premise of value creation, not the profit in nominal accounting. Therefore, NPV
and IRR are important as investment criteria including capital cost, not SPP.

The principles of investment criteria for corporate value evaluation and improvement are described below.

【Guiding principles on investment criteria on a firm's budget for capital expenditure】 .

1. Positive NPV is required.
2. IRR must be above capital cost.
3. NPV takes precedence over IRR.
4. Comparisons using PI (Profitability Index) are effective in some projects.
5. A real option is inserted if there is room to stop or change ("go or no-go" decision making).

NPV (Net Present Value) $= \Sigma \, (FCF_n)/(1+\text{discount rate})^n$ − present value of investment amount (FCF: Free Cash Flow, n = fiscal year).

IRR (Internal Rate of Return) = Discount rate to make NPV = 0.

PI (Profitability Index) = present value for the project cash flow ÷ present value for invested capital.

A more concrete example is given in Table 5.2, which is an image of investment criteria used for a budget for its capital expenditure for a project by IRC Corporation, a Japanese venture company that strives to be listed on the market.

IRC corporation, the unlisted venture company as an insurance consultancy firm (located in Tokyo), is working on management reform and considering doing a stock offering; even though unlisted on "Main Street," there are some companies that work to maximize shareholders' value as their mission. They share the investment criteria for value creation in all departments of the company, just like in the example given of IRC corporation.

Regardless of whether they are listed or unlisted, on Wall Street or Main Street, even such venture companies will have similarities in both missions and financial strategies striving to maximize their value.

Naoaki Aihara, CFO of the IRC corporation, set the discount rate for the project at 20%, according to the risk of the system project and by comparing peer-companies, which is based on his MBA experience in the U.S.

Hence, he applied NPV on management accounting as his major standards for determining criteria for investment acceptance, rather than the accounting profit. In this case study, IRC Corporation has secured a positive NPV calculated even without the terminal value of a going concern. Additionally, the IRR is 34.2%, which is far above the capital cost (20%) and the project's profitability is high.

SPP is calculated as 3.25 years as a reference, a comparatively short timeframe. Again, though the company is unlisted, it is watched by investment banks, commercial banks, consultants that are linked to outside investors who are potentially participating in future IPOs. Thus, the decision about value creation is made under the budget for capital expenditure that is applied through shareholders' value accounting such as NPV and IRR with the risk-adjusted hurdle rate.

Table 5.2 Example of investment criteria standards for value creation Capital expenditure of IRC corporation Business valuation Project X

	0 year	1st year	2nd year	3rd year	4th year	5th year	Perpetual value	Notes
1. Sales		18	126	252	414	594		
2. Cost		0	0	0	0	0		
3. Gross profit		18	126	252	414	594		
4. SG & A		44.1	100.2	112.2	124.2	136.2		
1. Labor cost		12	36	48	60	72		
2. PR cost		0	0	0	0	0		
3. Depreciation		18.6	37.2	37.2	37.2	37.2		
4. Running cost 584thusand/month		3.5	7	7	7	7		
5. Others		10	20	20	20	20		
5. Profit for sales		Δ26.1	25.8	139.8	289.8	457.8		
6. Current profit		Δ26.1	25.8	139.8	289.8	457.8		
7. Income before taxes		Δ26.1	25.8	139.8	289.8	457.8		
8. Taxes (effective tax rate)		0	10.5	56.9	117.9	186.3		=7 Income before taxes × Effective tax rate
9. NOPAT (Net Operating Profit After Tax)		Δ26.1	15.3	82.9	171.8	271.5		=5 sales profit -8 taxes

(continued)

Table 5.2 (continued)

	0 year	1st year	2nd year	3rd year	4th year	5th year	Perpetual value	Notes
10. Amount of investment	△186.0	0	0	0	0	0		Cost for developing system, cost and pre-investing for opening new store
11. Working Capital (WC)		6	15	27	42	57		Setting rough estimated value as X% of sales or in the case of impossible to estimate, 0 is usable
12. Increasing/decreasing WC		△6.0	△9.0	△12.0	△15.0	△15.0		

(continued)

Table 5.2 (continued)

	0 year	1st year	2nd year	3rd year	4th year	5th year	Perpetual value	Notes
13. FCF (Free Cash Flow)	△186.0	△13.5	43.5	108.1	194	293.7	14,868.40	
14. FCF cumulative amount	△186.0	△199.5	△156.0	△47.9	146.1	439.8		
15. Present value of each FCF	△186.0	△11.3	30.2	62.6	93.6	118	590.1	= 13 FCF ÷ (1 + discounting rate)^{year}
Rate of sales		−145.00%	20.50%	55.50%	70%	77.1%		= 5 Sales profit ÷ 1 Sales
Rate of current earnings		−145.00%	20.50%	55.50%	70%	77.1%		= 6 Current profit ÷ 1 Sales

(continued)

Table 5.2 (continued)

Index for valuation		Pre-condition		
NPV	1071 M yen	Effective tax rate	40.70%	=Effective tax rate in previous fiscal term only
NPV including perpetual value	697.2 M yen	Discounting rate	20.00%	=WACC (Weighted Average Cost of Capital)[a] =Hurdle rate[b]
IRR	34.2%	Perpetual growth rate	0.00%	=Effective tax rate in previous fiscal term only
Payback	3.25 year	←Required calculation by hand (the year that accumulated total is 0)		

[a]WACC: Weighted Average Cost of Capital including Cost of debt and Cost of Equity
[b]Hurdle rate: Required rate of return as minimum. *Source* IRC corporation

5.3   Utilizing Two Hundred Kinds of Hurdle Rates: Importance of the Risk Adjusted Hurdle Rate

NPV and IRR are the gold standards of investments in budget for capital expenditure. Cash flow estimation is made by business development departments of the company operation by frontline professionals, and the head office department of management accounting or finance verifies their work. However, the most critical part of the valuation is setting the discount rate appropriately, followed by implementing solid financial theory by the person in charge of management accounting. If the discount rate is changed even slightly, it will affect the judgment for making a decision to invest.

Nowadays, more and more companies are adopting NPV and IRR as investment criteria that is based on capital cost, but these are applied with across-the-board rates such as 5, 8 or 10%.

However, when reflecting on the actual situation, the risk of any individual project is always different.

Although this methodology of applying different hurdle rates depending on the project may sometimes cause criticism, the position of the author is to seek the possibility that the discount rate applied to investment criteria (hurdle rate) not be 8% across-the-board rate but rather an individual, risk-adjusted hurdle rate to further ensure value creation.

Obeying the "principle of conservatism" for investment projects, setting standards by adjusting the hurdle rate depending on the risk inherent in the project at issue, the country of investment, whether the target investment is located in the headquarters or a subsidiary, whether it is a listed or unlisted company could be used to support the presentation to shareholders and investors, noting that investment entails high risk.

Applying the discount rate after risk-adjustment suited to the project (risk-adjusted hurdle rate) would contribute to the improvement of corporate value.

At the author's suggestion, the image map of investment criteria considering the risk return by project is found below. It is based on NPV and IRR, but hundreds of hurdle rates could be set depending on the riskiness of each project.

Actually, the author, as CFO of a major Japanese pharmaceutical company (Eisai Co., Ltd.) listed on Tokyo Stock Exchange (TSE) with a market capitalization of more than 15 billion US dollars (as of the end of 2017), has been practicing this methodology in connection with valuation of investment cases raised within the company and gaining investor confidence ipso facto since his inauguration as CFO.

【Value-Creative Investment Criteria (VCIC)】 .

- Adapting to the investment criteria for creating shareholders' value
- Adopting investments with a positive NPV
- Adopting investments where the IRR is above the cost of capital
- NPV is a priority (when NPV conflicts with IRR)
- Apply PI (Profitability Index) when comparing many projects at once

- Apply real options if there is a choice ("go or not go" decision making leeway)
- Adopt a project-based hurdle rate considering the riskiness of the project at issue
- Respect the fact that shareholders and investors have choices (opportunity cost)
- Consider the opportunity cost of capital for management accounting which is not based on the black-ink bottom line of financial accounting
- Across-the-board unified hurdle rates are not enough if the company is aware of the true NPV
- Adjust the β (beta vale reflecting volatility) according to the project
- Change the risk-free rate according to the venue of the project (investee country)
- Risk premium is stable in principle (for example 6% as discussed in Chap. 4)
- Consider the risk premium of small companies (i.e., unlisted companies) due to liquidity

【Set the investment criteria concretely】 .

<Mandatory criteria>
NPV must be positive

- Accumulated DCF (discounting cash flow) less the present value of total investment amount must be greater than 0
  <Collateral criteria>

1. IRR > Hurdle rate +2% (the minimum earnings spread expected by investors in general)
2. Payback period under 5 years (in principle) = reference information (where applicable and possible).

   *Determine the advisability of the project considering both criteria completely; clearly stating the required criteria as an absolute condition, but judge that the specific investment may achieve overall corporate objectives using collateral criteria.

Consideration

- Is estimation of appropriate cash flow (profit) possible?
- Is setting the proper hurdle rate possible?

  - The management accounting or finance department will strictly check the suggested financial forecast (sales, expenses, profits) by the business department in charge for proper cash flow estimation in the strategic plan (This is the very fundamentals of the core business).
  - Premise of internal risk (β value as a proxy of the volatility of the project) of business should be individually specifically defined.
    Other components should be done by looking at the risk-free rate (the average value of yields on government bonds of each investee country on a long-term basis), then adding a risk premium of for example 6% (based on the analysis of the book as described in Chap. 4).

Most importantly, though, β (beta value as volatility risk) is fundamentally different for each individual investment project. However, it is challenging and bothersome in an actual business environment, enhances arbitrariness, leads to decreases in convenience. Therefore, the β value is set according to the three categories model as a simplified solution noted below:

(practical examples);

  *Level 3 High-risk profile category

Speculative project, venture project, new project.
(In case of pharmaceutical company, "R&D Phase 1 project" which is small scale clinical study mainly for safety or "R&D Phase 2 project" which is small scale clinical study mainly for efficacy)
Using β value of 2.0 (market average of high risk brands).

  *Level 2 Middle-risk profile category

Moderate risk, new project.
(In case of pharmaceutical company, "R&D Phase 3 project" or "project filed with regulatory agencies which is large scale clinical study mainly for efficacy as well as safety before regulatory approval)
Using β value 1.5 (market average of middle risk brands).

  *Level 1 Low-risk profile category

Expanding products already on sale, equivalent investment, building subsidiary
(In case of pharmaceutical company, "Approved project" or "Already marketed project)
Using β value of 1.0 (the individual hurdle rate of a listed company in the industry).

- Set individual β values based on average market rates that are found according to the categories with similar risk to the aforementioned three categories model.
- In the case of judging individual investment on subsidiary, or acquiring private company, for example adding a 30% premium due to insufficient liquidity, transparency, and disclosure level to the normal risk premium derived from each β value of the three categories.
- Do not consider liability or debt cost in the ordinal judging and assume as if 100% funded by equity money as a conservatism. However, in the case of special investing that is required to borrow under certain conditions or strictly tied to project financing by the bank, setting the WACC (Weighted Average Cost of Capital) is considered incorporating the interest rate at that time; always including the effect of tax savings.
- As for the risk free rate, the term of investment project is estimated to be within ten years and using the 10-year government bond yield that is different from the situation calculated by shareholders' capital costs for the whole corporation. Note that the exchange rate risk is not considered because it is hypothetical, and also offset by interest rate differentials in reliance on interest parity theory.

The image of a hurdle rate used for investment criteria for a global investment project is showed in Table 5.3, based on the notion of the Value-Creative Investment Criteria (VCIC) asserted in this Chapter.

As a CFO, I have been promoting this idea and using 200 kinds of hurdle rates in day-to-day businesses involving all the regional CFOs and finance professionals of the Eisai Group.

For example, the hurdle rate when a subsidiary builds the plan in Japan is 8.9% (Category 1, Japan, Subsidiary). In the case of a subsidiary for the release of new products in the U.S.A., the hurdle rate on NPV calculation is 13.5% (Category 2, USA, Subsidiary). When a headquarters purchases a venture company listed in the U.K., the discount rate for the DCF calculation is 15.0% (Category 3, UK, Public). Moreover, if a company purchases an unlisted venture company in China through a subsidiary, the hurdle rate is 17.3% (Category 3, China, Private). Likewise, when acquiring an unlisted venture company in India, threshold is 21.6% (Category 3, India, Private).

These are the simplified rates indicated for Japanese companies, verified and practiced by the author's experience as a CFO or USCMA (certified management accountant) and once endorsed and reconfirmed by global investors when the author worked as Executive Director of UBS. Many foreign investors highly support it as "conservatively secure shareholders' value creation" or "something that should be applied to M&A."

Surely it could be more refined and meticulous, but using an excessively complicated model precludes practical business and it would thus be difficult to apply or explain to the relevant department or business unit within a Japanese company; usefulness and accuracy are the relevant tradeoffs. (In general, few corporate finance textbooks address how to handle hurdle rates in concrete terms for actual NPV calculation or IRR valuation; many textbooks instead say the hurdle rate is fixed as a given figure (for example, unified 10% for all cases) to explain NPV and IRR; thus, it might even confuse a business professional. This book makes a simple but sophisticated solution, and provides concrete examples to readers.)

A fair caveat is that such a simplified standard for actual business and capital budgeting could be further improved depending upon each company's situation with appropriate modifications. Moreover, explaining investment policy in detail would play an important role in acquiring shareholder and investor confidence due to the fact that it shows the attitude of financial strategies focused on creating shareholders' value. That should be an engagement agenda between Japanese companies and global investors given the fact that the "overpay" in M&A by Japanese entities derived from lack of financial literacy sometimes poses an issue which could lead to value destruction or in severe cases to impairment losses.

Table 5.3 List of 200 kinds of discount rates by risk (example): as of June 30, 2013

Region	Country	RFR (%)[a]	Risk premium (%)	Category I			Category II			Category III		
				Beta	CoE (%)	Private (%)	Beta	CoE (%)	Private (%)	Beta	CoE (%)	Private (%)
Japan	Japan	*1.11*	6.0	1.0	7.1	8.9	1.5	10.1	11.9	2.0	13.1	14.9
Americas	USA	*2.75*	6.0	1.0	8.7	10.5	1.5	11.7	13.5	2.0	14.7	16.5
	Canada	*2.77*	6.0	1.0	8.8	10.6	1.5	11.8	13.6	2.0	14.8	16.6
	Mexico	*4.31*	6.0	1.0	10.3	12.1	1.5	13.3	15.1	2.0	16.3	18.1
	Brazil	*4.57*	6.0	1.0	10.6	12.4	1.5	13.6	15.4	2.0	16.6	18.4
EMEA	UK	*3.03*	6.0	1.0	9.0	10.8	1.5	12.0	13.8	2.0	15.0	16.8
	Germany	*2.59*	6.0	1.0	8.6	10.4	1.5	11.6	13.4	2.0	14.6	16.4
	France	*3.14*	6.0	1.0	9.1	10.9	1.5	12.1	13.9	2.0	15.1	16.9
	Netherlands	*2.92*	6.0	1.0	8.9	10.7	1.5	11.9	13.7	2.0	14.9	16.7
	Spain	*4.82*	6.0	1.0	10.8	12.6	1.5	13.8	15.6	2.0	16.8	18.6
	Italy	*4.72*	6.0	1.0	10.7	12.5	1.5	13.7	15.5	2.0	16.7	18.5
	Switzerland	*1.49*	6.0	1.0	7.5	9.3	1.5	10.5	12.3	2.0	13.5	15.3
	Sweden	*2.60*	6.0	1.0	8.6	10.4	1.5	11.6	13.4	2.0	14.6	16.4
	Portuguese	*6.89*	6.0	1.0	12.9	14.7	1.5	15.9	17.7	2.0	18.9	20.7
	Belgium	*3.57*	6.0	1.0	9.6	11.4	1.5	12.6	14.4	2.0	15.6	17.4
	Austria	*3.16*	6.0	1.0	9.2	11.0	1.5	12.2	14.0	2.0	15.2	17.0
	Australia	*4.61*	6.0	1.0	10.6	12.4	1.5	13.6	15.4	2.0	16.6	18.4
Asia	Singapore	*2.10*	6.0	1.0	8.1	9.9	1.5	11.1	12.9	2.0	14.1	15.9
	China	*3.52*	6.0	1.0	9.5	11.3	1.5	12.5	14.3	2.0	15.5	17.3
	Indonesia	*8.42*	6.0	1.0	14.4	16.2	1.5	17.4	19.2	2.0	20.4	22.2
	Malaysia	*3.86*	6.0	1.0	9.9	11.7	1.5	12.9	14.7	2.0	15.9	17.7
	Thailand	*3.65*	6.0	1.0	9.7	11.5	1.5	12.7	14.5	2.0	15.7	17.5
	Taiwan	*1.46*	6.0	1.0	7.5	9.3	1.5	10.5	12.3	2.0	13.5	15.3
	Korea	*4.38*	6.0	1.0	10.4	12.2	1.5	13.4	15.2	2.0	16.4	18.2
	Philipine	*5.39*	6.0	1.0	11.4	13.2	1.5	14.4	16.2	2.0	17.4	19.2
	India	*7.83*	6.0	1.0	13.8	15.6	1.5	16.8	18.6	2.0	19.8	21.6

[a]Risk free rate is average value of 10-year government bond by each country in past 5 years

5.4 Investment Criteria for Cross-Shareholdings that Correspond to Investor Criticism

Political investment among vested interests in Japan, in other words cross-shareholdings for the sake of entrenchment of incumbent management is also "investing" in securities, which explains investor complaints that the investment criteria should be deeply rooted in accountability.

Corporate Governance Code (CGC) stated as below;

Principle 1.4 Cross-Shareholdings

When companies hold shares of other listed companies as cross-shareholdings4, they should disclose their policy with respect to doing so. In addition, the Board should examine the mid- to long-term economic rationale and future outlook of major cross-shareholdings on an annual basis, taking into consideration both associated risks and returns. The annual examination should result in the Board's detailed explanation of the objective and rationale behind cross-shareholdings.

Companies should establish and disclose standards with respect to the voting rights as to their cross-shareholdings.

5.4.1 Griping of Foreign Investor: Cross-Shareholdings Is "the Root of All Evil"

Many government leaders or investors with high perceptions declare their opinions that the "fundamental problem is cross-shareholdings" and many investors are dissatisfied or have anxiety regarding them. When asking major asset management funds from the U.S. or the U.K. the reason why, they answer:

Cross-shareholdings, such an unfair policy, limits the right of vote by minority shareholders in fact.

Cross-shareholdings prevent us from voting on constructive shareholders' suggestions and make it possible to adopt antitakeover measures that are just for entrenchment of management.

Though cross-shareholdings on the surface accounts for only 10 to 20%, if one-side shareholdings or triangle-shareholdings are included, the rate of stable shareholders is estimated at approximately 30% which represents concerns about distorting the voting rights of general investors.

As Fig. 5.2 shows, many investors indicate cross-shareholdings worsen both governance and corporate value (Yanagi 2010).

Fig. 5.2 Does cross-sharing
of Japanese companies
aggravate corporate
governance and corporate
value? *Source* Yanagi (2010)

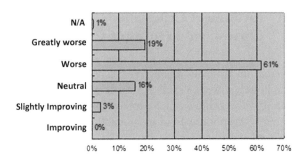

The result of a global investor survey[4] (targeted institutional investor from approximately 200 companies) was published in Yanagi (2010), as reported in Fig. 5.2. One result indicates that 80% of institutional global investors are concerned that cross-shareholdings in Japanese companies make governance and corporate value worse.

During the 2007–2008 period in Japan, cross-shareholdings were temporally revived again after the symbolic incident called the Bulldog case in 2007 whereby the U.S. activist fund Steel Partners tried a hostile takeover bid against Bulldog sauce manufacturer, which is a term that describes a hostile conflict between activist-shareholders and Japanese companies, along with the financial crisis that followed. In the 1980s the rate of stable shareholders, typically cross-shareholdings, reached more than one-half of all the share outstanding of corporate Japan as described in Chap. 1, including its stable stock level of one-sided shareholdings by life insurance companies. Normal shareholders virtually had no voting rights in Japan then. Thus, companies did not have to pay attention to the general shareholders who seek genuine return via corporate governance.

This rate of stable shareholdings, or cross-shareholdings, are becoming lower over time by bank-leading sell-offs (called "liquidations") in the wake of collapse of the "bubble economy" in Japan, to currently below 20%. The unwinding of cross-shareholdings has been progressing over the years.

However, cross-shareholding is still considered as mere entrenchment by investors. The fundamental matter that comes first is selling-buying of voting rights (purchasing stock in each other without contracts or even press releases in most cases). It limits the voting rights of general stakeholders, in fact.

That's why the Corporate Governance Code (CGC) in Japan requires companies to explain it.

At the end of the day, all the money invested in other companies (cross-shareholdings) is attributable to shareholders. Hence its investment return must exceed cost of equity or shareholders' opportunity cost, meaning that positive Equity Spread (ES) must be secured as a fiduciary duty or stewardship responsibilities of

---

[4]A survey conducted by Yanagi and UBS Securities in October 2007 included 192 respondents (101 overseas investors, and 91 Japanese investors), which appeared in *NIKKEI*, a news paper. The investment balance of the institutional investor as respondent is above 60 trillion yen (Estimated by UBS Securities).

corporate management. In general, investors requirements state: "We entrust our risk money with the CEO so that he can invest in his real business and make a return for us. Why does the CEO invest our money in the financial securities of his partners? If he invests our money in stock, please return our money. That's because we are the professional equity investors and this part of capital should be returned to shareholders if the company invests in securities."

The matter would deal with the engagement agenda as a discussion point in Japan's Stewardship Code (SC) or Corporate Governance Code (CGC). The concerns of investors are not dispelled unless highly-enhanced governance happens by something like introducing sufficient number of outside independent directors (making up more than half of the Board of Directors), and paying attention to built-in latent losses arising out of holding other companies' securities when demanded, as in the case of a decreasing stock price. In those contexts, criticizing cross-shareholdings have been deeply rooted.

There may be cross-shareholdings based on strategic collaboration with business partners, thereby leading to significant value creation for shareholders, in which cases it is not necessarily true that all cross-shareholding harm shareholder's best interests if there are both "good-shareholdings" and "bad-shareholdings." Japanese companies should thus disclose and explain cross-shareholdings in detail publicly. That means corporate Japan must stick to the global standards of not having such conflict of interest as cross-shareholdings, or explain the situation in each country and company (principle of "Comply or Explain").

However, many Japanese companies do not follow the exigencies of the required accountability in terms of the rationality of shareholdings. From the perspective of an investor, cross-shareholdings are a black box. Hence corporate governance discount emerges in connection with the valuation of the investment securities held (quasi-cash) by Japanese companies as well as cash holdings as explained in Chap. 2.

Even recently an interesting case emerged as of October 2017.

Thomson Reuters reported on October 25, 2017 (By Simon Jessop) as follows (summary):

Asset Value Investors (AVI), a London-based investor in Japan's Tokyo Broadcasting System Holdings (TBS) said it was pressing the company's board to sell stakes in other companies (cross-shareholdings) and return the resulting windfall to shareholders. The activist campaign is the latest attempt by a western investor to overhaul corporate governance in a Japanese company, a mission shared by the government of Shinzo Abe which sees such moves as a valuable spur to economic growth. AVI said, "It would be well received by shareholders and demonstrate the company takes the issues of corporate governance and achieving a high ROE (return on equity) and capital efficiency seriously,".

The author reconfirmed that actually, as of October 2017, the market capitalization of TBS was circa 4 billion US dollars and the value of the cross-shareholdings (investment securities) and cash held amounted to equivalent figure, meaning that core business value of TBS was valued at almost zero. In other words, value of cash and securities held by TBS was severely and deeply discounted due to corporate governance debacle as shown in Chap. 2.

5.4.2 Accountability for Investment Criteria of Cross-Shareholdings

I would like to suggest that companies should do self-disclosure with respect to the top-twenty ranked companies of cross-shareholdings in their notification of Annual General Meeting of shareholders (AGM) or Corporate Governance reports filed with the Tokyo Stock Exchange (TSE) based on the spirit of "Comply or Explain".

It is not only the number of shares, nor the investment value of shareholdings, the term of acquisition, but disclosing as follows would be ideal; that is disclosing the reason for acquisition in each case, estimated economic effects on management accounting (e.g., estimated calculation of NPV or IRR for shareholdings' synergy effect). Cross-shareholdings are "Investment".

That would be fair; disclosing whether economic effects are above capital costs or not could be a discussion target. Even if all aspects are not disclosed, in the companies' discussion enough is required.

Due to the fact that funding for purchasing business partners' securities as accounted for cross-shareholdings is borne by the money entrusted by shareholders, the companies have to fill out accountability in engagement declarations. If companies follow my suggestions, value creating "good cross-holdings" would be continuously approved by investors in many cases and "bad cross-shareholdings (cross shareholdings without rational explanation)" would gradually be eliminated during the negotiations.

Consider the CGC, an ideal example for self-disclosing, illustrated in Fig. 5.3 (author).

Some people assert that, "All cross-shareholdings should be banned without exception (since the business collaboration effect should be secured solely via written contracts with legally-binding force, otherwise why should they purchase the stock of counterparty?)." Yet the system has a built-in historical and cultural context in Japan, and thus prohibiting it all at once is very difficult for businesses.

In addition, I believe that some cross holdings are truly value creating through collaborative effects or by management integration in a very Japanese way.

【Suggested example for disclosure】
・Target: ABC company (Holding our stock by others 00000 stocks)
・Acquired original price: xxxxxxxxxxxxxxxxx yen
・Book-value in year-end: xxxxxxxxxxxxxxxxxx yen
・Market capitalization in year-end: xxxxxxxxxxxxxxxxxx yen
・The reason of holdings: Tie-up effect, intended to cost-cut by cooperating purchasing
・NPV trial calculation (Rough estimation): ±xxxxxxxxxxxxxx yen (trial calculation by tentative discounting rate X %)
・IRR trial calculation (rough estimation): xxx % (±X point to x % of our tentative stock cost)
・Term of Holdings and Result: Holding XX years in past, contributing to X yen cost-cut every year in average

Fig. 5.3 Ideal model for voluntary disclosure of rationale of cross-shareholdings. *Source* Yanagi (2015)

However, in fact, the investors' assertion must not be ignored; "Result of voting would be distorted by entrenchment" "Capital of shareholders would not be efficiently utilized (leads to be agency cost)." Still, filing accountability reports by Investor Relations (IR) or information disclosure is important, and in addition to the corporate governance issue, especially from the perspective of capital productivity, applying the suggested investment criteria in this chapter to estimate NPV and IRR for verifying the collaborative effect by cross-shareholdings is something corporate management is obligated to conduct as stewardship: These things are an ideal strategy at least for corporate accounting and financial professionals in Japan.

5.5   Focal Point for Japanese Companies: Is Value Creation Secured by M&A?

Consider the case for strategic acquisition or merger of other companies. In this book, I recommend that the company itself calculate its own intrinsic value as a precondition. On the strategy of M&A, in addition, valuation for an acquired company is required[5], but, in the case of practical M&A, Japanese companies normally rely on so-called "fairness opinion" as valuation done by their relationship investment bankers to determine the proceeds of acquiring value of investees or the merger ratio against peers based on the fair market value.

---

[5] There are several investment evaluation techniques, but the Discounted Cash Flow (DCF) method is commonly used. The future cash flow of a company is discounted by adopting a certain discounting rate; the discounted present value would be the theoretical stock price. This is called the income approach.

However, the management of the acquiring company side has "animal spirits" and excessively aspires to expand is scope in most cases. Or, they will tend to persist in the succession of companies' acquisition projects rather than strictly inspecting the creation of value by shareholders in general.

Moreover, conflicts of interest are sometimes generated, even on the side of the investing bank. In general, M&A advisory services are basically regarded as free of charge except contingent success fees for bankers. And participants do not fully get rewarded until the acquisition is completed in many cases. "Succeeded in the acquisition by any means." "Must buy." That desperate desire unintentionally aligns management interests with that of the investment banks, thereby inadvertently generating "overpay" situation in some cases.

Furthermore, it means there are concerns about the risks, especially that they are too concentrated on "complete the acquisition project per se for self-interest by any means" without protecting sufficient value for the general shareholders under such circumstances.

From such a perspective, overseas investors are skeptical about acquisitions by Japanese companies with weak corporate governance and afraid of value destruction by overpaying in M&A in many cases.

That induces an unfortunate situation; when the press release of an acquisition project is announced by a Japanese company, the acquired company's stock price immediately rises, while the stock price of the acquiring company often plummets. Event-driven hedge funds make such a long-short position for arbitrage transactions.

Considering the background, and the point of view of corporate management, outside directors should secure value creation as representative for the interests of general shareholders, and the IR officer must participate in the discussion by conveying to investors and shareholders, management's opinion.

In addition, companies should hire an in-house financial expert in order not to blindly follow the advice of the investment banks and the experts, but should rather contribute a self-determined opinion by his or her own corporate value estimates.

However, in the case of M&A, the point to be considered in addition to the investment criteria (e.g., a set hurdle rate) has to do with more. That focal discussion yields the synergy (mutual effect) and premium relationship with respect to the M&A at issue.

In general, the acquisition price is determined by the acquired company's stock price plus a fixed premium. Otherwise shareholders of the acquired company would not sell their shares to the acquiring company due to their fiduciary duty of the Board of Directors.

In the case of M&A through TOB (takeover bid) by cash, a 30% premium is the average value used in most cases as a rule of thumb. For shareholders of the acquired company, the only thing they have to do is to sell their stock; cash is everything for them. Simple. "The relationship will end when the money ends." On the other hand, obviously from the stand point of the shareholders of the acquiring company, overpaying comes with a certain premium. That is why the acquiring company should explain the synergy effect to justify the premium to shareholders when it comes to the acquisition.

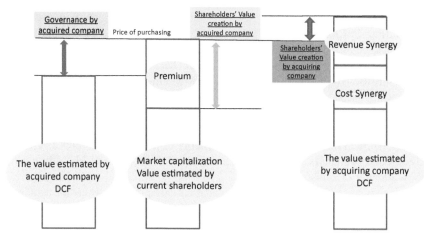

Price of Purchasing
= Market capitalization of acquired company + Surface premium of stock price comparison
= Intrinsic value by DCF + Actual Premium
= Intrinsic value by DCF + a part of synergy as advantage of acquired company's shareholders
  (The remaining synergy is the advantage of acquiring company's shareholders)

Synergy
= Shareholders of acquired company's advantage + Shareholders of acquiring company's advantage
= Cost synergy by fire off + Revenue synergy by increasing sales

Fig. 5.4 Golden rule (value creation for shareholders of both invetor and investee as corporate governence) of M&A. *Source* Author

However, in the case of M&A through exchanging stock, shareholders of the acquired company basically continue to be shareholders; the current stock is exchanged for the new company's stock at a given rate. The stake of shareholders of acquired entities as a continuous holder lies in the advantage to gain from expanding corporate value in the future. It is not that "the relationship will end when the money ends," since "they can acquire a new dream." If they have high hope for the future of the new company, the premium could be low. There also could be a discount case where the premium paid would be negative in some extreme cases.

In the case of cash or stock swaps, synergy targeted by M&A should justify the premium paid as future dreams. If there is no synergy, who can find the reason to integrate two companies?

Basically, synergy is of two kinds: one is "revenue synergy" secured by improving sales and profit going forward as positive aspects, and another one is "cost synergy" garnered by streamlining the redundant operations of two entities.

Based on the relationship between economic rationale for M&A and synergy vis-à-vis premiums, Fig. 5.4 shows the golden rule of company acquisitions.

As Fig. 5.4 shows, as long as both acquired and acquiring shareholders have an advantage, a win-win situation may be built, and the M&A would succeed without opposition.

Another point of discussion for the investment criteria of stock swap in an M&A, is the shifting of EPS[6] (Earnings Per Share: Net Income divided by the number of shares outstanding). The EPS migration criteria using PER (Price Earnings Ratio: share Price divided by EPS) should not be ignored, because PER as a common gauge is frequently used by market participants. In the M&A model of stock swap, company stock is being used as a currency of their own and a measure of that currency is PER.

In this model, the accretion means increasing EPS and dilution means decreasing EPS. For sure, simulating of EPS migration in the case of stock-for stock M&A situation and then inspecting the required synergy to justify the premium is critical because equity investors generally prefer accretion of EPS and dislike dilution of EPS as a matter of course.

For example, if an M&A to be consummated via cash proceeds where the acquired company is in the black, accretion of EPS is basically easy. The problem arises in the case of stock swap M&As.

The golden rule is, "dilution occurs if low-PER company acquires high-PER company in stock swap."

It is natural that if self-currency such as the U.S. dollar is highly-evaluated, it is an advantage. Reversely, in case your currency is devaluated, it is disadvantageous. For example, if the Japanese Yen goes up, Japanese companies could practice cross-border M&A at an advantage, and vice versa.

By the analogy of such foreign exchange situation of currency, company stock acts as a currency.

The higher the value of the currency (stock), the greater the advantage might be; for management, there is an incentive to enhance stock price from the viewpoint of M&A.

Table 5.4 shows the case of acquiring company A with 13.2 times PER that buys company B with 22.0 times PER. The currency (stock) of company A is less highly valued vis-à-vis that of company B as target. It may be a disadvantageous deal for company A's shareholders unless otherwise significant synergies can be created.

For example, in case of a simple stock swap with a premium of 0%, shareholders of company B exchange one share of stock of company B for 0.333 shares of stock in company A. If the premium is set at 40%, exchanging 1 share of company B will gain 0.467 shares of company A.

It is called exchange ratio or consolidation ratio (merger ratio) of stock swap on M&A.

In this case, even if the premium is 0%, EPS is diluted to 10%. It means that company A's current EPS is 333 yen, but if company A merges with company B, the new company's EPS would be 300 yen, which is 33 yen less.

Moreover, if a 40% premium is given, company A's EPS will be decreased from 333 yen to 273 yen with the difference being 60 yen. It is a significant 18% dilution.

---

[6]Currently, by Japanese standards, EPS on accounting is volatile, with or without amortization of goodwill, but this could change by adopting International Financial Reporting Standards (IFRS). Note that the investor is focusing more on cash EPS volatility.

Ordinarily, it is because approximately a 20–40% control premium is required that value creation hurdles would be raised by stock swaps used in company acquisitions.

The aforementioned golden rule may be applied: "If a company with low PER acquires a company with a high PER, dilution will occur." As long as it would be justified by creation of synergy, the shareholder of acquiring company A will not have to be convinced further.

Table 5.4 indicates the migration in EPS accretion or dilution with premium changes. In addition, it shows the required synergy amounts that prevent dilution from occurring. In this case, even if the premium is 0% for management integration, synergy creation at 6.7 billion yen is required. If the premium is 40%, as long as the synergy creation is above 13.3 billion yen obtaining the approval of company A's shareholders will be difficult.

In this chapter, I explained that "return above capital cost" is the resource of value creation for capital expenditure, M&A and policy investment while introducing the Value-Creative Investment Criteria (VCIC). Given the mentality of overseas investors, these things are important: setting well-qualified investment criteria with the capital cost-consciousness and operating budgets, as well as logically explaining the means of value creation figures (especially in the case of M&A) including synergy.

By these means, management can fulfill its fiduciary duty or corporate stewardship with proper financial literacy when investing the money attributable to and entrusted by shareholders. Therefore, the capital budgeting process including M&A endeavors should gather the attention of overseas investors more and more because it includes the important discussion points of corporate governance.

Given the fact that as of the end of December 2017 more than 1 trillion US dollars' worth of cash and securities held has been accumulated on the balance sheets of Japanese companies listed on the 1st section of Tokyo Stock Exchange (TSE), corporate Japan has to unlock the value via bolstering corporate governance and capital efficiency.

In order for companies to grow, investment in tangible and intangible assets including M&A will be the key to success. With that, Value-Creative Investment Criteria (VCIC) rooted in Equity Spread (ES) as described in Chap. 4 with NPV and IRR threshold based upon risk-adjusted hurdle rates should be a litmus test for corporate stewardship.

In summary, corporate governance is the premise of value creation as shown in Chap. 2 and three pillars of financial strategies described in Chaps. 4–6 such as Equity Spread (ES), Value-Creative Investment Criteria (VCIC) and optimal dividend policy will materialize the actual wealth in practice.

Given that this Chapter deals with the investment side, Chap. 6 will address the issue of repatriation of cash to shareholders in a bid to maximize value.

Table 5.4 Example of EPS accretion/dilution simulation in case of stock–for–stock M&A Cordinal rules of M&A through stock swap Diluted EPS in case low-PER company purchases high-PER company. Assuming aquiring company A obtains stocks of aquired company B 100% by stock swap

Acquiring company A		Acquired company B	
Current stock price (yen)	4400	Current stock price (yen)	1100
Market capitalization (Million yen)	660,000	Market capitalization (Million yen)	220,000
The number of stock (Thousand stock)	150,000	The number of stock (Thousand stock)	200,000
EPS (yen)	333	EPS (yen)	50
PER (times)	13.2	PER (times)	22
Expected net profit (Million yen)	50,000	Expected net profit (Million yen)	10,000

(continued)

Table 5.4 (continued)

Discount premium (%)	Discount 40%	Discount 20%	Premium 0%	Premium 20%	Premium 40%
Purchasing compensation (Million yen)	132,000	176,000	220,000	264,000	308,000
Consolidated ratio (per 1 stock of B company)	0.200	0.267	0.333	0.400	0.467
New issues of A company (thousand stock)	30,000	40,000	50,000	60,000	70,000
Total number of stock after acquisition (million yen)	180,000	190,000	200,000	210,000	220,000
Net profit after acquisition (million yen)	60,000	60,000	60,000	60,000	60,000
EPS after acquisition (yen)	333	316	300	286	273
Accretion/dilution (%)	0	−5	−10	−14	−18
Required amount of synergy (million yen)	0	3333	6667	10,000	13,333

Sensitivity analysis of EPS migration.
Source Author

References

Life Insurance Association of Japan. (2015). Survey results on approaches toward enhancing equity values *FY2014*. Life Insurance Association of Japan.

Yanagi, R. (2010). Improving manual for enhancing corporate value on managerial accounting. CHUOKEIZAI-SHA.

Yanagi, R. (2014). Managerial accounting and cash value of Japanese companies. *Melco Managerial Accounting, 7*(1), 3–14.

Yoshida, E., Fukushima, K., & Seno, T. (2009). Management accounting on Japanese companies (1) *Kigyo kaikei, 61*(9), 79–83.

Yanagi, R. (2015). The ROE revolution and financial strategy. Chuokeizai-Sha.

Chapter 6
Optimal Dividend Policy Based on Optimal Capital Structure

Abstract For purposes of maximizing corporate value, I have proposed "Three Pillars of Financial Strategies" such as Equity Spread and Value Creation, Value-Creative Investment Criteria, and Optimal Dividend Policy based on Optimal Capital Structure. After funding value-creative investments subject to threshold as specified in Chap. 5, Japanese companies have to think about cash repatriation to shareholders in order to optimize the balance sheet, thereby avoiding both undercapitalization and overcapitalization. Without proper corporate governance and sophisticated dividend policy, cash held by Japanese companies tend to be discounted as evidenced by Chap. 2. This chapter presents the third value-creation strategy related to optimal dividend policy based on optimal capital structure in a bid to unlock corporate value in Japan. Miller and Modigliani (J Bus 34:411–433, 1961) argue that dividends do not generally affect corporate value under perfect market premises, but they actually do in Japan (Ishikawa in Dividend policy for moving stock price-empirical analysis of collaboration effect. Chuokeizai-Sha, 2010), the land of stable dividends: 30% is corporate Japan's average dividend payout ratio, and the Life Insurance Association of Japan requires 30%. Japan's 30% myth persists because Japanese companies mistakenly believe that 30% parallels U.S. averages and stick to this average as a lockstep mentality. They fail to realize that U.S. counterparts set payout ratios according to their stage in their lifecycles. The book's survey results corroborate that investors focus on ROE (Return on Equity) and governance in conjunction with dividend policy as well. To break the chain of Japan's 30% myth, this chapter charts total repatriation ratios including not only dividends but also share buyback (TRR), not dividend payout ratios per se, for Japan and other countries. It finds that Japan's TRR is 33% versus 85% in the US and 63% in Europe. I therefore propose an optimal dividend policy based on an optimal capital structure as proven by investor surveys, interviews, comparisons of total return and empirical research. That optimal dividend policy considers companies' stages in their lifecycle and balance sheet management as well as issues of corporate accountability.

Keywords Myth of 30% payout ratio · Dividend puzzle · Payout ratio DOE · MM · Irrelevant theory · Corroboration effect · Signaling effect Catering effect · Residual theory · Free cash flow hypothesis Optimal capital structure · Pecking order · DDM

© Springer Nature Singapore Pte Ltd. 2018
R. Yanagi, *Corporate Governance and Value Creation in Japan*,
https://doi.org/10.1007/978-981-10-8503-1_6

6.1   Dividend Puzzle

The dividend is a puzzle. The harder we look at the dividend picture, the more it seems like a puzzle, with pieces that just don't fit together. (Black 1976)

The above quote is taken from Professor Black who first developed the famous Black–Scholes model for option pricing (Black 1976). From this perspective, does it affect the companies' stock value as to how the dividend, if any, is distributed? From the viewpoint of individual investors, dividend income might underpin future pension values or instead it might be more important to receive cash in the short term. In general, corporate stocks that tend to pay out high dividends often outperform the benchmarks for their industry; especially, the correlation between dividend payment and stock value is strong for the Japanese economy.

However, in corporate finance theory, the dividend should not affect corporate stock value under a perfect market assumption. This dividend-irrelevant theory is often described as the MM proposition following the work of the Noble prize-winning scholars Miller and Modigliani (1961). Equally there are other reasons for a firm to set low or no dividends. If it can internally invest and earn high ROE (IRR) then this could provide more substantial long-term rewards. As an example, early stage investors in Microsoft did not seek dividends but instead hoped that the growth of the corporation would yield even greater capital gains rather than immediate income gains. In effect, this strategy is attractive to a growth investor.

The inverse of this growth oriented thinking is a stable or aggressive dividend policy whereby a firm focus on maintaining or increasing dividends. My caveat is that we should not be trapped with "short-termism" whereby companies either do not expect internal growth or are prepared to sacrifice long-term growth under excessive myopic pressure. Having said that, as part of corporate governance, listed companies are supposed to address the needs of owners (shareholders) if they prefer dividends as a catering effect (or clientele effect). In addition, dividend policy disseminates significant messages to the stock market, which is called a signaling effect.

For many companies, there is a need to find some balance between these two options. Such a hybrid policy that mixes the residual dividend policy repatriating cash only after funding all the necessary growth investments (or even no dividend) and a stable policy maintaining a dividend (or even increasing a dividend), is perhaps more common in Europe or North America. Thus, the value of the dividend is not the only way to assess corporate success and often different companies face different challenges depending upon their lifecycle or capitalization between using funds for dividends or investment. As Professor Black said, "dividend is a puzzle" in the real world unlike the perfect market premised by the MM proposition.

Even at the level of setting and evaluating dividends, there are a number of different indices. Since these are referred to in the rest of this chapter, the main classifications are set out below:

[Major Dividend index]

- Dividend payout ratio = Dividends paid/Net profit (%);
- Dividend yield = Dividend/Stock price (%);
- Share buyback ratio = The amount of share buyback/Net profit (%);
- Total Return ratio = Dividend payout ratio + Share buyback ratio (%);
- Dividend on Equity ratio (DOE) = Dividend paid/Shareholders Equity (%) = ROE × Dividend payout ratio;
- Theoretical stock price by Dividend Discounted Model (DDM) = Dividend per share/(capital cost − permanent growth ratio).

6.2   Dividend Payout Ratio of Japanese Companies Has Caught up with the U.S.: All Problems Are Solved?

In the past, there were criticisms that Japanese companies did not match the dividend level of U.S. counterparts due to the traditional lack of shareholder respect or "investor-phobia" backed by cross-shareholding partners as described in Chap. 1, but this perception has steadily changed over recent years. As Fig. 6.1 shows, in the wake of transition from "bank-governance to shareholder-governance" as described in Chap. 1, the dividend payout ratio of Japan on average is about 30% and is now the same as that in the U.S. (The Life Insurance Association 2015). This has led some commentators to argue that the "key goal is a dividend payout ratio of 30%" and that the "dividend policy has finally caught up with U.S." so that "the dividend policy of Japan is now enough." Given the historical comparison with the U.S. and Europe, it can be noted that Japan has caught up with the U.S. but is still below the dividend payout ratio for Europe (Fig. 6.2).

However, practically, both investors and companies in Japan mostly pay attention to the dividend payout ratio (Figs. 6.3 and 6.4). The dividend payout ratio of

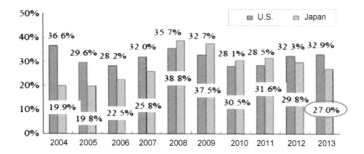

Fig. 6.1 Transition of Japan–U.S. dividend payout ratio on average in the past decade. *Source* Life Insurance Association of Japan (2015) Japan: TOPIX constituent company U.S.: S&P500 constituent company (Universe Company for which data could be continuously acquired in past decades, excluding red-ink companies)

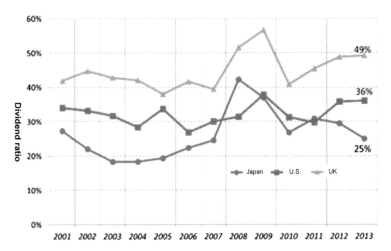

Fig. 6.2 Migration of average dividend payout ratios for Japan, U.S., U.K. *Source* Author based on FACTSET

Fig. 6.3 Japanese investors hope that companies disclose the numerical target of dividend payout ratio at most. *Source* Life Insurance Association of Japan (2015)

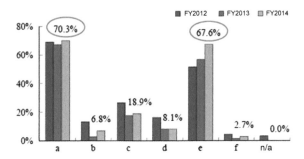

a. Dividend payout ratio
b. Dividend yield
c. DOE (Dividend on Equity) (DOE = ROE × Dividend payout ratio)
d. Dividend total amount or divided amount per stock
e. Total return ratio (Dividend + Share buyback) / Net income
f. Other
(A number of respondents: FY2014: 74, FY2013:74, FY2012: 68)
* Multiple answers allowed.

Japanese companies focuses on 30% (as a herding effect), which is the average value for both Japan and the U.S. as Fig. 6.5 shows. The dividend payout ratio of 30% reflects on Japanese investors' hope (Fig. 6.6). In addition, The Life Insurance Association (2015) has noted that "based on the situation, our association requires that a sustainable dividend payout ratio is above 30% as a mid-to-long term standard." In effect, there is a general expectation of payments of around 30%, to the extent that "dividend payout of 30% is now the magic number in Japan."

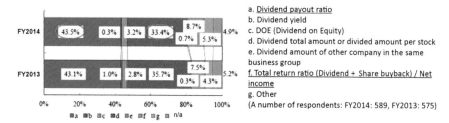

Fig. 6.4 Japanese companies' priority is dividend payout ratio at most. *Source* Life Insurance Association of Japan (2015)

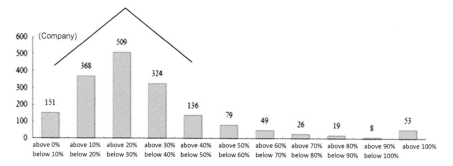

Fig. 6.5 Payout ratio of Japanese company is concentrated at 30%. *Source* Life Insurance Association of Japan (2015)

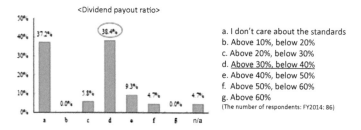

Fig. 6.6 Japanese investors also hope that dividend payout ratio is 30%. *Source* Life Insurance Association of Japan (2015)

Finance theory asserts that in a "perfect market," if the MM proposition is correct, then the size of the dividend should not affect corporate valuation. However, as Ishikawa (2010) pointed out, the dividend effects on share price are real and prevalent.

Professor Ishikawa at Osaka City University conducted an empirical study with 8921 samples from April 2007 to February 2009, using Nikkei data and looking at indicators of cumulative average abnormal return to benchmark TOPIX during 10 days before and 30 days after the announcement of fiscal forecast of net profit and dividends by the listed companies in Japan. His study found instances of a signaling effect (called the "corroboration effect" by Professor Ishikawa) whereby, for example, a dividend hike against the previous year conveys a message to the market that "management has strong confidence in future financial forecast" and this is well received by the market as a positive signal. As a consequence, this leads to a rise in share price in many cases.

According to Ishikawa (2010), overall excess return of 30 days from the dividend announcement was about +8% against TOPIX in the case of increasing both profit and dividend compared with the previous term. Moreover, even if the profits remained intact vis-à-vis last year, the excess return turned out to be about +4% when raising the dividend. In addition, it is confirmed that in the case of a decreased dividend combined with a decreased profit, the result should have been a decline of 8% in share price as it is, but it turned out at around only negative 2% return if only they maintain the dividend at the level identical to previous year, with adverse effect being mostly contained by the signaling effect (these figures are an approximation by the author).

Due to this compelling empirical research, it can be argued that the dividend of Japanese companies is positively correlated to their share price and a strong signaling effect is observed. Thus, at least in the short term, stable or consecutive dividend policy has a positive effect on share price.

Currently, 77% of Japanese companies aim to take a consistent approach (stable dividend policy) to their dividends and 81% of them aim to maintain their dividend even in the face of descending profit. Furthermore, 44% agree with the 30% dividend payout ratio requested by the Life Insurance Association (The Life Insurance Association 2015). Hanaeda and Serita (2009) indicated that 84% of Japanese companies do not intend to slash their dividend at any rate.

This has led to a synergistic effect and a kind of consensus between Japanese companies that maintain dividends and Japanese investors that evaluate dividends positively as a corroborating effect. In reality, given the compelling signaling effect or corroboration effect, the consensus forces companies toward accepting the stable dividend myth with the norm of a "dividend payout ratio of 30%." Thus, dividend is sort of a "sanctuary area" in Japan, a country of "stable dividend" and "dividend payout ratio of 30%." Hence many Japanese companies follow suit with similar dividend policy arising out of a herding effect or lockstep mentality (sometimes called "groupism" under peer pressure deeply rooted in the homogeneous society of Japan).

In fact, the average value of Japanese dividend payout ratio is much the same as in the U.S., but could we conclude that all problems are solved? Whereas Japanese investors require the dividend payout ratio of 30%, overseas investors are less sure in my assumption and claim that they "value the cash holdings in Japan as just half" as shown in Chap. 2. I am afraid that Japan has deviated from the U.S. or global standards in substance.

6.3 Fallacy of Boilerplate Dividend Policy by Japanese Companies

Even if the dividend payout ratio on average is the same as that of the U.S., using the measure of the total of shareholder return including not only dividends but also share buybacks, it cannot be said to be the "same." While the dividend myth has become deeply rooted in Japan, the U.S. is actually more focused on share buybacks than dividend. Therefore, we have to use the total return ratio (payout ratio of both dividend and share buyback) for meaningful international comparisons (Fig. 6.7).

Using this indicator, it is evident that the total return ratio in Japan is not just inferior to Europe and the U.S., but in fact is just half. Even if Japan could catch up with the U.S. in terms of dividend payout ratio on average, the overseas investor remains unsatisfied with the total repatriation of cash by Japanese companies owing to their usage of this standard for international comparison. Given such discrepancy, it is useful to explore once again carefully whether the U.S.–Japan dividend payout ratio is really the same in substance.

Using the same gauge of dividend payout ratio but analyzing the distribution chart by company in detail, quite different results would be indicated despite the fact that dividend payout ratio in average is the same on the surface. It is clear that there is a substantial dichotomy in the distribution. Japanese companies may remain focused on the 30% dividend ratio, but in the U.S., there is much more diversity. The "no-dividend" company is common, and the dividend payout ratio varies in the U.S. according to the lifecycle of the firm (Kondo and Yanagi 2013). In practice, investors do not look for or demand a dividend from a growing company that is investing in its own growth with high IRR (Internal Rate of Return) but requires even more

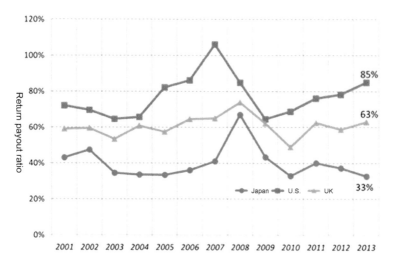

Fig. 6.7 Total Repatriation Ratio to shareholders in the U.S. is more than double of that in Japan. *Source* Author based on FACTSET

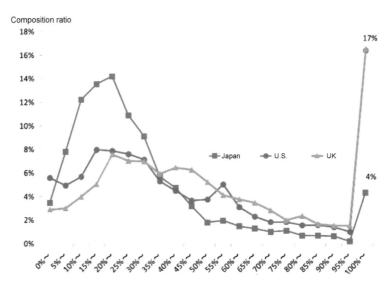

Fig. 6.8 Distribution of dividend payout ratio (FY2013). International comparison, "distribution" of dividend payout ratio. *Source* Author based on FACTSET

than 100% shareholders' return out of net profit in connection with an excessively cash-rich and overcapitalized entity.

In effect, the optimal capital structure for each company has to be considered in a bid to maximize shareholder value. A dividend payout of 10% is too high for one company with undercapitalization but even 300% may be too low for another corporation with overcapitalization. Hence, a "one target fits all approach" or "boilerplate approach" is not appropriate. This range of options is set out in Fig. 6.8. In turn, Fig. 6.9 provides an international comparison for the total return ratio distribution and the cash repatriation for a number of companies, in Europe and the U.S., are above 100% of the net profit.

The reason why investors are still unsatisfied with Japanese dividend policy, regardless of whether the dividend payout ratio on average is likely to catch up with the U.S., is probably that a low PBR (Price Book-value Ratio) depends on stagnant ROE and excess cash holdings as described in the preceding chapters. The concepts of "stable dividend policy" and the "unified 30% dividend payout ratio" are not sufficient to convince overseas investors unless Japanese companies also focus on their capital efficiency and clarify their shareholder return policy in terms of their desired optimal capital structure from the viewpoint of stewardship responsibility.

Composition ratio

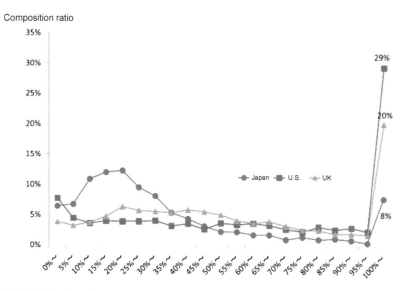

6.4 Dichotomy Between Japanese Companies Groupism and Investor Perspectives

The next step in this analysis[1] is to research the links between dividend policy and investor expectations, using the consolidated financial results filed with TSE (Tokyo Stock Exchange), to confirm the hypothesis that "Japanese companies prefer a stability-oriented boilerplate dividend policy and have strong groupism (herding behavior arising out of lockstep mentality deeply rooted in historically homogeneous nation or agricultural society subject to peer pressure) compared to the perspective of investors.

My first move was to count the number of letters in the dividend policy description in the financial results filed with TSE to reconfirm the distribution of writing. The average number of letters was 416, the median value was 398, and the standard deviation was 176 (Fig. 6.10).

In addition, analyzing the characteristics of descriptions about dividend policy in TSE filing documents, I identified that 53% of the companies mentioned "stable dividend" and 48% of companies explained the reason to hold cash as "retained

[1] The subjects are 83 companies whose financial data of the past 3 years (FY2008–2011) are available in public and whose financial results, analyst valuation, and financial data can be verified. These companies are the subject for evaluation of "Awards for Excellence in Corporate Disclosure (FY2010) selected by securities analyst" by SAAJ (Securities Analysts Association of Japan) from Japanese representative listed companies "TOPIX100." Please check the details in Kondo and Yanagi (2013).

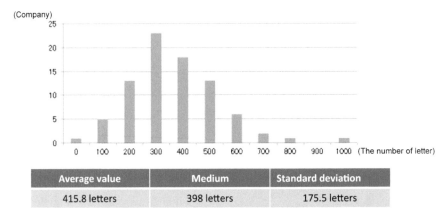

Average value	Medium	Standard deviation
415.8 letters	398 letters	175.5 letters

Fig. 6.10 The number of letters as for the dividend policy description in TSE filing. *Source* Author

	The number of company	Ratio
Stable dividend	44 companies	53.0%
Capital Efficiency	7 companies	8.4%
Cash Flow	6 companies	7.2%
Retained earnings for investing	40 companies	48.2%

Approximately more than half of companies describe as for "Stable dividend" or "Retained earnings for investing."

Many companies seem to consider "Stable dividend" and "Retained earnings for investing" as required subject by shareholders

Fig. 6.11 Distribution of narrative contents as for dividend rationale. Description of dividend in the financial results filed with TSE. *Source* Author

cash for the future investment, if any, or an unexpected situation, just in case, but without sophisticated financial theory." From this, it is concluded that approximately half of the Japanese companies have a "stable dividend policy" and a tendency of "cash-hoard mentality".

In contrast, the ratio of "dividend policy in relation to capital efficiency," was described by only 8% and merely 7% of the Japanese companies mentioned "dividend based on cash flow generated" (Fig. 6.11).

Table 6.1 Dichotomy between Japanese companies' description of dividend policy and investors' evaluation

Contents of financial result		Disclosure total score	Governance score
Description of stable dividend	○	71.4	66.8
	×	*74.0*	*69.6*
Description of retained earnings	○	71.8	67.6
	×	*73.4*	*68.6*
Description of cash flow	○	*75.3*	*74.5*
	×	72.4	67.6
Description of Capital efficiency	○	*75.2*	*72.4*
	×	72.4	67.7

Source Author
○, described; ×, un-described

Table 6.1[2] shows that the research outcome of my analysis of the relationship between the descriptions of financial results filed with the TSE by Japanese companies and the evaluation by analysts and investors of these Japanese companies. This is based on the individual score of companies for their disclosure evaluation as developed by the Securities Analysts Association of Japan (SAAJ) where all the major sell-side analysts and buy-side investors participate in an annual survey.

In this case, the average rating of the companies that prefer a "stable dividend" and "cash-hoard mentality" derived from boilerplate approach with groupism is actually lower than that for the companies that do not set out these unified concepts. In contrast, the average score of the company that identifies "dividend policy in relation to capital efficiency" and "dividend based on cash flow generated" is higher than that for the companies that do not address these issues.

These tendencies remain intact whether evaluated on the basis of the corporate disclosure level or the quality of corporate governance (in the meaning of reflecting the shareholder-friendly capital policy) in connection with the investees on which relevant market participants made judgement.

It can be concluded that analysts and investors evaluate the companies that explain their dividend policy with respect to capital efficiency and cash flow more highly than those companies that pay attention to a stable dividend or retained earnings as their strategy. This implies that there is a dichotomy between the preferences of Japanese companies and the perspective of investors.

---

[2]Suda (2004) proves the negative correlation between "disclosure total score," released by SAAJ that is utilized to the qualitative analysis in the chapter, and capital cost with statistically significant difference.

6.5   Global Investors Demand Dividend Policy Based on Optimal Capital Structure

6.5.1   The Result of Global Investor Survey: Most Overseas Investors Answer that Companies Have to Focus on Capital Efficiency and ROE

I also conducted a global investor survey in conjunction with Japanese companies' dividend policy to reconfirm the perspective of overseas investors. This strand of the research was a qualitative analysis based on the comments of opinion leaders like the ACGA (Asia Corporate Governance Association). The result of the global investor survey is particularly concerned with ROE as Fig. 6.12 Question 3 shows.[3]

The result of the survey also supports the hypothesis that many investors are unsatisfied with the dividend policy of Japanese companies and implies that overseas investors pay more attention to the dividend policy in relation to corporate governance and ROE than to a stable dividend from lockstep mentality.

6.5.2   Global Investors' Perspectives About the Dividend Policy of Japanese Companies

The survey data above can be deepened by considering the specific comments of some overseas investors as additional qualitative evidence. This helps us to understand the reasons why they are sometimes dissatisfied with the dividend policy of Japanese companies.

Overseas investor A

Sure, we interpret companies' holding cash as somewhat understandable as indicative of the opacity of managerial environment or concerns of financial arrangement. There are, however, too many Japanese companies holding excess cash as a "saving-box-type company." The management should be aware that it is not ideal.

---

[3]The author and UBS Securities conducted the global survey as below:

(The term of research) Three month from November 1, 2011 to January 31, 2012.
(The conductor) The author and Japanese stock sales team of UBS Securities. Basically, UBS Securities was in charge of the Japanese investors and the author was in charge of overseas investors.
(Subject of research) Conducting the survey with the global major institutional investor (UBS core200). Respondents: Japanese investors' companies: 57, overseas investors' company: 58. Total 115 companies. (valid response ratio 57.5%) In addition, we can collect the comment in detail from ACGA, overseas investors' opinion leader. The detail is in Yanagi (2013), Kondo and Yanagi (2013).

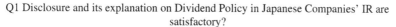

Q1 Disclosure and its explanation on Dividend Policy in Japanese Companies' IR are satisfactory?

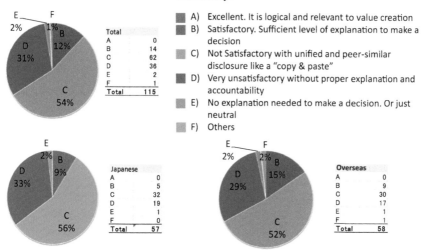

A) Excellent. It is logical and relevant to value creation
B) Satisfactory. Sufficient level of explanation to make a decision
C) Not Satisfactory with unified and peer-similar disclosure like a "copy & paste"
D) Very unsatisfactory without proper explanation and accountability
E) No explanation needed to make a decision. Or just neutral
F) Others

Total	
A	0
B	14
C	62
D	36
E	2
F	1
Total	115

Japanese	
A	0
B	5
C	32
D	19
E	1
F	0
Total	57

Overseas	
A	0
B	9
C	30
D	17
E	1
F	1
Total	58

Q2 What do you think as an investor is the important elements in connection with Dividend Policy in Japanese Companies?

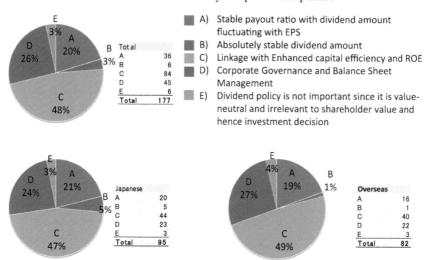

A) Stable payout ratio with dividend amount fluctuating with EPS
B) Absolutely stable dividend amount
C) Linkage with Enhanced capital efficiency and ROE
D) Corporate Governance and Balance Sheet Management
E) Dividend policy is not important since it is value-neutral and irrelevant to shareholder value and hence investment decision

Total	
A	36
B	6
C	84
D	45
E	6
Total	177

Japanese	
A	20
B	5
C	44
D	23
E	3
Total	95

Overseas	
A	16
B	1
C	40
D	22
E	3
Total	82

(NOTE) Two or more answers are accepted here

Fig. 6.12 Global investors' perception as for dividend policy of Japanese companies. *Source* Yanagi (2013)

Q3 Are you generally satisfied with ROE level of Japanese investees?

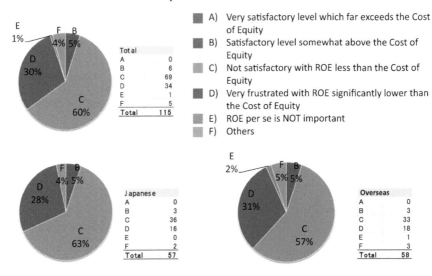

A) Very satisfactory level which far exceeds the Cost of Equity
B) Satisfactory level somewhat above the Cost of Equity
C) Not satisfactory with ROE less than the Cost of Equity
D) Very frustrated with ROE significantly lower than the Cost of Equity
E) ROE per se is NOT important
F) Others

Total

A	0
B	6
C	69
D	34
E	1
F	5
Total	115

Japanese

A	0
B	3
C	36
D	16
E	0
F	2
Total	57

Overseas

A	0
B	3
C	33
D	18
E	1
F	3
Total	58

Q4 Are you generally satisfied with Corporate Governance of Japanese investees?

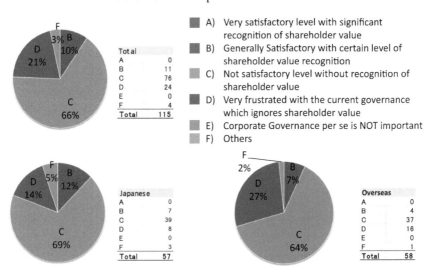

A) Very satisfactory level with significant recognition of shareholder value
B) Generally Satisfactory with certain level of shareholder value recognition
C) Not satisfactory level without recognition of shareholder value
D) Very frustrated with the current governance which ignores shareholder value
E) Corporate Governance per se is NOT important
F) Others

Total

A	0
B	11
C	76
D	24
E	0
F	4
Total	115

Japanese

A	0
B	7
C	39
D	8
E	0
F	3
Total	57

Overseas

A	0
B	4
C	37
D	16
E	0
F	1
Total	58

Fig. 6.12   (continued)

Overseas investor B

I think Japanese companies operate for their self-defense in-group rather than for maximizing shareholders' value. In general, the contents of capital policy or efficiency in Japanese companies are less than our expectation.

Overseas investor C

The quality of Japanese dividend policy is not great. They hold too much cash to justify and the balance sheet is inefficient. Needless to say, cross-shareholdings for no-profit are out of discussion. Japanese companies have to understand the difference between a "strong balance sheet" and an "inefficient balance sheet." They lose sight of essentials for listing—committing to the creation of shareholders' value. Most Japanese companies seem to be just a "saving box" and are not aware why they are listed on the stock market.

Overseas investor D

In general, Japanese companies' management should sincerely strive to improve their corporate governance and to enhance overall transparency and disclosure levels. They need to recognize the position of the shareholder and produce high-quality dividend policies and accountability.

Overseas investor E

Though Japanese companies tend to have the obsession of groupism, setting a 30% average dividend payout ratio as the goal is not really identified as a problem in the mass media, but it is a problem for investors. The dividend payout ratio is just an index for accounting and it has to depend on the balance sheet and cash flow in particular. Each company has its own lifecycle and the necessity for reinvesting is different depending on the company's situation, so the average dividend payout ratio is meaningless.

Overseas investor F

As shareholders' return, we hope for higher dividends due to concerns about the agency cost—Japanese companies rarely implement share buybacks or efficient M&A. However, our concern is fundamentally about low ROE. A serious problem of Japanese corporate governance stems from this lack of awareness about the importance of ROE.

Overseas investor G

We prefer DOE which secures value (shareholders capital to dividend ratio) and a stable dividend payout ratio. DOE decreases the risk premium for the income gain-oriented investor and it leads to higher corporate value. It is not just about the profit for one term but about reflecting on the companies' overall balance sheet. That is why it is informative about the companies' long-term performance.

Overseas investor H

We are unsatisfied about the level of dividend on the accumulated cash by the Japanese companies. The Olympus incident implies that the risk of holding excessive cash leads to investing in other companies' securities. Every time this happens, it reveals corporate governance structures and a lack of transparency of management that is below international standards and inadequate check-balance of management which negatively impacts the shareholders' trust of Japanese companies.

Overseas investor I

The management of the Japanese companies has to consider that we, as long-term investors, require improvements in capital efficiency and the fact that pension funds rely on the dividend. Fulfilling the accountability sufficient for capital efficiency, that would lead to the high roads for good-quality corporate governance.

Overseas investor J

We believe that Japanese companies do not fulfill their accountability in respect of not only the dividend policy but also management strategy or corporate governance. Too many corporate management teams do not understand the concept of capital cost or shareholder value.

They even don't understand what the purpose of listing is or for whom management works. The attitude to the shareholders will never change unless the management truly realize what "shareholders' return" is.

Overseas investor K

Many Japanese companies disclose target dividend payout ratio such as 30%, but they do not understand the meaning of dividend or share buybacks. For investors, relevant ROE and corporate governance are a priority over dividend per se.

Overseas investor L

Many companies have continuously paid the same dividend without an understanding of the shareholders' return in substance. They just keep focusing on paying a stable dividend while ignoring the relationship with ROE and the shifting of financial conditions. The majority of investors are unsatisfied with Japanese companies' low ROE. ROE in Japan is still lower than equity cost. The Japanese market will be inferior to others on the global market competition if the situation is not changed.

Overseas investor M

Japanese companies burn their cash for the self-defense or entrenchment of the incumbent management team. We have no choice but to link Japanese companies' excessive cash holdings with bad performance of corporate governance at approximately 50% discount due to the inherent agency cost. Such agency cost causes the discounting and it could be connected with too much holding cash above market capitalization.

Oversea investor N

Accountability of management or IR (Investor Relations) affects capital cost. In the case of companies that lack sufficient accountability, we calculate the applied capital cost higher as a risk factor. Because corporate governance and dividend policy has a mutual relationship, balance sheet management is important. Japanese companies just tend to accumulate cash without a clear purpose and do not utilize it efficiently. As a result, it is difficult to value cash as cash.

Overseas investor O

The dividend policy of Japanese companies is based on a wrong concept: "companies' owners are not shareholders." Management intentionally avoids shareholders' involvement rather than maximizing shareholders' value. Therefore, Japanese corporate governance is of poor quality.

Overseas investor P

Tendencies such as having lackluster low ROE or lack of unequivocal explanations for their dividend policy are all caused by low management capability. Japanese management is required to have the ability of theoretical understanding: how to create profit from the limited management resource in-house and return it to the shareholders.

Overseas investor Q

We do not feel there is consistency of shareholders' return as a strategy in superficial boilerplate "stable dividend policy." The shareholders' return problem, needless to say is also linked to the issue of accountability of corporate management. When this is obscure, they cannot explain value creation for shareholders. The opacity of all the stakeholders-targeting as excuse causes the weakness of Japan's corporate governance and the unconsciousness of shareholders' wealth.

Overseas investor R

Many Japanese companies are resting on their laurels due to accumulated excessive cash. They ignore the lifecycle hypothesis and are mistakenly consistent to stable dividend. From the stand point of international standards, the main cause is accumulated excessive cash on the balance sheet. Raising the threshold of dividend policy is not only rewarding shareholders for income gain but also improving ROE for long-term value creation.

Overseas investor S

We request above 10% of ROE in order for us to invest in Japanese stock and if their corporate governance performance is bad, we set the valuation of company's cash at 50%. That is because of agency cost. How should they improve corporate value to ease the agency cost? This is what we would like them to do.

Overall, these quotes emphasize the overseas investors' concern that Japanese companies are captured by "stable dividend policy" and the "dividend payout ratio 30%" based on groupism or lockstep mentality. Moreover, the research also implied that the priority of the investors is the relationship of dividend with capital efficiency or corporate governance rather than boilerplate stable dividend policy per se. Such a perspective is related to the background of discounting valuation of excessive cash holdings by Japanese companies (as shown in Chap. 2).

6.6 Optimal Dividend Policy Based on Optimal Capital Structure: Fulfill Their Own Accountability

6.6.1 What Is the Optimal Dividend Policy Based on Optimal Capital Structure?

From the perspective of the corporate governance changes and the capital efficiency required by overseas investors as identified in the global investor survey, Japanese companies need an optimal capital structure that reduces the agency cost implied by the free cash flow hypothesis.[4] This is more important than maintaining a stable dividend.

Some overseas investors declare that they value the cash and securities held by Japanese companies as 50%. Even if they have similar cash holdings, the cash held by the companies with good corporate governance would be regarded as "real option" and evaluated much higher given the fact that such cash is expected to be used for capital investment with IRR higher than capital cost or be returned to shareholders.

On the contrary, the cash held by companies with bad corporate governance is considered an agency cost; in other words, some investors think that "Japanese companies make value-destructive investing without awareness of capital efficiency or capital cost." They believe that some companies "accumulate cash for self-defense or entrenchment of incumbent management and that might destroy shareholder value as agency cost."

The approaches to holding cash, investing opportunities, lifecycle, capitalization, and dividend policy are closely related to each other, and this makes a focus on a particular figure for dividend payout ratio such as 30% relatively meaningless. Even if there was a 10% dividend payout policy, this would be too high for some undercapitalized companies and a payout ratio of 300% may be too low for others with overcapitalization. Therefore, constructing an "optimal dividend policy based on optimal capital structure (Yanagi 2015)" considering corporate governance and

---

[4]It seems like it is established by Jensen (1986). Shareholders as a principle fund risk money and entrust this to management as agency, but capital-rich companies' management might use it for self-protection or value destructive investing. It is called agency cost.

capital efficiency leads to improve market valuation of cash held by Japanese companies.

For example, optimal capital structure is theoretically set based on the trade-off theory (balance is the key, because excessive utilization of leveraging effect makes the risk of bankruptcy too high whereas incurring debts decreases the capital cost) and pecking order theory (finance theory mandates that as a sequence of funding, in principle, company utilizes cash first, debt second, and equity-financing last). I propose the "credit rating analogy approach" as appropriate as a simplified method as follows.

Some financial experts believe that the credit rating BBB (lowest investment grade before falling into speculative rating), constructed for taking advantage of the trade-off theory with KPI (Key Performance Indicators) of credit-worthiness such as Equity to Total Assets ratio, DER (Debt Equity Ratio), Debt/EBITDA multiple, and Interest Coverage Ratio, is a suitable or even ideal state as a definition of optimal capital structure. Considering the funding availability in this case, the credit rating A level, which is one notch higher than rating BBB as based on revised pecking order theory by Myers[5] (1983), including financial slack, would be a more ideal goal for adjusting capital structure[6] by dividend (or share buyback) as one of the financial strategies in a bid to maximize corporate value. Based on this approach, the optimal dividend has to be collectively determined, also considering future investing opportunity, capitalization, lifecycle, signaling effect, catering effect, stable dividend, ROE target, and Equity Spread. Just blindly maintaining stable dividends and ignoring capital structure would invite investors to doubt the strategy. This is not just an issue for overseas investors as even Japanese investors seem to be actually unsatisfied with the companies' explanation about equity level and excessive cash (Fig. 6.13).

In effect, Fig. 6.13 stresses that companies do not explain sufficiently the rationale behind holding too much equity and cash reserves.

Given such a situation, what can be done to address the problem? The answer is to create an optimal dividend policy based on an optimal capital structure as suggested in this chapter. The global investor survey by Yanagi (2014b) implies that optimal capital structure (balance sheet management) would be the most important criteria in setting an acceptable dividend policy (Fig. 6.14).

In Fig. 6.14, the most important thing for dividend policy is an optimal capital structure from the viewpoint of global investors.

---

[5]Myers (1983) affirms capital structure is a "puzzle" the same as dividend policy and there is no absolute answer. Moreover, he also mentioned dynamic pecking order theory in addition to the static trade-off theory. That means he affirms that a company should determine capital structure considering minimization-oriented capital cost, information asymmetry, and bankruptcy risk and keeping financial slack (borrowing capacity for future investing).

[6]Some people advocate share buybacks that could be flexibly adjusted and that holding cash is suitable for this. However, whereas a dividend confirms the intent to meet the stockholders, share buyback has the possibility of un-implementation by considering insider information, liquidity, level of stock price, and commitment of management, though the number could be confirmed. In this chapter, there is a deliberate focus on describing dividends as a tool to prevent inviting fallacy of investors by consecutive dividend.

Perception on the level of capitalizaion of Japanese
companies (Investor)

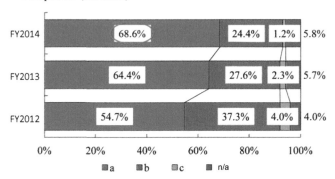

            a   b   c   n/a

Considering the level of capitalization as
a. overcapitalized
b. adquate
c. undercapitalized
(Respondents: FY2014: 86, FY2013: 87, FY2012:75)

Rationale on the level of capitalizaion (Investor)

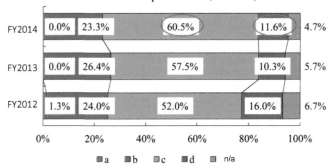

            a   b   c   d   n/a

The standards of equity is

a. sufficiently explained
b. explained somehow
c. insufficiently explained
d. hardly explained

(Respondents: FY2014: 86, FY2013: 87, FY2012:75)

Fig. 6.13 Investor perception on cash holding and its explanation by Japanese companies. *Source*
Life Insurance Association of Japan (2015)

If the concept of an "optimal dividend policy based on optimal capital structure
(Yanagi 2013, 2014a)" is mapped onto issues of corporate governance, the results
are as shown in Fig. 6.15.

Perception on the level of cash holdings (Investor)

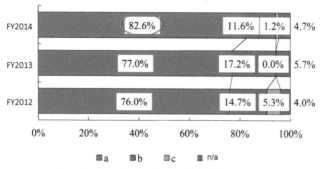

◼a   ◼b   ◻c   ◼ n/a

Considering the level of cash holdings as

a. excessive
b. adequate
c. not sufficient

(Respondents: FY2014: 86, FY2013: 87, FY2012:75)

Rationale on the level of cash holdings (Investor)

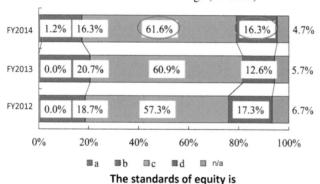

◼a   ◼b   ◻c   ◼d   ◻ n/a

The standards of equity is

a. sufficiently explained
b. explained somehow
c. insufficiently explained
d. hardly explained

(Respondents: FY2014: 86, FY2013: 87, FY2012:75)

Fig. 6.13 (continued)

A concrete KPI for optimal dividend policy based on optimal capital structure could be DOE (dividend on equity ratio) (Yanagi 2008).[7] DOE is appropriate for

---

[7]DOE could be explained as a hybrid policy, because it is decomposed to the product of ROE and dividend payout ratio. In other words, a growing company with a high ROE would mainly be reinvesting and the dividend payout ratio would be low. On the contrary, a matured company that is

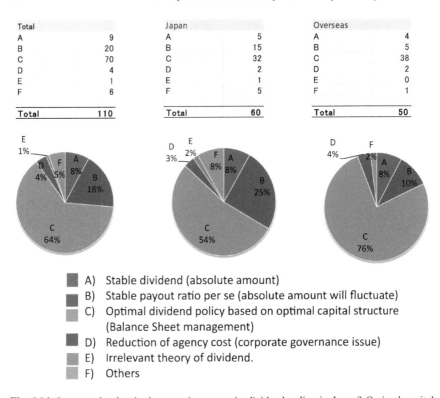

Total		Japan		Overseas	
A	9	A	5	A	4
B	20	B	15	B	5
C	70	C	32	C	38
D	4	D	2	D	2
E	1	E	1	E	0
F	6	F	5	F	1
Total	110	Total	60	Total	50

A) Stable dividend (absolute amount)
B) Stable payout ratio per se (absolute amount will fluctuate)
C) Optimal dividend policy based on optimal capital structure (Balance Sheet management)
D) Reduction of agency cost (corporate governance issue)
E) Irrelevant theory of dividend.
F) Others

Fig. 6.14 In general, what is the most important in dividend policy in Japan? Optimal capital structure is important for dividend policy (not dividend payout ratio). *Source* Yanagi (2014b)

balance sheet management, because this indicates the ratio of dividend total amount to shareholders' equity base entrusted by shareholders. In addition, for setting up the optimal capital structure, retained earnings are one of the important concepts that should be considered. In this respect, the investor Warren Buffet (Cunningham 2008) argues that a "worthwhile company is able to show that every dollar of retained earnings equates to at least one dollar or more of market value." Behind this argument is the concept that if "the profit belonging to shareholders" is being retained within companies, then companies have to prove they can increase the value via their business and, if not, it should be returned to shareholders in principle.

"Make my one dollar more than one dollar, or return it to me!" That essentially is what Warren Buffet said.

---

cash-rich should have a high dividend payout ratio. Moreover, DOE is appropriate for balance sheet management and will even show the cash dividend to capital cost, because it indicates the ratio of dividend to shareholders' equity. Based on such advantages, DOE is also appropriate as a KPI for a "dividend policy based on optimal capital structure." The insightful investor Scott Callon, CEO of Ichigo Asset Management, assertively supports it use. Note that Japanese companies average is just 2% and greatly inferior to the U.S. average level of 5%. (Life Insurance Association 2015)

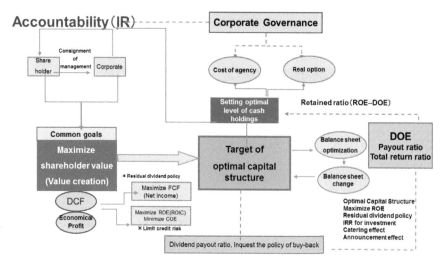

Fig. 6.15 Schema of optimal shareholders' return policy based on optimal capital structure. *Source* Author based on Yanagi (2013, 2014a)

Retained earnings that are not returned to shareholders (including accumulated profit) are the same as funding by equity financing.[8] That is why if the company has to keep retained earnings for some reason, they have to create additional shareholders' value with positive NPV (Net Present Value), or positive Equity Spread by investing shareholders' money as fiduciary duty (Brealey et al. 2002). Therefore, companies have to consider optimal retained earnings level, optimal capital structure, optimal cash holdings, and ensuing optimal dividend policy.

The Ito Review says the following;

> Needless to say, it is important to capital markets that companies provide follow-up information based on the relevance of the matter, in addition to satisfying disclosure obligations at initial deal launch. In order to ensure that transactions are not value destructive, such as only pursuing expansion of scale, it is imperative that clear targets for corporate value-creation be included in transaction criteria.

6.6.2   Japanese Companies Have to Fulfill the Accountability for Dividend Policy

With respect to the accountability of dividend policy, Warren Buffet's assertion explained above has profound implications in identifying that "many companies

---

[8]Written in the Ito Review. In short, in the point of (potential) increasing shareholders' equity, equity finance and decreasing dividend or retained earnings (below 100% dividend payout ratio) are the same. In addition, in the point of (potential) decreasing shareholders' equity, share buyback and increased dividend or shareholders' return that is above 100% dividend ratio mean the same.

Explanation for dividend policy (Company)

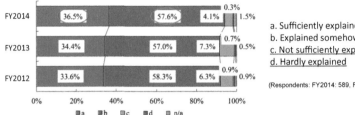

a. Sufficiently explained
b. Explained somehow
c. Not sufficiently explained
d. Hardly explained

(Respondents: FY2014: 589, FY2013: 575, FY2012:57

Explanation for dividend policy (Investor)

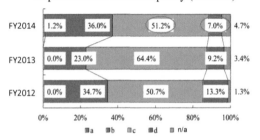

a. Sufficiently explained
b. Explained somehow
c. Not sufficiently explained
d. Hardly explained

(Respondents: FY2014: 86, FY2013: 87, FY2012:75)

Fig. 6.16 Explanation for dividend policy by Japanese companies. Dichotomy exists between Companies and Investors in terms of explanation. *Source* Life Insurance Association of Japan (2015)

announce the ideal goal of dividend payout ratio such as 30% in public, but few companies explain why it is the very best for shareholders value maximization" (Cunningham 2008). Japanese companies believe that they have already explained their dividend policy sufficiently, but ironically more than half of Japanese investors are not satisfied with such explanations (Fig. 6.16).

This chapter started with the argument that dividends should, in a perfect market premise, have no effect on stock market value. However, it is verified that the dividend actually does impact stock price in the real world and that it can contribute to "creating value" in some cases and "destroying value" in others.

The dividend policy has to be determined considering issues such as investing project, stage of company growth, profits, standards of cash reserves, capital structure and capital cost, shareholders' distribution and dividend preference, market trends, and bankruptcy remoteness. All these strands need to be drawn together. Based on this discussion, companies are accountable to shareholders and an explanation of dividend policy is the basis for the "purposeful dialogue between companies and investors (engagement agenda)" required by the Stewardship Code (SC) and Corporate Governance Code (CGC) in Abenomics reforms.

Before concluding this chapter, in terms of stipulating dividend policy, the Ito Review (excerpted from Kondo and Yanagi 2013; Yanagi 2013) provides some useful insights:

From a statistical perspective, most Japanese companies have a dividend payout ratio centered at the average value of 30%, which is reflective of the tendency to "follow the crowd" and employ a "stable dividend" policy. Although the average dividend payout ratio is also 30% in the US, there is a large variance depending on the life-cycle theory of corporate growth, and in fact the data between 2007 and 2010 indicate the largest statistical group was non-dividend-paying companies. It seems every company consciously plans an optimal dividend policy. (Kondo and Yanagi 2013)

On this point, there is a survey showing that Japanese companies have a strong tendency to include the expressions "stable dividend" and "retained earnings for future investments" in their earnings briefings. On the other hand, the survey shows that global investors attach paramount importance towards "capital efficiency" among dividend policies of Japanese companies, and that they are dissatisfied with Japanese companies' disclosure of dividend policies and IR briefings. There was also a comment from a domestic investor that Japanese companies fail to rationally explain policies on dividends and shareholder returns under the context of ROE and the cost of capital. (Yanagi 2013)

It is important to consider dividend policies based on optimal capital structure. Minimization of the cost of capital without sacrificing financial soundness, and KPI-conscious capital structure adjustments through dividends and share buybacks are topics that can help the financial strategies of a company and dialogue with investors. Companies should determine a dividend policy upon holistically considering future investment opportunities, liquidity needs, and signaling effects. (Yanagi 2013)

References

Black, F. (1976). The dividend puzzle. *The Journal of Portfolio Management, 2*(2), 5–8.

Brealey, R. A., Myers, S. C., & Allen, F. (2002). *Principles of corporate finance global edition* (10th ed.). McGraw-Hill.

Cunningham, L. A. (2008). *The essays of Warren Buffet for corporate America*. Pan Rolling. (Translation supervised by Masuzawa, H.)

Hanaeda, H., & Serita, T. (2009). Survey research for payout policy: Mainly comparing Japan and US. *SAAJ Journal, 2009*(8).

Ishikawa, H. (2010). *Dividend policy for moving stock price-empirical analysis of collaboration effect*. Chuokeizai-Sha.

Jensen, M. C. (1986). Agency cost for free cash flow, corporate finance, and the take-overs. *American Economic Review, 57*(2), 283–306.

Kondo, K., & Yanagi, R. (2013). *Financial, IR & SR strategies for improvement of corporate value*. Chuokeizai-Sha.

Life Insurance Association of Japan. (2015). *Survey results on approaches toward enhancing equity values FY2014*. Life Insurance Association of Japan.

Miller, M. H., & Modigliani, F. (1961). Dividend policy, growth and valuation of shares. *Journal of Business, 34*, 411–433.

Myers, S. C. (1983). The capital structure puzzle. *The Journal of Finance, 39*, 575–592.

Suda, K. (2004). *Strategies and effect of disclosure*. Moriyama-shoten.

Yanagi, R. (2008). Utilizing dividend on equity ratio (DOE) on management accounting. *Kigyo kaikei, 60*(1), 90–96.

Yanagi, R. (2013). Study for dividend policy and IR activities. *Investor Relations, 2013*(7), 58–77.

Yanagi, R. (2014a). Importance of optimal dividend policy based on optimal capital structure. *Kigyo kaikei, 66*(7), 44–51.

Yanagi, R. (2014b). Study for Japanese-version Stewardship code and capital efficiency. *Investor Relations, 2014*(8), 48–62.

Yanagi, R. (2015). *The ROE revolution and financial strategy*. Chuokeizai-Sha.

Chapter 7
Synchronization of Non-financial Capital and Value Creation: Japan Should Show ROE of ESG

Abstract Japanese companies prefer to discuss non-financial information such as ESG (Environment, Social, Government) and CSR (Corporate Social Responsibility) when they set agendas for talks with investors. Investors, however, want to discuss information in the financial statements. Both types of information indicate potential for growth and creation of corporate value, and they can be synchronized through market value added (MVA). The author specifies that MVA as defined as portion with PBR (Price Book-value Ratio) above 1 equals to Intangibles (non-financial capital such as ESG/CSR). The equation responds to assertions in Japan's Corporate Governance Code (CGC), Stewardship Code (SC) and the Ito Review, which promote discussions of capital efficiency (i.e., improved ROE) and non-financial information in a broad sense. It is a sort of pursuing "ROESG (Return On ESG)" concept. In this context, the author provides empirical research proving this correlation with statistical significance between ESG and ROE as well as a global investor survey. The book's three financial strategies bring investors and corporations together in a quantitative dialogue as shown in Chap. 4. This chapter suggests an agenda for that dialogue taken from results of the investor survey, and how to synchronize financial and non-financial value in a quantitative dialogue. The chapter includes the integrated report of Eisai (one of the largest pharmaceutical companies in Japan for which the author serves as CFO) as a case study and shows that financial and non-financial information can be synchronized by reporting the MVA and Equity Spread (ES) as evidenced by Yanagi (2017a). Overseas investors severely criticize Japanese corporate management, as the author proves through surveys, interviews, and quantitative analysis. However, remember one of the Aesop's Fables "The North Wind and The Sun" anecdote. "The North Wind," only criticism does not blow the conventional way of corporate governance in Japan. "The Sun," constructive dialogue is the ideal and effective way to unbutton the old wears as The Sun got win through gentleness in the anecdote. Corporations and investors both must seek for a win-win. That is "Synchronization of non-financial capitals (ESG) and Equity Spread (or ROE)" as my value proposition. And this chapter is the author's conclusion.

Keywords Non-financial capital · ESG · CSR · Intangibles
Equity spread · MVA · RIM · Synchronization

© Springer Nature Singapore Pte Ltd. 2018
R. Yanagi, *Corporate Governance and Value Creation in Japan*,
https://doi.org/10.1007/978-981-10-8503-1_7

7.1 The Purposeful Dialogue Between Companies and Investors Recommended by the Japanese Stewardship Code and the Corporate Governance Code

Abenomics corporate governance reforms in Japan are ongoing. The important *Stewardship Code (SC)* binding investors, and the *Corporate Governance Code (CGC)* for companies have been called "Double-Codes". In addition, the *Ito Review* emulating the UK's Kay review is designed to educate the entire investment chain including asset owners, asset managers, and companies. Sometimes, the *Stewardship Code*, the *Corporate Governance Code* and the *Ito Review* are called "Three pillars of Abenomics corporate governance reforms" in Japan, all of which are touting the merits of a "purposeful dialogue between companies and investors," or engagement.

The Japanese Stewardship Code defines "purposeful dialogue" as follows:

> "Stewardship responsibilities" refers to the responsibilities of institutional investors to enhance the mid-to-long-term investment return for their clients and beneficiaries by improving and fostering the investee companies' corporate value and sustainable growth through constructive engagement, or purposeful dialogue, based on in-depth knowledge of the companies and their business environment. This Code defines principles considered to be helpful for institutional investors who behave as responsible institutional investors in fulfilling their stewardship responsibilities with due regard both to their clients and beneficiaries and to investee companies.

Overseas investors with a long-term horizon have tried to build relationships with Japanese companies for many years. The *Japanese Corporate Governance Code* has in turn defined "purposeful dialogue" as noted below:

> In order to contribute to sustainable growth and the increase of corporate value over the mid-to-long-term, companies should engage in constructive dialogue with shareholders even outside the general shareholders' meeting.

> With the establishment of Japan's Stewardship Code, institutional investors are encouraged to engage in purposeful dialogue (engagement) based on the in-depth knowledge of investee companies and their business environment.

> Regularly engaging in dialogue with shareholders to gain their understanding of specific business strategies and business plans and taking appropriate action when there are concerns being extraordinarily useful for companies to strengthen the foundations of management legitimacy and support their efforts to generate sustainable growth.

These two codes work closely together and aim to promote purposeful dialogue between shareholders (including overseas investors) and companies.

Furthermore, the *Ito Review* suggests being an "advanced nation in terms of dialogue" as the following manner:

> If sustainable corporate value creation is to be realized through the "collaborative creation" of companies and investors, then both sides must forgo any preconceived notions, prejudices, and apprehensions, and work to build a relationship of mutual trust.

How should Japanese companies engage in "purposeful dialogue" with investors, especially overseas ones, to improve corporate value? What themes are appropriate

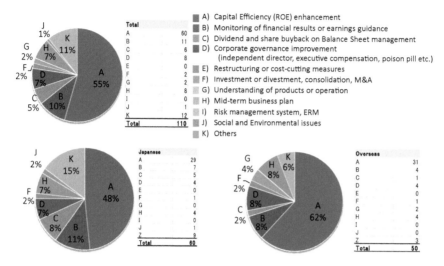

Fig. 7.1   What is your top priority engagement agenda in Japan? *Source* Yanagi (2014b)

for purposeful dialogue (i.e., engagement agendas) that generate a win-win situation for both sides? This section considers the theme for dialogue as engagement agenda based on a global investor survey.

I conducted a global investor survey regarding the Japanese Stewardship Code in FY 2014 (Yanagi 2014b), and asked investors to cite the major themes for dialogue (Fig. 7.1).

Overseas investors answered that capital productivity or capital efficiency in 62% of replies—in other words, ROE—was their top priority engagement agenda. This result is reasonable considering the contents of this book, which serve as a corollary to the fact that ROE is a proxy for shareholder value creation.

In 2015, I also conducted a global investor survey of the Corporate Governance Code (Yanagi 2015a, b, c), asking investors about their expectations of it (Fig. 7.2).

Indeed, overseas investors expected an improvement in ROE over the mid-to-long term through awareness reform by the Corporate Governance Code.

Even though it is obvious that capital efficiency drew the greatest attention of overseas investors concerned about ROE's correlation with shareholders' value, Japanese companies also hope that these concerns could be an ideal engagement agenda to promote investors' understanding. Japanese companies, therefore, are seeking a mid-to-long-term perspective, non-financial information, intangibles, ESG (Environment, Social, Governance) or CSR (Corporate Social Responsibility) and contributions to society.[1]

---

[1] For the purposes of this chapter, "ESG (Environment, Social, Governance)," "CSR (Corporate Social Responsibility)," "non-financial capital," "non-financial information," "intangible," "invisible," and other related terms will not be distinguished according to their strict definitions.

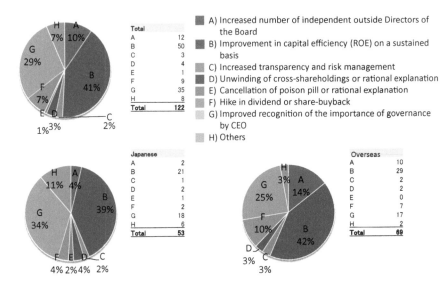

Fig. 7.2 What do you expect most in wake of Japan's Corporate Governance Code? *Source* Yanagi (2015b)

7.2 ESG (Environment, Social, Governance) Impact on Corporate Value Global Investor Survey Pertaining to ESG as Qualitative Evidence

The double codes commonly include "capital efficiency" and "capital policy" for sustainable growth and improvement of corporate value objectives, and, as the global survey result given in the previous section indicates, the priority of investors both overseas and in Japan is ROE.

However, it also is essential that then Corporate Governance Code takes into account the balance between ROE (financial information) and non-financial information like "Stakeholders other than shareholders," "Engagement with ESG (Environment, Social, Governance)," and "disclosure of non-financial information," which reflects on the mid-to-long term perspective of companies along with the possibility of sustainability. The priority of companies is generally non-financial information such as corporate philosophy and ESG/CSR from the standpoint of the mid-to-long-term horizon.

In fact, according to the questionnaire for corporate IR (Investor Relations) by the JIRA (Japanese Investor Relations Association), the number one ranked agenda for IR activities—indicated by 57% of the respondents—is "explanation of corporate value that is not transparent on the basis of financial information (non-financial information)". Moreover, 54% of companies said that they conducted IR activities considering ESG.

How should companies explain their non-financial capital such as ESG that is related to value creation? One useful tool for more assertive disclosure by companies might be an "Integrated Report." A globally accepted framework for integrated report disclosure was published by the IIRC (International Integrated Report Council) in December 2013.

The IIRC defines the six capitals in The International Integrated Reporting Framework (IIRC 2013) as "Intellectual capital", "Human capital", "Manufactured capital", "Social and relationship capital", "Natural capital" (together called five non-financial capitals), and financial capital.

I conducted a global investor survey[2] from May to September in 2013 about the definition of corporate value, the relationship between ESG—as non-financial information—and corporate valuation, investment criteria, and the adoption of integrated reporting by Japanese companies. The result is shown in Fig. 7.3.

In Question 2, the majority of investors answered that ESG has an impact on corporate value as non-financial information. The impact roughly falls into two categories: reduction of equity costs and improvement in the degree of earnings forecasting. In other words, theoretically, ESG impacts the reduction of equity cost[3] and, practically, improvement in the degree of business forecasting.[4]

However, in Question 4, one may see arguments for and against integrated reporting by Japanese companies. The results may imply that although most investors admit that non-financial information is valuable, they would neither value integrated reporting nor its explanation unless these are of sufficiently high quality as to indicate the proper relationship between ROE and corporate value.

For example, as for Question 1, fifteen respondents answered D, "corporate value can't be measured by figure (more conceptual, philosophical)," but 12 of 15 respondents consist of Japanese investors. As we can see, overseas investors tend to think that corporate value can be measured by the figures.

In Question 4, a majority of Japanese investors demonstrated their understanding of integrated reporting, answering that "Integrated reporting is favorable and it should be left to each companies' decision," whereas 35% of overseas investors asserted that "Shareholder-oriented annual financial reporting is preferred over integrated reporting."

Overall, overseas investors seem to require "the high level of financial reporting" first rather than non-financial information such as ESG.

Note that the number of Japanese institutional investors is more than overseas investors in this questionnaire.

---

[2]The result is reprinted with permission of UBS. The targets of the surveys are all major customers of UBS Securities, which is composed of 200 UBS core companies. Respondents are that; overseas companies 31, Japanese companies 97, valid response total is 128. (Rate of response: 64%)

[3]Dhaliwal el al. (2011) report that companies with excellent CSR in the U.S. publish CSR reports and in the first fiscal year calling for non-financial information, reduce cost of equity by approximately 1%.

[4]Nissay Asset Management (2014) indicated that its investee ESG ranking was reflected in the accuracy of analyst performance forecasts, and that there was a positive correlation between ESG ranking and stock performance.

Q1 What is corporate value?

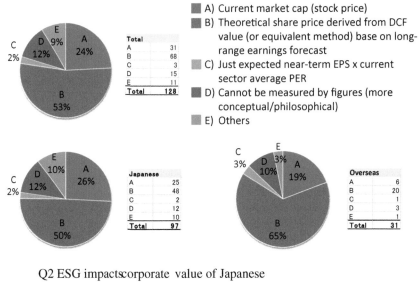

A) Current market cap (stock price)

B) Theoretical share price derived from DCF value (or equivalent method) base on long-range earnings forecast

C) Just expected near-term EPS x current sector average PER

D) Cannot be measured by figures (more conceptual/philosophical)

E) Others

Q2 ESG impacts corporate value of Japanese

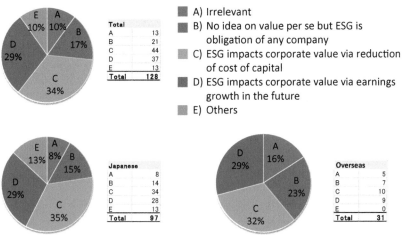

A) Irrelevant

B) No idea on value per se but ESG is obligation of any company

C) ESG impacts corporate value via reduction of cost of capital

D) ESG impacts corporate value via earnings growth in the future

E) Others

Fig. 7.3 Result of global investor survey related to ESG and corporate value. *Source* Yanagi (2015b)

Q3 Investors should factor ESG in investment decision?

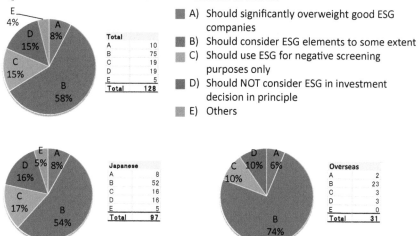

A) Should significantly overweight good ESG companies
B) Should consider ESG elements to some extent
C) Should use ESG for negative screening purposes only
D) Should NOT consider ESG in investment decision in principle
E) Others

Q4 Adoption of Integrated reporting in Japan?

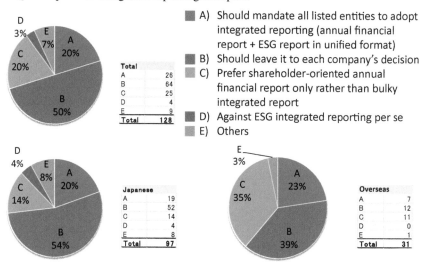

A) Should mandate all listed entities to adopt integrated reporting (annual financial report + ESG report in unified format)
B) Should leave it to each company's decision
C) Prefer shareholder-oriented annual financial report only rather than bulky integrated report
D) Against ESG integrated reporting per se
E) Others

Fig. 7.3 (continued)

To make sure the true intention of investors regarding non-financial information such as ESG, I conducted a global investor survey again in 2017 and asked the following ESG-related questions:

(Survey Period: 2017, January 10 to February 22, Respondents: Japanese Investors 77, Overseas Investors 62, and Total 139 respondents whose assets under management of Japan equity investment amounts to 100 trillion yen in the aggregate as of March 31, 2017) (Fig. 7.4).

*These charts are excerpts of the latest global investor survey in 2017, which is fully quoted in the Appendix of this book.

In the Question regarding Japanese Companies' ESG, 73% of investors are demanding that Japan should explain the value-relevance between their ESG and ROE (corporate value). On the other hand, it should be noted that 27% of overseas investors are critical by saying "Japanese companies must put first priority on capital efficiency before ESG since Japan's ROE lags far behind its international peers."

Thus, global investors seek not "ESG for ESG" but instead "ESG for value creation". Japan should show ROE of their ESG. In this context, Professor Kunio Ito of Hitotsubashi University, who is the chair of the Ito Review Committee, asserts the importance of "ROESG" in his recent assertions.

In return, in the Question, "How do you factor ESG of Japanese companies in your valuation/investment decision?", there seems to be no unified methodology on the part of investor constituency with the most common answer being "we will consider ESG to some extent but rather ambiguously and subjectively". In this chapter, I will try to show the value-relevance model connecting ESG with ROE as a new value proposition.

7.3 Engagement Agenda Between Japanese Companies and Overseas Investors: Achieving a Good Balance Between Social Value and Economic Value

"Dialogue with shareholders" is the basic principle of the Japanese Corporate Governance Code, and the Japanese Stewardship Code emphasizes that "purposeful dialogue" must be maintained between companies and investors. Both Codes also focus on ROE.

Moreover, as confirmed in this chapter (by means of the global investor survey), global investors require the improvement of ROE though governance reform.

Indeed, in contrast, Japanese companies advocate the importance of non-financial information such as ESG or CSR from the mid-to-long-term perspective.

Of course, long-term oriented global investors certainly recognize and seek the relationship between ESG and corporate value.

The Corporate Governance Code includes factors reflecting on such a situation: corporate philosophy, consideration to stakeholders other than shareholders, engagement with respect to ESG, and disclosure of non-financial information.

What do you think about Japanese Companies'
ESG (Environment, Social, Governance) and its disclosure (by integrated reports) ?

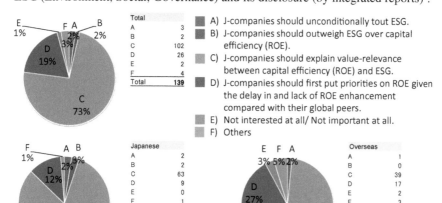

A) J-companies should unconditionally tout ESG.

B) J-companies should outweigh ESG over capital efficiency (ROE).

C) J-companies should explain value-relevance between capital efficiency (ROE) and ESG.

D) J-companies should first put priorities on ROE given the delay in and lack of ROE enhancement compared with their global peers.

E) Not interested at all/ Not important at all.

F) Others

How do you factor ESG of Japanese companies in your valuation/investment decision?

A) I do NOT factor it in at all.

B) ESG is used for negative-screening ONLY.

C) ESG is used for positive-screening ONLY.

D) ESG is reflected in the level of capital cost (DCF discount rate) applied to valuation of each Japanese company.

E) ESG is reflected in the confidence level of earnings forecast (DCF discount rate) applied to valuation of each Japanese company.

F) ESG is factored in the level of multiples (PBR, PER) applied to each Japanese company.

G) ESG is somewhat influencing my subjective investment judgment albeit ambiguously and roughly.

H) Others

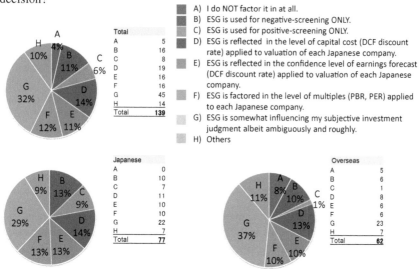

Fig. 7.4 Result of latest global investor survey related to ESG and corporate value. *Source* Yanagi (2017b)

Companies have a variety of important stakeholders besides shareholders. These stake-holders include internal parties such as employees and external parties such as customers, business partners and creditors. In addition, local communities form the foundation for the on-going business activities of companies. Companies should fully recognize that appropriate cooperation with these stakeholders is indispensable in achieving sustainable growth and increasing corporate value over the mid-to-long-term. Given the recent and growing interest in social and environmental problems worldwide, taking positive and proactive measures toward ESG (environmental, social and governance) matters may also be included as part of this cooperation.

The appropriate actions of companies based on the recognition of their stakeholder responsibilities will benefit the entire economy and society, which will in turn contribute to producing further benefits to companies, thereby creating a virtuous cycle.

Considering the matter further, I have interviewed global investors many more times and gave a presentation titled, "The Theme of Suggestive Dialogue" at the "IR conference 2014" by JIRA-sponsored. The main points are basically introduced in the interim report of the "IR Round Table" (Chairman: Shoichi Tsumuraya, Associate professor, University of Hitotsubashi) by JIRA.

The Proposed Agenda of "dialogue with shareholders" on Corporate Governance Code suggested by the author is noted below:

【Engagement Agenda】

- Corporate Philosophy (Social value and economic value)
- Vision of management in the mid-to-long-term (financial information plus non-financial information)
- The goal and strategies of ROE in the mid-to-long-term (The goal of each factor and improvement strategy by DuPont Analysis)
- Premise of ROE
- Disclosure and discussion of Equity Spread (ROE over cost of equity)
- Optimal capital structure (balance sheet management)
- Optimal level of cash holdings
- The goal and rationale of shareholders return policy
- Quantitative Investment criteria on capital budgeting (NPV and IRR threshold)
- Current situation of corporate governance
- ESG (Environment, Social, Governance)
- The policy of IR activities.

In fact, investors request improvement of ROE while companies seek sustainability. Therefore, in short, "sustainable ROE" is important and non-financial information also plays an important role in securing "sustainable ROE."

The idea could be synchronized with the perspective of long-term oriented investors if companies engage with the dialogue regarding suggestive agenda. As proof, the agenda basically corresponds to the policy by Hermes, the famous U.K. pension investment management (Hermes Responsible Ownership Principles, Chap. 2, What we expect of listed companies).

【Hermes quotation "what we expect of listed companies"】

- Listed companies should be willing to have an open, ongoing and high-level dialogue with shareholders on the issues.

- Companies should generate sustainable returns in excess of the cost of capital.
- Companies should ensure that all investment plans have been critically tested in terms of their ability to create long-term shareholder value. If a company is considering diversifying from or rapidly expanding its core business, especially if by acquisition, it should apply significantly higher hurdles within such tests to reflect the greater risks inherent in such a strategy.
- Companies should have an efficient capital structure which will minimize the long-term cost of capital. Where the capital structure is inefficient taking the particular circumstances of the company concerned into account, the balance of debt and equity should be reconsidered.
- Companies should manage effectively relationships with their employees, suppliers and customers and others who have a legitimate interest in their activities with a view to maximizing long-term shareholder value.
- Companies should manage effectively environmental and social factors that affect their business and society at large with a view to enhancing their long-term sustainability.
- Companies should be guided by boards that are made up of members with an appropriate and diverse range of competencies, knowledge and experience to enable them effectively to carry out their duties and responsibilities. These include selecting, guiding, monitoring, challenging and where necessary, replacing management and thus require an ability to step back and act objectively and independently in the long-term interests of the company and its shareholders. The leadership structure of boards should reflect these objectives. Ideally, boards should be led by an independent non-executive chair. Where a different approach is preferred, this should be explained and justified. Boards should establish and maintain an appropriate corporate culture and assume responsibility for remuneration policies and oversee the risk management function.

7.4 The Integrated Report as a Tool of "Purposeful Dialogue": Case Study of Integrated Report by Eisai Co., Ltd.

7.4.1 The Character of the Integrated Report

According to the results of the global investor survey by Yanagi (2014b), the agenda that the investors strongly required for a dialogue with Japanese companies is ROE, whereas the survey by JIRA (2014) said that companies hope to explain most "non-financial information" during the dialogue.

Accordingly, the keywords for companies were "sustainable ROE" and "the mid-to-long-term perspective" and "non-financial information," including ESG. These ideas should be synchronized with the perspective of long-term investors.

In order to construct a win-win situation for sustainable improvement and corporate value, an integrated report would play an important role as a tool for assertive disclosure to promote social value and economic value that asserts disclosure and explains the information according to the dialogue under consideration.

In general, most integrated reports are edited by combining ordinal annual reporting with Corporate Social Responsibility (CSR) reporting. It should not be just a standardized fact, but an explanatory tool for disclosing information that organically connects financial information and non-financial information for sustainable corporate value by means of the six types of capitals defined by IIRC: (1) financial, (2) manufactured, (3) intellectual, (4) human, (5) social and relationship, and (6) natural capital, within the business model. (IIRC 2013)[5]

7.4.2 Case Study of the Integrated Report of Eisai Co., Ltd.

In response to the published framework set forth by IIRC, Eisai Co., Ltd., a TSE-listed pharmaceutical company in Japan, published an integrated report for the first time in September 2014 as a pilot study that is in accordance with the aforementioned framework,[6] and has since continued a "purposeful dialogue" with global investors (Yanagi 2015a, b, c).

Though it might not always be the best practice in Japan, as the published material example for a case study of an integrated report the significant points are summarized below with Figures (Annual Report in FY2014 called "Integrated Report Pilot Study," according to the webpage of Eisai):

7.4.2.1 Unique Policy that Linked the IIRC Framework and the Balanced Scorecard

Figure 7.5 shows the structure of the integrated reporting by Eisai, based on this IIRC framework published in December 2013 (IIRC 2013). It included not only financial information but also non-financial information to explain the sustainable generation

---

[5]A summary of the six capitals as defined by the IIRC follows: "Intellectual capital" indicates value from R&D activities, including intangible assets such as patents and other intellectual property. "Human capital" refers to people's skills and experience, and their motivations to innovate. "Manufactured capital" refers to buildings, equipment, and manmade infrastructure used in the production of goods or the provision of services. "Social and relationship capital" is the relationships of trust established within and between each community, various stakeholders, and other networks. "Natural capital" is the environmental resources and processes affected by an organization's activities. Additionally, and distinct from these five non-financial capitals, financial capital is broadly defined as the financial base that supports the corporate activities of an organization; in a narrow sense, it refers to be the book value of shareholder's equity on an accounting basis.

[6]Integrated Report in fiscal year 2014 was made of rearranged Annual Report by IIRC framework as pilot study case, that's why CSV reporting is also existing. In FY2015, Eisai Co., Ltd. actually integrated both reports.

Fig. 7.5   Eisai's value creation process and flow. *Source* Ito (2014)

of social value and economic value, while considering all stakeholders under the six categories of capital given by IIRC (i.e., financial, manufactured, intellectual, human, social and relationship, and natural capital).

The "flow of value creation," or how to create value by business, is based on the four perspectives of the Balanced Scorecard (Kaplan and Norton 1996), which takes its standpoint from learning and growth, customer, internal process, plus financial[7] and ends up focusing on the financial perspective to show the route to enhancing corporate value while still considering all stakeholders.

A combination of IIRC's six capital model and Balanced Scorecard with four perspectives is well-suited for explaining the flow of value creation from both financial and non-financial viewpoints.

---

[7]Ito (2014) implies the integration of Integrated Report and Balanced Scorecard.

7.4.2.2   Corporate Philosophy Called Human Health Care (hhc), Is Defined by the Notion that Economic Value Should Result from Social Value, Which Is Its Mission and Priority

Eisai is a unique company that shares its corporate philosophy with its shareholders by the special resolution passed by majority vote in the Annual General Meeting of Shareholders, thereby setting forth the principles in Articles of Incorporation. Companies with such characteristics are uncommon in Japan. The philosophy called *hhc* is defined as being that "the company gives first thought to patients and their families." This was established in the corporate Articles of Incorporation over twenty years ago.

CSR is defined as a social responsibility, whether charity, voluntary activities or social contribution activities, that are not always connected with economic value.

Moreover, CSR (Creating Shared Value) is the business model[8] that realizes social and economic value simultaneously, with the result being an advanced business model of common value.

Though the *hhc* philosophy is similar to CSV, *hhc* has only one mission: contribution to patients as the first priority. Economic value is the consequential result of these contributions. This sequence is stressed, and that is the difference vis-à-vis CSV.

Eisai declares in the Articles of Incorporation that "The Company's mission is the enhancement of patient satisfaction. The Company believes that sales and earnings will be generated as a consequence of the fulfillment of this mission. The Company places importance on this positive sequence of the mission and the ensuing results."

This means that *hhc* is the management model that generates economic value (like sales and profits) that result from creating social value, whereas enhancing patient satisfaction is the only purpose, accomplished by continuous organizational transformation of its activities. Moreover, Eisai places importance not only on patient value and employment value, but also on shareholder's value, and engages with disclosure, enhancing corporate value, and shareholder's return. However, its "social value first" motivation, placing importance on the sequence described above, differs at certain points with CSV in which the priority is generating social value and profit at the same time (Fig 7.6).

7.4.2.3   Pipeline as Intellectual Capital (i.e., the Value of Research and Development)

The corporate value of pharmaceutical companies relies on its pipeline of new drugs and intellectual value, as part of non-financial capital. Therefore, integrated reporting devotes many pages to explaining the current situation of R&D and also R&D systems that are related to human capital. Moreover, with respect to the expected

---

[8]Referring to Porter and Kramer (2011) as for CSV.

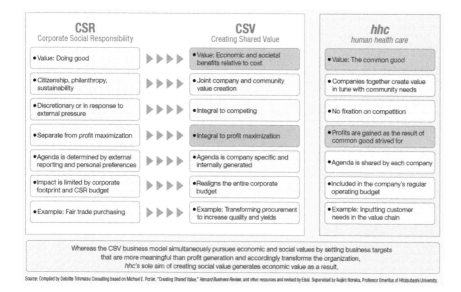

Fig. 7.6 Comparing CSR, CSV, and the corporate philosophy *hhc* (human health care). *Source* Integrated Report 2014 by Eisai Co., Ltd.

pipeline of drug discovery in-house, it encourages the writing of the background of the development or the scientific mechanism of action in detail in order to promote the valuation for a new drug, such that a growing base of long-term investors is acquired ipso facto.

7.4.2.4 Promoting Long-Term ROE Management as a Part of a Companies' Financial Capital in the Wake of Intangibles

As Fig. 7.7 shows, Eisai has been engaged with long-term ROE management related to creating sustainable shareholder value since the 2000s, and has been seeking ten-year average ROE above cost of equity (positive Equity Spread) while overcoming short-termism especially when it comes to R&D investment for the future.

ROE management aims at an ROE and Equity Spread that fulfill global standards for the long-term by means of improving margins, financial leverage, and turnover.

The ROE target is calculated using the average over a decade due to the fact that R&D from long-term projects and upfront investments supporting R&D projects is mandatory and should gain consent from long-term investors.

In addition, hypothesizing that the cost of equity is 8% (i.e., the risk-free rate of 2% plus a risk premium 6% with a beta 1.0) ahead of other companies and spontaneously disclosing its Equity Spread aims at creating shareholder value on a long-term basis (over a decade).

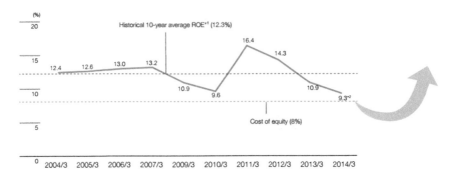

Equity spread (%): ROE − Cost of equity (CoE)
Proxy variable for shareholder value creation
Historical 5-year average: ROE 12.1% - CoE 8% - Equity spread 4.1%
Historical 10-year average: ROE 12.3% - CoE 8% - Equity spread 4.3%
*Assume cost of shareholders' equity of 8% (risk-free rate of 2% + risk premium of 6%)
*[1]Results for the fiscal year ended March 2008 are not included
*[2] Number excludes impact from an extraordinary loss due to a voluntary early-retirement program
**They have been removed as they do not serve as an appropriate reference due to the extraordinary impact of the MGI
Pharma, Inc. acquisition

Fig. 7.7 Eisai's ROE migration and value creation by equity spread–Self-disclosure of Equity
Spread and engagement with investors. *Source* Integrated Report 2014 by Eisai Co., Ltd.

For your reference, along with Eisai, Anritsu Corporation, an electronics-
manufacturing company listed on TSE and SATO Holdings Corporation, has obtained
a high reputation from overseas investors via disclosure of equity spread or equivalent.

7.4.2.5   MVA (Market Value Added): Materialization of Non-financial Capitals (i.e., the Breakdown of PBR)

The standard level of PBR that describes the market value creation of Japanese companies is not very high at the international level, leading to investor dissatisfaction.
However, the market value of Eisai over the past decade has largely been above
double the equity book value (net assets) though the standard levels of PBR in Japan
being just one, because Eisai has been engaged with "ROE management" since the
2000s as mentioned beforehand. In other words, market value (i.e., market capitalization) exceeds its net assets (book value), and Eisai generates steady MVA (market
capitalization equals net asset plus MVA). Net assets are related to "financial capitals" whereas MVA is related to the aforementioned five "non-financial capitals" by
IIRC (Fig. 7.8).

Thus, integrated reporting at Eisai has linked financial and non-financial information. This connection has played an important role and tool for "purposeful dialogue,"
as well as explaining corporate value creation that has promoted a fruitful discussion
with long-term investors.

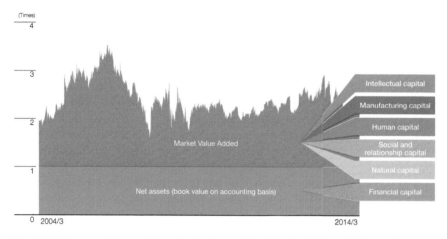

Fig. 7.8 Relevance of six capitals and valuation by Eisai-Eisai's PBR model. *Source* Integrated Report 2014 by Eisai Co., Ltd.

7.5 All Japan Case from the Viewpoint of IIRC-PBR Model

7.5.1 Inconvenient Truth

Japan's inconvenient truth is the lack of value creation in recent years. In Japan, CSR/ESG and non-financial information are booming now with nearly 300 listed companies having adopted on Integrated Report Format in 2016. Given the fact that Japanese corporate managers are traditionally inclined to provide their companies' intangibles such as human resource data and social contribution information rather than financial metrics like EPS and ROE which investor constituency naturally places importance on as a source of valuation. According to the global investor survey conducted by author (Yanagi 2017b), as mentioned beforehand, the vast majority (73%) of investors in Japan and abroad demand an explanation of value-relevance between ESG and ROE in connection with non-financial information described in Japanese companies' integrated reports. Under such circumstances, how can we prove the relationship between non-financial information (intangibles) and corporate value (ROE)?

In this section, "non-financial information" is defined as referring to the six capitals in *The International Integrated Reporting Framework* (IIRC 2013) published by the International Integrated Reporting Council (IIRC), but excluding "financial capital" to use only the five "non-financial capitals," particularly "human capital" and "intellectual capital."

Furthermore, as briefly touched upon in the Eisai case study in the previous section, PBR (price-book value ratio) which is market capitalization divided by equity book value is adopted as a standard proxy variable for corporate value; PBR indicates a company's market capitalization over its net assets (equity) on an accounting basis, but when this is less than one, the situation is interpreted as being one of "value destruction," or that below liquidation value. On the contrary, in connection with PBR, the portion above PBR one or the amount that exceeds book value is considered to be a listed company's additional "value creation" or the value added.

In other words, from the standpoint of corporate value creation, "market value added" (MVA), market capitalization minus equity book value) is of great importance. Approaching this from a different angle, MVA is in other words "self-created goodwill" that cannot be recorded on an accounting basis, an added value that management should create to improve long-term corporate value, and a "hidden value (intangible value)."

However, in recent years, Japan's PBR has been stagnant and hovering around one without meaningful MVA as shown in Fig. 7.9. Japan's inconvenient truth is lack of value creation despite its allegedly affluent intangibles. Will the SUN rise again in the wake of Abenomics?

For your reference, major financial metrics are shown below:

*PBR (times) = Market capitalization ÷ Book value net assets on accounting basis = Stock price ÷ Book value net assets per share
*MVA (amount) = Market capitalization – Book value net assets on accounting basis = Amount of the portion in excess of PBR 1
*PBR = ROE x PER
*ROE (%) = Net profit in accounting book ÷ Book value shareholder's equity on accounting basis
*PER (times) = Market capitalization ÷ Net profit on accounting basis = Stock price ÷ Net profit per share (EPS)

7.6 IIRC-PBR Model and Synchronization of Non-financials and Equity Spread

First, under the Intrinsic Value Model described in Yanagi (2009), market value added (MVA) is defined as intangibles like "organizational value," "human value," "customer value," and "ESG/CSR value (cost of capital reduction effects)."

In contrast to this, Yanagi (2015a, b, c) introduces the IIRC–PBR Model, which comprises the six capitals defined by the IIRC aforementioned in previous section (Eisai example) and their relationship with PBR as a proxy variable of corporate value. Based on the assumption that "shareholder value equals long-term market capitalization, which equals Book Value of Shareholders' Equity (BV=net assets) plus MVA," the model positions BV (part with PBR of less than one time) as "financial capital" and MVA (part with PBR of one time or more) as the five non-financial capitals related. Such IIRC-PBR model is shown in Fig. 7.10 citing Eisai's latest number.

Incidentally, the IIRC suggests that approximately 20% of corporate value is related to the value of "physical and financial assets," with the remaining approxi-

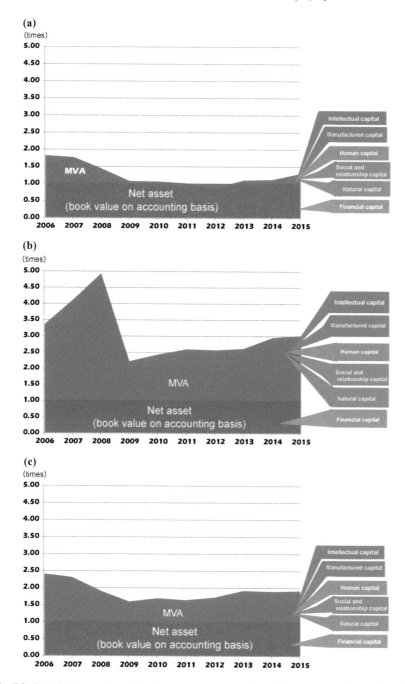

Fig. 7.9 Japan's inconvenient truth by peer comparison. *Note* Average value. *Source* Based on Bloomberg (Yanagi) **a** TOPIX PBR Migration (2006–2015), **b** Dow Jones Industrial Average PBR Migration (2006–2015) **c** FTSE100 PBR Migration (2006–2015)

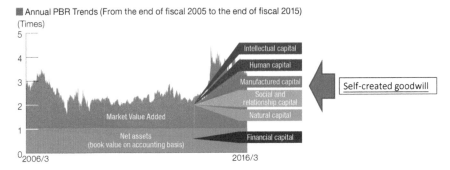

■ Annual PBR Trends (From the end of fiscal 2005 to the end of fiscal 2015)

Fig. 7.10 IIRC– PBR Model. Proposed Relationship Between Five Non-Financial Capitals and Market Value Added (Self-Created Goodwill) in the case of Eisai (one of the largest Japanese pharmaceutical companies) for which I serve as CFO. *Source* Reproduction of figure on page 60 of *Integrated Report 2016*, published by Eisai Co., Ltd.

mately 80% being related to the value of "intangible factors." Based on this indication as well as the assumption that asymmetry of information is overcome, it is possible to potentially see value added creation with PBR of up to five times. IMA's Strategic Finance May 2017 article (*The Power of Intangibles by Cokins and Shepherd*) proves the same in the case of US companies.

In addition, following the Residual Income Model (RIM; Ohlson 2001), it can be said that a company with a high PBR has a strong long-term Equity Spread (ROE minus Cost of Equity) prediction, but on the other hand, this can also be explained as the market incorporating the value of non-financial capital (also called "pre-financial capital") converted into future financial value.

In conjunction with the RIM model, based on its relationship whereby market value added converges to the total discounted present value of long-term stream of Residual Income (Equity Spread), I present below the value relationships of all three models: the abovementioned RIM, the IIRC-PBR Model, and the Intrinsic Value Model.[9]

Intrinsic Value Model (Yanagi 2009):

Market value added (MVA) = the part with PBR of more than one
=non-financial capital related (intangibles)
="organizational value" + "human value" + "customer value" + "ESG/CSR value (cost of capital reduction effects)"

IIRC–PBR Model (Eisai case):

---

[9]Although the equation does not hold up in reality because stock price reflects market noise and asymmetry of information, it still is able to provide an indication of long-term market capitalization as a proxy for corporate value. Furthermore, although non-financia capital (converted into future financial capital) and market added value do not always match, it remains a conceptual framework that suggests that there is a relationship.

Shareholder value = long-term market capitalization
=Book Value of Shareholders' Equity (BV) + market added value (MVA)
BV =the part with PBR of less than one = "financial capital"
MVA = the part with PBR of more than one
=non-financial capital related (intangibles)
= "intellectual capital" + "human capital" + "manufactured capital" + "social and relationship capital" and "natural capital" as IIRC defines
(=delayed and converted "future financial capital" which equals self-created goodwill).

Residual Income Model (RIM):

Shareholder value = long-term market capitalization
=Book Value of Shareholder's Equity (BV) + market added value (MVA)
MVA = the part with PBR of more than one
=the sum of the present values of stream Equity Spread which is ROE minus cost of shareholder's equity x BV (=Residual Income)

Based on these equations, "MVA" based on PBR as a proxy variable of corporate added value is a common characteristic, and Equity Spread as total present value of residual income and the IIRC's five non-financial capitals are mutually complementary. Figure 7.11 shows a model that integrates the value relationships indicated by the three models—the IIRC–PBR Model, the Intrinsic Value Model, and RIM—that associate non-financial capitals with Equity Spread via MVA.[10] I advocate that these "Non-Financial Capitals and Equity Spread Synchronization Model" as my value proposition also be adopted in integrated reporting.

7.7 Case Study of Non-financial Capitals and Equity Spread Synchronization Model

7.7.1 Eisai Case: Supplying DEC Tablets Free of Charge

Based on the evidence introduced in this chapter, the concept of equity spread should be well disseminated and utilized by corporate management, which leads to improvement of corporate value. Investors also should emphasize the relevance of equity spread and performance.

In order to show a concrete example of this ESG-ROE integration model, Eisai (one of the largest Japanese pharmaceutical companies) case study from their 2016 integrated report is noted below:

Eisai has announced in a joint declaration that they have entered into an agreement with the WHO (World Health Organization) to provide 2.2 billion tablets (DEC

---

[10]The author presented this model as Eisai CFO at the ICGN–IIRC Conference in London in December 2016, and it was met with consent from IIRC representatives.

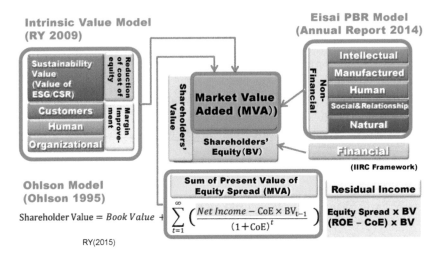

Fig. 7.11 Non-Financial Capitals and Equity Spread Synchronization Model. (Source) Yanagi (2015b)

tablets) for the treatment of lymphatic filariasis, a neglected tropical disease, free of charge to patients in emerging countries until 2020. This social contribution to access to medicines (ATM) is not a donation and does not merely stop at CSR (corporate social responsibility), but is an aspect of "ultra-long-term investment" that is also accepted by investors and shareholders. In other words, it is the combination of social value and economic value (CSV: Creating Shared Value). Following the IIRC model, Eisai explains the input, output, and outcome of this in its 2016 integrated report (Fig. 7.12).

This is indeed an attempt aimed at "high value–added management" and is value creation through the S (social contribution) in ESG. At first, as a project in the red ink, it was a negative factor on short-term profits and ROE, but in the ultra-long term, NPV (net present value) can actually be calculated as having become positive through factors such as brand value in the company's business operations in emerging countries in the future, increased productivity and improved skills and motivation of employees through higher capacity utilization rate at Eisai's India plant.[11] In a sense, this is an "ultra-long-term investment" that is both a win-win situation for long-term investors and justifiable from a financial theory standpoint. In other words, this project is not just a partial example, but arguably a concrete case of the "non-financial capital and equity spread synchronization model" being implemented that has led to increased ROE as a long-term and delayed outcome (Fig. 7.12).

---

[11]Reference: *The Nikkei*, July 26, 2016. "Market Dynamics, Chosen Companies, and below, Growth and Co-existence on a Single Axis" (Author: Takahito Fujiwara et al.)

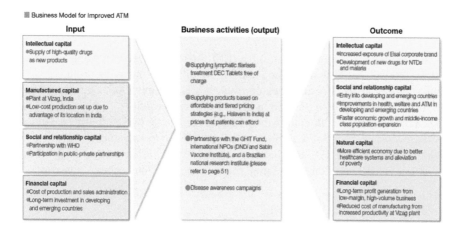

Fig. 7.12 Value creation via free distribution of anti-filariasis drug. *Source* Page 47 of *Integrated Report 2016*, by Eisai Co., Ltd. (Republished with permission from company website)

7.7.2 SAP Case: Employee Satisfaction Translated into Profit

In addition, to prove the IIRC-PBR model from a human capital perspective, SAP (Germany) case study (from SAP's 2015 Integrated Report) is introduced as below;

SAP is the largest IT software corporation in Europe. Mainly as a representative variable of "human capital," it analyzes points of engagement index of internal employees and correlation of operational profit and discloses them in its 2015 integrated report. The case studies SAP introduces as methods for measuring non-financial capital performance are of great interest.

For example, SAP's employee engagement index (EEI) is an index that measures company loyalty, work ethic, pride, and sense of belonging at SAP. The EEI is based on the results of an employee survey, and this index is applied and measurements implemented based on the stance that the corporation's growth strategy is essentially employee engagement as "human capital."

To measure its effectiveness, SAP implements a "people survey" (employee survey) from October to November each year to analyze how financial and non-financial performance correlates with employee engagement. As a result, when the EEI changes to 1%, SAP calculates that it brings about a positive influence of EUR 40 million to EUR 50 million to the corporation's objectives of "growth accompanied by profit acquisition" and "customer loyalty."

SAP has also devoted close attention to building a framework for a concrete, mutually correlative establishment of financial capital and non-financial capital performance. As a result, it measures impact on operating profit using four environmental and social (the "E" and "S" of ESG) indices, namely, the business-health-culture index (BHCI), the employee engagement index (EEI), employee retention rate, and

CO_2 emissions volume. (It also calculates return on invested capital based on a causal relationship.)

*When the employee engagement index (EEI) increases by 1%, it brings about a positive influence of EUR 40 million to EUR 50 million to operating profit.
*When the employee retention rate improves by 1%, it brings about a positive influence of EUR 45 million to EUR 55 million to operating profit.
*When the business-health-culture index (BHCI) optimizes by 1%, it brings about a positive influence of EUR 75 million to EUR 85 million to operating profit.
*When the volume of CO_2 emissions is reduced by 1%, it brings about a positive influence of EUR 4 million to operating profit (cost reduction becomes possible).

This is also a good example to verify the efficacy of the IIRC-PBR model or Integration of ESG and ROE as win-win.

7.8 Correlation Between Five Non-financial Capitals and PBR: Empirical Research as Quantitative Evidence

Is it possible to confirm the "relationship between the IIRC-defined five non-financial capitals and PBR" or "Non-Financial Capitals and Equity Spread Synchronization Model" by demonstrating a statistical correlation in Japan? In this section, the author will introduce previous academic study results. I also will show empirical research of correlation study results where I was involved as latest research applied to Japanese companies.

7.8.1 Existing Empirical Research Implying Correlation Between Non-financial Capitals and Shareholder Value as Quantitative Evidence

7.8.1.1 The ESG (Environment, Social, and Governance) of a Company Reduces Its Capital Cost

In a previous study that indicated a "negative correlation" between information disclosure as accountability (Investor Relations: IR), or corporate governance in the broader sense (the "G" in ESG), and capital cost, Botosan (1997) conducted a regression analysis sampling annual reports published by 122 US manufacturers in 1990. The analysis suggested that levels of disclosure considered high by the study's standards led to a reduction in expected shareholders' cost of equity in the Ohlson model (with a difference in capital cost of about 0.28% between those companies with excellent disclosure and those companies without). In addition, Agarwal et al. (2008) found that companies awarded Best IR Programs in the U.S. between 2000 and 2002 indicated reduced asymmetric information, increased liquidity, and an excess return on stocks.

Among Japanese companies, too, Otokawa (2000) used comprehensive disclosure scores from "Award for Excellence in Corporate Disclosure" choices by the Securities Analysts Association of Japan for fiscal years 1998 and 1999 to suggest companies with a high level of disclosure had reduced shareholders' cost of equity. Furthermore, Suda (2004) similarly examined the relationship between "Award for Excellence in Corporate Disclosure" rankings for fiscal years 1995–2000 and shareholders' cost of equity, reporting that the shareholders' equity cost of companies in each sector with an IR evaluation ranking within third place was about 0.3% lower than that of companies ranking in fourth place or lower; that the shareholders' equity cost of companies ranking in first or second place was about 0.5% lower than that of companies ranking in fourth place or lower; and that the shareholders' equity cost of companies ranking in first place was about 0.8% lower than that of companies ranking in fourth place or lower.

For example, given a clean surplus and steady-state conditions, if the shareholders' equity of a company was 8% and its net profit was 100 billion yen, and considering that the shareholder value of the company is represented by PER (reciprocal of capital cost minus growth rate: r-g), then 100 billion yen divided by 8% equals 1.25 trillion yen. In this case, assuming that based on the above, better quality IR would reduce capital cost by circa 0.3%, and then the shareholders' equity cost would drop to 7.7%, and, hence, the company's shareholder value would improve to 100 billion yen divided by 7.7%, that is, 1.3 trillion yen (an increase of 50 billion yen). This is the market interpreting non-financial capital, or "invisible value of governance (the "G" of ESG) in the broader sense (IR)," as being related to corporate value.

Regarding ESG overall, on the other hand, Dhaliwal et al. (2011) report that U.S. companies with award-winning CSR programs had reduced capital cost by about 1% in their first fiscal year publishing non-financial information in their CSR reports. Incidentally, regarding Japanese companies, Nissay Asset Management (2014) suggests that its investee ESG rating is reflected in the accuracy of its analyst earnings forecast, and that there is a positive correlation between ESG rating and stock price performance. In addition, Saka and Oshika (2014), Oshika (2008, 2013) all demonstrate that the "E" (CO_2 reduction), "S" (human resources investment), and "G" (ensuring active general shareholders' meetings) have a positive influence on corporate value.

7.8.1.2   Incorporating ESG Factors into Valuation

SMBC Nikko Securities' Chief Quants Analyst Keiichi Ito's report[12] published on April 25, 2016, provides a fascinating analysis of the impact of ESG on stock prices. Introduced here with his permission, the report proves that the "G" (corporate governance as defined by SMBC Nikko Securities scores) of Japanese companies reduces capital cost, but unlike in Europe and elsewhere, ESG factors overall has yet to be fully incorporated in valuations in Japan. Although the report did examine the influence of ESG factors on corporate value in each region, namely, Japan, North America, Europe, and the Pacific (excluding Japan), using a regression model that added ESG information to the PBR–ROE model, no results were obtained indicating that ESG factors had any significant influence on corporate value in Japan, while the influence of ESG factors in Europe, the Pacific (excluding Japan), and elsewhere has been strengthening in recent years. This result is consistent with the MSCI[13] ESG indexes outperforming the MSCI regional indexes in Europe and the Pacific (excluding Japan) recently.

As factors that are ineffective in Japan, there are differences between those items to which MSCI is paying attention, especially in governance, and those items that are actually drawing attention in Japan, and little time has passed since ESG operations began to attract attention in the country. In Japan, this can be interpreted as being because environmental and social information has not yet been sufficiently incorporated as information. I believe that in the future, ESG evaluation will be included in valuations in Japan as well, and through this process, I argue that valuations of highly evaluated brands will rise and valuations of poorly evaluated brands will fall, with ESG evaluation itself becoming the source of excess return.

Meanwhile, an article[14] in The Nikkei published on July 31, 2016, described the introduction of "ESG investment" by the GPIF (Government Pension Investment Fund), a public annuity in Japan, to equity investment activities, in a policy that incorporates not only profit but environmental, social, and governance into corporate evaluation as well. In addition, Schroders, a UK investment fund, has begun sales in Japan of investment trusts that incorporate the ESG viewpoint, stating, "ESG leads to a good relationship with all stakeholders and not only shareholders, and the type of governance in which all members participate is not at odds with the interests of shareholders, but actually enables sustainable growth and contributes to long-term shareholder returns," and, "For example, although a wage increase might be considered "S," investors will think positively if long-term employee motivation contributes to improved productivity, even while the company presses for short-term profits."

---

[12]SMBC Nikko Securities Inc. April 25, 2016. Equity Research Division Report/Japan/Quants "Quants: Prospects for Investment Methods Using ESG Related Information".

[13]Globally recognized representative stock price index calculated and published by MSCI Inc. in the US. To measure the performance of international securities investments, the majority of institutional investors worldwide have adopted it as a benchmark for equity investment.

[14]*The Nikkei.* July 31, 2016. "*Economic Exposition, GPIF (Government Pension Investment Fund) adopted ESG indices, New normal for sustainable growth* " (by Ryujiro Kodaira, senior staff writer).

Next, let's look at the performance of MSCI ESG indexes according to the SMBC Nikko Securities report (Fig. 7.13). According to an analysis of data from September 2010 onward, the ESG indexes have steadily outperformed the regional indexes in Europe and while volatility is high in the Pacific (excluding Japan), as a general trend, there has been a continuing tendency to outperform regional indexes. The information ratio in Europe, where awareness of ESG is widespread, is as high as 0.88 in terms of the annualized rate, and the excellent performance of the ESG indexes is evident. Meanwhile, North America has continued to steadily underperform during this period. Although not much disparity is seen in Japan, there is a tendency to outperform from the middle of 2013, albeit a weak one. Because the performance of North America, with its large composition ratio, is not good, when based on a world index, the tendency to underperform while the weak ESG index is confirmed.

It is likely that the ESG of Japanese companies will be increasingly evaluated and reflected in stock prices after earning the appreciation of investors. In other words, conversion of non-financial capital (ESG) into financial capital (stock price) is expected to accelerate. There is a high probability that the importance of high value-added management according to the "Synchronization Model of Non-financial Capital and Equity Spread" proposed in this chapter will only increase.

7.8.1.3 Patent Information as Intellectual Capital Leads to Mid-to-Long-Term ROE Improvement

Next, I would like to introduce academic research results that suggest patent information, which is intellectual capital (non-financial capital), being transformed with delay into mid-to-long-term ROE and stock price (financial capital). In the October 2016 issue of the Securities Analysts Journal, Mr. Shingo Ide, Chief Financial Strategist at the NLI Research Institute, and Professor Hitoshi Takehara, a professor at Waseda University, published a very insightful study under the theme of "Dissemination of Patent Information into Stock Prices," from which I quote below with their permission.

In the study, patent information (non-financial information) is delayed and converted into a profitability indicator (ROE), suggesting that market participants incorporate changes in profitability into stock price returns (R).[15] See Fig. 7.14.

---

[15] For the data used, the patent information was prepared and provided by Kudo & Associates (data acquisition period: January 2000–December 2013), with exclusive technology usage rights calculated as a YK value (index developed by Kudo & Associates, the value obtained by measuring the aggregate cost invested in the termination of exclusive usage rights of third parties, after considering technological deterioration incurred over time). In addition, sources used for information other than patent information: Nikkei NEEDS, Financial Data Solutions/NPM. The target of the analysis was YK momentum, that is, (as of the end of June, when financial information becomes public information) the data for each industry type was sorted by ascending order according to ΔYK/TA, the change rate in YK value relative to total assets, and then categorized in groups numbered 1 (Low ΔYK/TA) through 5 (High ΔYK/TA). Regarding Groups 1 through 5, P1 (Low)–P5 (High) are constructed as an iso-weighted portfolio for quintile analysis. For P1 through P5, ROE changes in 1, 2, and 3 years after portfolio construction over the past 2 years were measured to calculate

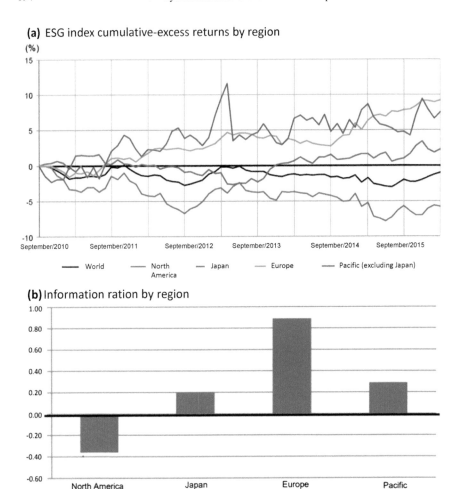

(a) ESG index cumulative-excess returns by region

(b) Information ration by region

Fig. 7.13 Performance of MSCI ESG indexes. **a** ESG index cumulative-excess returns by region. *Note* Cumulated monthly return including dividend (gross) of MSCI ESG index by region and spread of regional index (0 indicates the baseline, as of end of September 2010) Pacific (excluding Japan) refers as follows; Hong Kong, Singapore, Australia and New Zealand. **b** information ration by region. *Note* Calculated each index that is based on monthly return (October 2010–March 2016) and risk is calculated by annualized rate. Return is geometric mean. Active return is the difference between return of the ESG index and return of the original index. Active risk is calculated based on the difference of monthly return of the ESG index. *Source* MSCI, Bloomberg, Nikko Research Center, SMBC Nikko Securities Ltd. (April 15th 2016)

a cumulative portfolio. Analysis period: From June 2000 to June 2012 (stock prices were July 2000–June 2016), the analysis of the TSE 17 industries includes companies specializing in food, construction and other materials, chemicals, automobiles, transportation; analytical target included

> **Hypothesis**
> Development of technological competitiveness (intellectual capital) has positive correlation to ROE migration after 3 years . Afterward, the development is gradually factored into permeates stock price.

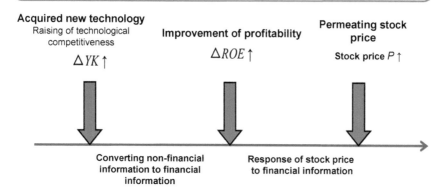

Acquired new technology
Raising of technological competitiveness

$\Delta YK \uparrow$

Improvement of profitability

$\Delta ROE \uparrow$

Permeating stock price

Stock price $P \uparrow$

Converting non-financial information to financial information

Response of stock price to financial information

Fig. 7.14 Patent information (intellectual capital) delayed to improve ROE and contribute to stock price penetration. *Source* Ide and Takehara (2016) Analysis of permeating process patent intelligence through stock price. 24th Annual Meeting of Nippon Finance Association on May 22, 2016, Yokohama National University

- (Study result) Changes in ROE
- After rise in patent value (YK value), positive ROE change correlation in cumulative three-year period
- Difference in cumulative change rate (P5–P1) increases with time

- Inadequate penetration of information into ROE in two years after patent value (YK value) rise
- Difference significantly increased to 2.901 in cumulative three-year period, significant 5% level (p value $= 0.041$)[16]
- YK patent momentum (intellectual capital) had a statistically significant positive influence after three years

Note: The study proved statistical significance that intellectual capital (patent value) was delayed and converted into financial capital (ROE) after three years (Tables 7.1 and 7.2).

It was suggested that patent information as intellectual capital was delayed and positively correlated with ROE improvement (Table 7.1) and subsequent stock price penetration (Table 7.2). In other words, the current non-financial capital (intellectual

---

iron and steel/non-ferrous metals, machinery, electric machinery, and precision instruments as of March 31.

[16]The p value refers to "the probability that when an event can happen by chance, it is equivalent to or more extreme than the observed value." In general, the standard is $p = 0.05$, which means that the possibility of "being mistakenly deemed 'significant' despite actually being a mere coincidence" is 5% or less.

Table 7.1 Relationship between intellectual capital and ROE

	ΔROE (t $-$ 2, t)	ΔROE (t, t + 1)	ΔROE (t, t + 2)	ΔROE (t, t + 3)
P1 (Low)	2.035	-0.333	0.174	-0.081
P2	0.376	0.566	0.432	1.387
P3	0.292	-0.695	1.088	2.117
P4	-0.384	0.495	1.306	1.470
P5	1.275	0.688	1.331	2.821
Difference (P5 $-$ P1)	-0.759	1.021	1.157	**2.901**
P-value	0.700	0.483	0.519	**0.041**

Source Ide and Takehara (2016)
Study result Stock return response
R is the return due to the rise in stock price. Although the return spread (the difference in profits obtained from the equity investment in the top patent value group, P5, and bottom group, P1) was not statistically significant, there was a trend to expand in three to five years after portfolio construction
Note This can be interpreted as R having been incorporated into stock price formation after confirming the increase in ROE

Table 7.2 Relationship between intellectual capital and shareholder return

	R (t, t + 1)	R2(t, t + 2)	R (t, t + 3)	R (t, t + 4)	R (t, t + 5)
P1 (low)	3.851	11.440	22.509	37.673	44.072
P2	3.065	12.622	26.171	40.923	47.236
P3	5.111	12.796	25.096	40.773	48.460
P4	3.760	12.810	25.272	39.864	46.506
P5 (high)	4.318	12.199	26.218	42.310	49.697
Difference (P5 $-$ P1)	0.467	0.759	3.709	4.637	**5.625**
P-value	0.809	0.832	0.417	0.307	**0.244**

Source Ide and Takehara (2016)

capital) was delayed and converted into future financial capital. In order to improve long-term, sustainable corporate value, it is important that Japanese companies do not become short-sighted, but actively invest in R&D. This should also be consistent with the perspective of long-term investors. This is also a valuable work of empirical research supporting high-added value management following the "Synchronization Model of Non-financial Capital and Equity Spread" proposed in this chapter.

7.8.1.4 Indicating Potential Research Value Using the Real Options Model and PI

Regarding the synchronization of quantitative value-added with R&D (including intellectual capital and human capital taking into account the capabilities of researchers), since Yanagi (2009), I have emphasized that in the short term, R&D is charged to expenses (as if being "sunk cost") in accounting GAAP and becomes a negative factor on operating profits. However, the research will bring value on a long-term basis. Therefore, I have used real options and PI (Profitability Index) for the valuation of basic research at the stage where the product value of a specific project is not visible. For example, emphasizing a model where $1 of research expenses today is worth $1.10. This is also a conceptual framework that highlights high added-value management following the "Synchronization Model of Non-financial Capital and Equity Spread" outlined below.

Regarding the calculation of the potential value of basic research, I introduce a simple model in Fig. 7.15 and summarize the logic behind it. R&D expenditure on currently ongoing projects and pipelines can be factored into future DCF value as cost-effective, but the value of potential basic research not yet able to visualize any product is, in the short term, merely charged to expenses in accounting on normal DCF. Is basic research (intellectual capital) worthless? However, there are many cases where high market value added (MVA) is allotted to bio ventures in the red-ink and in many cases PBR is 10 times or more. This is a valuation that is made through incorporating future long-term Equity Spread (or ROE) improvements.

Basic research should be worthwhile. I would like to quantify the value as a real option from a company's past performance and use this model to estimate its intrinsic value.

For example, as seen in Fig. 7.15, from the track record of previous R&D success cases, following the pattern typical of major Japanese pharmaceutical companies (average of peers in the same industry across multiple fiscal years), I assumed that the business value when one product is launched is 130 billion yen, and the capital cost for drug discovery is 25% of the global average number used for bio ventures valuation overall. In addition, it is also assumed that it takes three years for drug discovery and another six years for clinical trials, based on the industry average. On the other hand, I assumed based on the industry average that R&D expenditure will cost more than 50 billion yen until a new product is released to the market.

When adjusting for the harsh probability average of success in the industry and considering the average present value, the projected value of this case estimated from these assumptions is 17.4 billion yen. On the other hand, the present value of the net total R&D expenditure amount is 52.4 billion yen. Therefore, simply put, the net present value (NPV) is a negative 35 billion yen, in which case it is concluded that companies should avoid basic research (intellectual capital). The Profitability Index (PI) of the cost-effectiveness comparison of NPV is 0.33, so $1 today is therefore calculated as only being worth 33¢.

However, R&D has the option of either 'Go' or 'No Go,' and an "option value" should exist. When calculating the real option value to 36.2 billion yen, taking the 200% average volatility of the bio venture's stock price into account and incorporating it into the corporate valuation, the NPV with option becomes positive by 1.2 billion yen and the cost input is therefore justified. In other words, since the PI, obtained by dividing the present value of the investment effect by the present value of the investment, comes to 1.09, $1 of R&D investment today is actually worth $1.09.

DISCOVERY STAGE VALUATION (IMA Corporation)

Unit	00M(JPY)

<Assumption of business value>

Business value per product at the time of launch	1,300.0
Caotal cost	25.0%

<Assumption of clinical stage>

Term of clinical development	6	year	OK	* 10	no-description in case of beyond 10 year
Effecitive tax rate	35.0%				

Term (Clinical stage, based on year)	1	2	3	4	5	6
Phase	P-I	P-IIa	P-IIb	P-III	P-III	NDA
Cost of clinical development per drug (before tax, investing at beginnning of the period)	16.3	13.5	20.7	57.4	57.4	5.0
Cost of clinical development per drug (after rax, beginning of the period)	10.6	8.8	13.5	37.3	37.3	3.2
Total cost of clinical development per drug (before	170.2					
Probability of success for next step (measured at the end of period)	70.0%	60.0%	65.0%		80.0%	90.0%
Probabiliry of success for next step (Blanked space modified: no-descripton)	70.0%	60.0%	65.0%	100.0%	80.0%	90.0%
Launch date	19.7%	28.1%	46.8%	72.0%	72.0%	90.0%
Cost of clinical development per drug (after tax)	53.8	31.3	28.8	51.8	51.8	3.6
Cost of clinical development per drug launch (after	221.0					

<Assumption of Drug discovery stage>

Term of drug discovery research	3	year	OK	* 6	no-description in case of beyond 10 year
Required total cost of drug discovery for starting clinical test per drug (before tax)	100.0			* Probability of success for drug discovery is including the value	
Required total cost of drug discovery for starting clinical test per drug (after tax)	65.0				

Term (Stage of drug discovery, based on year)	1	2	3
Required total cost of drug discovery for starting clinical test per drug (before tax)	33.3	33.3	33.3
Required total cost of drug discovery for starting clinical test per drug (after tax)	21.7	21.7	21.7
Required cost of drug discovery research for launch per drug (before tax)	110.2	110.2	110.2
Required cost of drug discovery research for launch per drug (after tax)	330.7		

<Assumption of optional value calucuration>

Underlying assets price (PV(Business value))	174.5
Volatility (per year)	200.0%
Risk-free interest rate (per year)	2.0%
u (Appreciation rate of underlying asset price)	7.38906
d (Decline rate of underlying asset price)	0.13534
p (Risk-neutral probability of appreciation rate)	12.2%
1-p (Risk-neutral probability of decline rate)	87.8%

< Result of potential value calculation>

Business value (Simple PV)	174.5
Present value of R&D	524.0
Simple NPV	-349.6
Simple PI (Profitability index)	0.33

NPV with option	12.3	100%
Simple NPV	-349.6	-2844%
Net option value	361.9	2944%

Business value (after adjusting OP exercise probability)	151.5
Present value of R&D investment (after adjusting OP probability)	139.2
NPV with option	12.3
PI with option	1.09

Present value of research investment of 100 billion yen over ten years assuming PI = 1.09 (Billion, yen)

Year	1	2	3	4	5	6	7	8	9	10
Investment of fundamental research	100	100	100	100	100	100	100	100	100	100
Incremental value by PI1.09	9	9	9	9	9	9	9	9	9	9
Total present value of incremental value for a decade	¥60.4									

Fig. 7.15 Quantification model of potential research value (intellectual capital) by real options and PI. *Source* Yanagi (2009)

(There are many such cases in the Nasdaq market in the U.S. And the fact that the bio venture has just been listed and in deficit, but also with considerable market capitalization means that the market both consciously and unwittingly incorporates the value of these real options).

It is possible to quantify the potential value of intellectual capital investment by using a new basic research budget not specifically attached to late stage project, assuming that this PI is a value creation driver of general intellectual capital. For example, net present value (NPV) when investing 100 billion yen in potential research over a 10-year period, assuming a PI of 1.09, is over 60 billion yen as shown in Fig. 7.15. Although it is a simplified model, it suggests that added value creation by conversion of non-financial capital (intellectual capital and human capital) into financial capital has been established. Embodied in this conceptual framework is the delayed effects of R&D on future ROE improvement, and in the long term, the possibility of gaining market understanding, leading to high stock price performance.

7.8.1.5   Empirical Analysis on Delayed Penetration Effect on ROE, Stock Price from R&D Investment in Japan

Yanagi et al. (2016), intending to create evidence for the "Synchronization Model of Non-financial Capital and Equity Spread," conducted an empirical analysis on the question of "When companies increase R&D investment (intellectual capital and human investment), how does it affect the future ROE and stock price (shareholder value)?" I tried to prove the relationship between R&D (non-financial) and financial value together with quants analysts. Analysis (1) analyzed the relationship between changes in R&D expenses over sales and changes in ROE, while Analysis (2) analyzed the relationship between changes in R&D expenses over sales and stock price performance. For the analysis, the nature of the references used, such as the statistical test with a wide significance margin of 20% and the small sample number, while sufficient as references were also sufficient as evaluation materials.

   Analytical data:

 – Universe: From among TOPIX component stocks, those companies in the manufacturing industry that settle their accounts at the end of March. The manufacturing industry is defined as the following sectors included in the TSE's 33 sectors: Foods, Textiles and Apparels, Pulp and Paper, Chemicals, Pharmaceutical, Oil and Coal Products, Rubber Products, Glass and Ceramics Products, Iron and Steel, Nonferrous Metals, Metal Products, Machinery, Electric Appliances, Transportation Equipment, Precision Instruments, and Other Products.
 – Financial data: With priority given to consolidation, I did not use information on interim settlements but only data on the relevant settlements.

Analysis   (1):   Relationship   between   R&D   investment   over   sales difference three years before and ROE two years ahead

   In this analysis, I examined whether the future ROE of companies with increased R&D investment over sales improved with quants analysts. Specifically, I calculated coefficient relationships regarding (A) the difference between R&D investment over sales in the base year and R&D investment over sales three years before the base year,

Table 7.3 Correlation coefficient and statistical significance in change in R&D investment over sales in the past three years and change in ROE in the following two years

Base year	R&D ÷ Sales difference in 3 years ago × ROE 2 years ahead		Test	Significant ratio of p-value
	Correlation figure	p-value		
2002	0.007	0.426	10% one-sided test	25%
2003	0.288	0.000	20% one-sided test	50%
2004	−0.010	0.393		
2005	0.135	0.000		
2006	0.027	0.239		
2007	0.067	0.037		
2008	0.038	0.160		
2009	0.033	0.198		
2010	0.007	0.424		
2011	0.046	0.117		
2012	0.004	0.458		
2013	−0.026	0.246		

Note Calculate the correlation figure (R&D ÷ Sales difference in previous 3 years and ROE of 2 years ahead) Conducted one-sided test and calculated significant ratio (the number of year that p-value is below 10%, or below 20% ÷ Total sample). However, minus basic year is excluded
Source Yanagi et al. (2016) Prepared by Daiwa Securities based on Toyo Keizai, Nikkei, etc

and (B) the difference between ROE two years ahead of the base year and ROE in the base year. In addition, I conducted a statistical test (one side) of those correlation coefficients to investigate their significance. The base years were from fiscal 2002 to fiscal 2013.

The analysis results are shown in Table 7.3. The significance of the correlation coefficients were verified with a significance ratio. The significance ratio was calculated as "the number of samples for which the correlation coefficient was statistically significant, divided by the number of all samples overall" and found the fiscal year of "correlation coefficient > 0 and p-value < significance margin" to be significant. In other words, the higher the significance ratio, the more positive the correlation coefficient and the more statistically significant the fiscal year.

First, the significance ratio when the significance margin was 10% on one side was 25%. In addition, although provided only as reference, the significance ratio when the significance margin was 20% on one side was 50%. From the significance ratio, it can be observed that although a statistically significant correlation was not completely confirmed in the differences between R&D investment over sales three years before and between ROE two years ahead, a certain positive relation was. I was able to observe the tendency of R&D investment as intangibles to delay and lead to improved ROE, which resulted to a certain extent in supporting the synchronization of non-financial capital (R&D investment) and Equity Spread (ROE) (Table 7.3).

Analysis (2): Relationship between difference in R&D investment over sales five years before and a spread return divided into ten groups for ten years later.

As the ratio of R&D investment increased, together with the quants team, I examined whether future stock returns would rise. The specific procedure used to verify this was as follows: First, (A) Take the difference between R&D investment over sales in the base year and R&D investment over sales five years ago from the base year and place in one of ten groups (largest in tenth, smallest in first). Next, (B) for the stock group in the tenth group (P10), we calculated the return[17] from the base year to ten years later and also for stock in the first group (P1) too, I calculated the return for ten years later using the same method. Finally, I calculated the spread return (High–Low) by subtracting the net average return of P10 from the net average return of P1." The base years were from fiscal 2004 to fiscal 2006.

The analysis results are in Table 7.4. It should be noted that the samples are over a three-year period, but the average of the High-Low spread returns from fiscal 2004 to fiscal 2006 was +16.9% and the average value over standard deviation was 2.956, which means that a positive effect was observed on the future returns. Because stock returns move in anticipation of the future, longer delay penetration effects are clearer than financial information (ROE). The result suggests one form of the "Synchronization Model of Non-financial Capital (R&D investment) and Equity Spread (leading to shareholder value following the Residual Profit Model)," showing R&D investment is, in the long term, delayed and leads to valuation.

From the two empirical studies of analysis (1) and analysis (2) above, the probability that R&D investment as intellectual capital and human capital has a positive correlation with a company's future performance (ROE) and in the long term, in its further delay with penetration of shareholder value (stock price). However, the empirical analysis in this section is merely a reference showing the trend, and I would like to conduct detailed empirical analysis as a future research topic.

7.8.1.6 The "Relationship Between Intangibles and Financial Value" Indicated in Previous Research (Ito and Sekiya 2016)

In previous research by academic papers, Ito and Sekiya (2016) discuss the relationship between corporate reputation and corporate financial performance, the results of which are highly suggestive. I will pick up the relevant parts as evidence to support the central aspect of this chapter, that is, the "Synchronization Model of Non-financial Capital and Equity Spread" that converts non-financial capital into financial capital and creates added value.

Although in this chapter I discuss "non-finance capital" as a comprehensive concept in the broad sense to also include "intangibles," Lev (2001) adopts other syn-

---

[17]((Stock price in ten years/base-year stock price) − 1) × 100, calculated at the end of June, when disclosure for the fiscal year ended in March issue will have been published.

Table 7.4 Relationship between change in R&D investment over sales during the preceeding five years and spread return in the following 10 years term

		P1 (Low)			P10 (High)			High-low spread return		
		Average	Standard deviation	Average/SD	Average	Standard deviation	Average/SD	Average	Standard deviation	Average/SD
Return of next 10 years	FY2004-FY2006	31.4%	34.8%	0.902	48.3%	29.2%	1.655	16.9%	5.7%	2.956

Source Yanagi et al. (2016). Prepared by Daiwa Securities based on TOYO Keizai, Nikkei, etc

onyms for "intangibles," namely, "intellectual assets," "intellectual capital," and "intangible assets." According to Lev (2001), intangibles consist of innovation, which is a factor in the creation of intangibles, unique competence, and human resources. For example, he includes patents, brand, a unique organizational structure to reduce costs, and other factors as also being intangibles. Furthermore, in Sakurai (2008), "corporate reputation (stakeholders' perceptions)" which is one of the intangibles, is defined as being a "sustainable competitive advantage derived from various stakeholders surrounding enterprises, based on the result of past actions by management and employees, the present, and future forecast information."

The connection to the "Synchronization Model of Non-financial Capital and Equity Spread," which is the conceptual framework of this chapter, is valuable in that, according to research by Fombrun and Shanley (1990), a significant correlation was found to exist between "corporate reputation" and "corporate financial performance." In Fombrun and Shanley (1990), the surrogate variable of "corporate reputation" used corporate reputation rankings data based on Fortune magazine's "World's Most Admired Companies" survey conducted in 1985. The survey included quality of management, products and services, long-term investment value, innovation, financial soundness, and the degree of attractiveness, training, and turnover for talented employees; corporate citizenship and environmental responsibility; and the use of corporate assets, with eight categories of questions evaluated on an 11-point Likert scale.

In this previous study, the "scale" used was the value obtained by logarithmically converting sales from 1984. "Corporate performance" was the return on invested capital (ROIC) at the end of 1984, the market value to book value ratio (PBR) in 1985, and the stock price dividend yield in 1985. For "risk," the accounting risk was measured by the variation coefficient (standard deviation divided by average value) of ROIC from 1975 to 1983, and the market risk was measured by the company's beta value in 1985. "Stockholding by institutional investors" was measured by the shareholding ratio of institutional investors such as banks, insurance companies, trust banks, and other organizations in 1985. "Visualization" describes exposure to media, as measured by the number of articles written about the company in 1985. "Differentiation" is considered as the degree of ads cost concentration, and was measured by total ads expenditure in 1984 after company size adjustment. "Diversification" measured the degree of diversification using annual sales data by segment from financial data for 1985.

The result of the correlation analysis of 557 companies suggests that return on invested capital (ROIC), differentiation, and scale share a positive relationship with corporate reputation. It was also found that risk is in a negative relationship with corporate reputation. Similarly, as a result of the regression analysis, it was apparent that ROIC, differentiation, scale, the shareholding ratio of institutional investors, and PBR share a positive relationship with corporate reputation. In contrast, risk was shown to be negatively related to corporate reputation. The correlation between corporate reputation and corporate financial performance was a highly valuable study in that it proved the viability of "Synchronization Model of Non-financial Capital and Equity Spread" from a different angle.

This previous study demonstrates that non-financial capital (intangibles) shares a positive correlation with Equity Spread (theoretically leading to ROIC and PBR) and one set of evidence for supporting the "Synchronization Model of Non-financial Capital and Equity Spread."

7.8.2 Latest Empirical Research Regarding the Relationship Between Non-financial Capitals and PBR in the Case of Japanese Healthcare Companies to Support the IIRC-PBR Model

In this section, I introduce the latest empirical research in Japan which was conducted for a research project at a Chuo University graduate school of accountancy where I served as advisor. Professor Yoshikazu Tomizuka, of the same graduate school and who served as editor on the project, provides a research summary on the direct relationship between the IIRC's five non-financial capitals and PBR in the July 2017 issue of *Kigyō kaikei* (Tomizuka 2017).

In this study, Japanese healthcare sector was analyzed. The reason for choosing healthcare companies was because the proportion of companies that refer to the IIRC's international integrated reporting framework when compiling integrated reports in that industry is high. Most companies compile their integrated reports by referencing the IIRC framework. In order for the study to analyze non-financial capital using a scoring system based on non-financial information disclosed in integrated reports, it was therefore reasonable to analyze healthcare companies, which have the largest percentage of referencing the IIRC framework. As the analytical method, they verified the relationship between the five non-financial capitals and corporate value (PBR) through a unique evaluation of non-financial information (using a scoring system) based on the IIRC's five non-financial capitals. To prove the relationship between the five non-financial capitals and corporate value, the following hypotheses were set with reference to the previous study.

Hypothesis 1: There is a relationship between the five non-financial capitals combined as a single indicator and corporate value.

Hypothesis 2: Intellectual capital, human capital, manufactured capital, social and relationship capital, and natural capital each have a positive relationship with corporate value.

The results of an empirical analysis showed the five non-financial capitals when combined as a single indicator (combined total of five non-financial capital evaluations) and human capital to have a correlation with one-percent p-value to PBR, social and relationship capital and natural capital to have a correlation with five-percent p-value, and intellectual capital to have a correlation with ten-percent p-value. Thus it can be said that there were significantly positive correlations with PBR. Especially the evaluation score of five non-financial capitals in the aggregate showed the highest correlation coefficient of 0.733 with PBR which is statistically significant with 99%

◆Result of Regression Analysis

Corporate value variable	Confirmatory non-financial capital	Analysis coefficient	
		β	t
PBR	Total of capital evaluation	0.733	(3.73)***
PBR	Intellectual capital	0.484	(1.91)*
PBR	Human capital	0.708	(3.47)***
PBR	Manufactured capital	0.390	(1.46)
PBR	Social・relationship capital	0.616	(2.71)**
PBR	Natural capital	0.607	(2.65)**

***p<0.01, **p<0.05, *p<0.10

◆Path diagram for PBR and 5 non-financial capitals

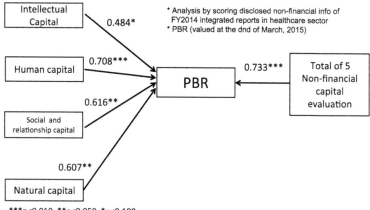

***p<0.010, **p<0.050, *p<0.100
***p<0.010: statiscal significance with 99% confidence level
**p<0.050: statiscal significance with 95% confidence level
*p<0.100: statiscal significance with 90% confidence level

Fig. 7.16 Correlation of Non-Financial Capitals and PBR. *Note* The analysis was to universe of 14 companies (Astellas Pharma, Eisai, Ono Pharmaceutical, Kyowa Hakko Kirin, Kyorin Holdings, Sawai Pharmaceutical, Shionogi, Daiichi-Sankyo, Taisho Pharmaceutical Holdings, Sumitomo Dainippon Pharma, Takeda, Mitsubishi Tanabe Pharma, Chugai Pharmaceutical, and Nippon Shinyaku) in the pharmaceutical sector that published their integrated reports for fiscal 2014 in accordance with the IIRC's framework. Furthermore, Asuka Pharmaceutical's PBR at the end of the fiscal year ending March 31, 2015, was below one, and Chiome Bioscience had lack of disclosed information. Hence these two companies are excluded from the universe.* Kyowa Hakko Kirin and Chugai Pharmaceutical settle business years at the end of December* The analysis was conducted by first converting disclosed non-financial information from integrated reports into objective numerical scores, using a score-based system * PBR as of March 31, 2015

confidence level, meaning that significant portion of corporate value is attributable to IIRC-defined non-financials. *Meanwhile, the correlation with manufacturing capital was not significant on a stand-alone basis.

Therefore, this suggests that companies with a high valuation of intellectual capital, human capital, social and relationship capital, natural capital, and all five non-financial capitals combined also have a high corporate value (PBR). A summary of the analysis results is shown in Fig. 7.16.

Thus, using the Japanese healthcare sector as a sample, a significant positive correlation was suggested between the IIRC's five non-financial capitals and PBR. It is a result that supports the IIRC-PBR model. (Source) Chuo Graduate School of Accounting "Integrated Report Project." Edited by Professor Yoshikazu Tomizuka advised by Dr. Yanagi. *Bulletin of Chuo University* (2017) in publication

7.8.3 Latest Empirical Research on the Relationship Between Intellectual Capital/Human Capital Versus MVA in Japan to Prove the Synchronization Model of Non-financial and Equity Spread

Furthermore, in this section, in a bid to further prove the "Non-Financial Capitals and Equity Spread Synchronization Model" in Yanagi (2015a, b, c) with the samples of Japanese companies across-the-board, an empirical study in Yanagi and Yoshino (2017) is introduced below.

By confirming the IIRC-PBR model or Intrinsic Value Model described in Yanagi (2009) of which it is partly comprised, we have the following (reproduced) formula:

IIRC–PBR Model:

Shareholder value = long-term market capitalization
=Book Value of Shareholder's Equity (BV) + market added value (MVA)
MVA = the part with PBR of more than one
=non-financial capital related (intangibles)
="intellectual capital" + "human capital" + "manufactured capital" + "social and relationship capital" and "natural capital" as IIRC defines

First, when estimating from financial data published about the value of people, one approach can be to consider its relationship to personnel expenses (human capital). Furthermore, R&D expenses can also be considered as financial data relating to the formation of comprehensive corporate intangibles, including the value of the organization and its personnel. From the perspective of a company's long-term growth and its formation of relevant technical knowledge assets, too, the relationship between R&D expenses and intangibles runs deep (intellectual capital). Therefore, the empirical analysis dealt with in this section describes the relationship between MVA (market capitalization minus equity book value) and personnel expenses (human capital) and R&D expenses (intellectual capital).

For our analysis, we adopted the following two regression models to pool company and year data. Both models are pool regression models that are widely used in empirical analysis.

(Validation model 1)

(Market capitalization − equity)/equity = a0 + a1 × personnel expenses/equity (BV)

(Validation model 2)

(Market capitalization − equity)/equity = b0 + b1 × R&D expenses/equity (BV)

Under these regression models, if a1 and b1, which are regression coefficients of personnel expenses divided by equity and R&D expenses divided by equity, respectively, become statistically significant, it would show then that intangibles such as human capital have a huge influence on the formation of MVA.

The two regression models use equity book value (BV) to deflate market capitalization and either personnel expenses or R&D expenses. This is aimed at dealing with uneven distribution of residual items.

A breakdown of the analysis data follows: First, the target period is from fiscal 1999 to fiscal 2015. The method of accounting used for R&D expenses in Japan has undergone a historical change. Since the fiscal year starting April 1, 1999 (fiscal 1999), R&D expenses are to be treated as expenses at the time of occurrence (in the past they were treated as deferred assets); the periods set in our analysis in this section are based on consistent standards and available data as far as possible.

The companies selected for analysis are those companies listed in the first section of the TSE (Tokyo Stock Exchange) that settled their accounts on March 31st as the end of the fiscal year. Regarding personnel expenses and R&D expenses, the level is different between the non-manufacturing industry and the manufacturing industry. R&D expenses in particular are important in the formation of technology assets in the manufacturing industry. The reasoning behind only targeting those companies that settled their accounts on March 31st was that although dummy fiscal years could be included to control for fiscal-year effects, if sample data was added containing different fiscal year-end dates, the market capitalization acquisition times when calculating the explained variables would be different. Even for companies with the same fiscal year-end date, market capitalization would also be affected by changes in the overall market. In other words, if the sample contained any companies other than those with their fiscal year ending on March 31st, the fiscal year dummy control would not have been adequate.

We also only used companies with a positive MVA. That is, companies with a PBR of more than one; because a discussion of the relationship between intangibles and negative MVA is complicated, any companies with PBR of less than one were excluded from the sample.

Furthermore, in actual regression analysis, with respect to independent variables and dependent variables, data of brands that exceed 1% above and below the upper and lower limits are subjected to outlier processing that rounds upward and downward to 1%.

The analysis results are shown in Table 7.5.

From the empirical model results, the regression coefficients for personnel expenses over BV (0.4975) and R&D expenses over BV (2.9801), respectively, were significantly positive (p-value below 1% means statistical significance with 99% confidence level). In other words, a positive relationship was made evident, where the more a company's intangibles were formed from personnel expenses (human capital)

Table 7.5 Relation between R&D/personnel investment and MVA

	Model 1	Model 2
	Investment for human resources	Investment for R&D
Regression coefficient	0.4975	2.9801
t value	11.24	13.01
p value (%)	<1	<1
R^2	0.1047	0.1081

Note p-value is calculated by two tailed test

and R&D expenses (intellectual capital), the higher its MVA accordingly. In addition, R^2(determination coefficient) were 0.1047 for personel invest and 0.1081 for research invest respectively, meaning that 10.47% of MVA is attributed to human capital while 10.81% of MVA is derived from intellectual capital. Hence more than 10% of MVA is explainable by R&D investment and personnel investment respectively. This can be interpreted as compelling and direct evidence supporting the IIRC-PBR model or "Non-Financial Capitals and Equity Spread Synchronization Model", even expanding the research universe to all the companies listed on the 1st section of TSE across the board. (Yanagi and Michels-Kim 2018).

7.9   Conclusion: Synchronization Model of Non-financial Capital and Shareholders Return

As introduced by Yanagi (2015a, b, c), according to a global investor survey, at the top of the agenda for company–investor dialogue is ROE, and both Japan's Corporate Governance Code and the Ito Review (emulating UK's Kay Review) also call for the issue of capital efficiency to be addressed. Meanwhile, in the questionnaire survey of the Japan IR Council (JIRA 2017), companies that engage in investor relations activities point out "disclosing and explaining non-financial information in connection with corporate value (55.9%)" as a challenge in non-financial information disclosure. How are ESG and the other "invisibles" emphasized by Japanese companies related to "visibles," such as ROE, on which investors place emphasis? Addressing this question is also extremely important within the context of the ESG boom in Japan. It is clear even in the latest investor survey that the market is not demanding "ESG for ESG" but "ESG for corporate value creation" (as shown in this chapter).

Therefore, in this chapter, in addition to such global investor survey, the statistical correlation was examined from the hypothesis that non-financial capital is related to PBR. A latest empirical study of the Japanese healthcare sector (Tomizuka 2017) has shown that MVA (the part with PBR of more than one) has a positive relationship with the non-financial capitals—that is, "intellectual capital," "human capital," "manufactured capital," "social and relationship capital," and "natural capital"—based on the assumption that shareholder value matches the sum of BV and MVA according to the Residual Income Model (RIM). In the latest empirical study as to Japanese companies across-the board shown by Yanagi and Yoshino (2017), we expanded the applicable universe to all the general corporations in Japan and found that R&D expenses (intellectual capital) and personnel costs (human capital) had a statistically significant positive correlation with MVA (corporate value).

Non-financial capital or intangibles is leading to the added value that management should create as self-created goodwill (hidden value) that cannot be accounted for on a financial accounting basis, and is related to MVA. On the other hand, RIM indicates that shareholder value is the total of equity book value (BV) plus the sum of present value of future residual incomes (with its KPI as Equity Spread). Since Equity Spread is ROE minus cost of equity capital, theoretically MVA is a variable for future ROE.

From this relationship, non-financial capital should be able to be synchronized with long-term ROE, and the viewpoint of companies focusing on management philosophy, the value of human resources, social contribution, and other non-financial information in fact coincides with that of investors seeking ROE and should be considered as a win-win by both sides ("ROESG: Return on ESG" concept as stated by Prof. Ito at Hitotsubashi University and chair of the Ito Review).

Of course, the premise of "Non-Financial Capitals and Equity Spread Synchronization Model" as shown in Fig. 7.11 is the long-term time axis, and in "purposeful dialogue" between companies and investors which Japan's Corporate Governance Code mandates, the long-term corporate value that excludes short-term–oriented discussions are desired. In addition, the empirical research supporting this model, including the empirical research introduced in this chapter, specifically suggests correlation although it does not prove causality by any means. Again, in addition to empirical research, disclosure of concrete examples such as Eisai and SAP through integrated reporting and a comprehensive approach that includes accumulated engagement between Japanese companies and long-term investors, avoiding traditional "investor-phobia", will help provide further momentum.

It is the wish of the author that "purposeful" dialogue between Japanese companies and global investors will also be further enhanced to overcome the challenging task of "making invisibles visible" and to maximize corporate value over the long term. And also that is what the Abenomics corporate governance reforms are for.

The key to success toward that goal is "Non-Financial Capitals and Equity Spread Synchronization Model" as my value proposition and conclusion in this book.

References

Agarwal, V., Liao, A., Taffler, R., & Nash, E. (2008). The impact of effective investor relations on market value. SSRN. Working Paper.

Botosan, C. A. (1997). Disclosure level and the cost of equity capital. *The Accounting Review., 72*(3), 323–349.

Cokins, G., & Shepherd, N. (2017). The Power of Intangibles. *Strategic Finance, 2017(5)*, 32–39.
Dhaliwal, D. S., et al. (2011). Voluntary nonfinancial disclosure and the cost of equity capital: The initiation of corporate social responsibility reporting. *The Accounting Review, 2011*(1), 59–100.
Fombrun, C., & Shanley, M. (1990). What's in a name? reputation building and corporate strategy. *Academy of Management Journal, 33*(2), 233–258.
Ide, S., & Takehara, H. (2016). Analysis of infiltrating process to stock price by patent Information—Technical competitiveness as mid-term alpha driver. *SAAJ Journal, 54*(10), 68–77.
IIRC. (2013). *The international IR framework*. International Integrated Reporting Council.
Ito, K. (2014). Integrated report from the perspective of managerial accounting. *Kigyo kaikei, 66*(5), 83–88.
Ito, K., & Sekiya, H. (2016). Constructing the theoretical model relevant to intangibles and corporate value. *Kaikeigaku kenkyu, 42,* 1–32.
Japan Investor Relations Association (JIRA). (2014). *Survey results of annual shareholder's meeting and investor relations*.
JIRA. (2017). IR survey 2017. JIRA.
Kaplan, R. S., & Norton, D. P. (1996, January–February). Using the balanced scorecard as a strategic management system. *Harvard Business Review*.
Lev. B. (2001). Intangibles: Management measurement, and reporting. Brookings Institution Press.
Nissay Asset Management. (2014). *Management strategies to enhance corporate value in a Stewardship Code era.* CHUOKEIZAI-SYA.
Ohlson, J. (1995). Earnings, book values, and dividends in equity valuation. *Contemporary Accounting Research, 11,* 661–687.
Ohlson, J. (2001). Earnings, book values, and dividends in equity valuation: an empirical perspective. *Contemporary Accounting Research, 18*(1), 107–120.
Oshika, T. (2008). Management attitude to disclosure and responses of stock market—Stimulate general shareholders meeting and efficiency of accounting information. *SAAJ Journal, 46*(5).
Oshika, T. (2013). Relevance of expenditure of human resource and corporate value—Does payment-cut contribute to improve corporate value? *Waseda Commerce Report, 434,* 289–311.
Otokawa, K. (2000). Capital cost reduction effect for IR activity. *Kaikei, 158*(4), 543–555.
Porter, M. E., & Kramer, M. R. (2011). Creating shared value. *Harvard Business Review, 6,* 8–31.
Saka, C., & Oshika, T. (2014). Disclosure effects, carbon emissions and corporate value. *Sustainability Accounting, Management and Policy Journal, 5*(1), 22–45.
Sakurai, M. (2008). *Corporate reputation*. CHUOKEIZAI-SYA
Suda, K. (2004). *Strategies and effects of disclosure*. Moriyama-shoten
Tomizuka, Y. (2017). Are non-financial capitals connected with corporate value? Empirical research on Japanese healthcare sector. *Kigyo kaikei, 69*(7), 116–122.
Yanagi, R. (2009). *Financial strategies for maximizing corporate value*. Doyukan.
Yanagi, R. (2014b). Study for Japanese ver. Stewardship code and capital efficiency. *Investor Relations, 2014(8)*, 48–62.
Yanagi, R. (2015a). *The ROE revolution and financial strategy*. CHUOKEIZAI-SHA.
Yanagi, R. (2015b). Eisai's Integrated Report pilot study. *Kigyo kaikei, 67*(4), 106–113.
Yanagi, R. (2015c). Corporate governance code and "Engagement with shareholders"—Implications of global investor survey and study for equity spread. *SAAJ Journal, 2015*(9).
Yanagi, R. (2017a). *ROE management and Intangibles*. CHUOKEIZAI-SHA.
Yanagi, R. (2017b). How are global investors looking at Japanese Companies? Implications from the global investor survey in 2017. *Kigyo kaikei, 69*(5), 108–114.
Yanagi, R., Meno, H., & Yoshino, T. (2016). Study of synchronization for non-financial capital and equity spread. *Gekkan shihon shijyo, 2016*(11), 4–13.
Yanagi, R., & Yoshino, T. (2017). Relation bet. Human/Intellectual Capitals and Corporate Value (PBR). *Gekkan shihon shijo 2017*(10) (No. 386), 4–13.
Yanagi, R. & Michels-Kim, N. (2018). Integrating Non-financials to create value. *Strategic Finance, 2018*(1), 27–35.

Appendix
Latest Investor Survey 2016 and 2017

Introduction

I have been conducting a large-scale, ongoing questionnaire survey of investors for a period of several years. In this book, the investor surveys in 2014 and 2015 are mainly quoted. This appendix is to provide readers with the latest investor survey in 2016 including not only quantitative answers, but also qualitative comments in detail. In addition, the brief results of the 2017 survey are also included. We can see some improvement in the wake of Abenomics corporate governance (CG) reform in Japan, but there is still a long way to go in order to catch up with global standards in conjunction with corporate governance and capital efficiency, thereby leading to value maximization.

© Springer Nature Singapore Pte Ltd. 2018
R. Yanagi, *Corporate Governance and Value Creation in Japan*,
https://doi.org/10.1007/978-981-10-8503-1

Questionnaire Survey of Investor Perspectives on Corporate Governance Reform 2016

In order to survey global perspectives on CG reform in Japan from the vantage point of overseas investors in Japanese stocks, I conducted a questionnaire survey with the cooperation of UBS Securities from November 2015 to January 2016, targeting major institutional investors in Japanese stocks from Japan, the Americas, Europe, and Asia.[1] The findings of the survey are included below. Please kindly note that as the focus this time was on obtaining the frank opinions of overseas investors in particular, the ratio of Japanese investor respondents to overseas investor respondents was 1:2.[2]

What Do You Most Expect from the CGC (Corporate Governance Code)?

In **Question 1**, I asked investors worldwide what they most expected from Japan's CGC. Fifty percent responded that they most expected capital efficiency (return on equity, ROE) to improve, making this the most common response again (Yanagi 2015: 40%). Among overseas investors specifically, 55% expected improved ROE.

---

[1]Survey period from November 2015–January 2016. 183 respondents in total; 61 Japanese investors and 122 overseas investors. Investors were from 115 companies in total; 35 Japanese companies and 80 overseas companies. All investors were major institutional investors (pension and asset management companies) with managerial positions or higher, selected from 200 core UBS companies worldwide. They included executives, CIOs, fund managers, and analysts and all were acquaintances of either the author or a UBS sales representative. For the purposes of the survey, overseas companies based in Japan were also categorized as overseas investors. Investor strategies are highly confidential and global surveys of this scope are therefore rare. However, investor opinions are subject to change with changes in environmental factors and therefore surveys must also be ongoing. Before compiling this report, the author had previously conducted similar large-scale surveys (Yanagi 2010, 2013, 2014, and 2015), with the Yanagi 2010 and 2013 survey findings also referenced in the Ito Review. With no significant changes in recent trends, the survey analyzed in this report is both consistent and robust in its findings.

[2]The p-value for the the the null hypothesis that "Japanese and overseas investors had the same response rates" is indicated in each response. With a significance level of 1%, there was judged to be a significant difference between the opinions of Japanese investors and overseas investors where the p-value was less than 0.01; and no significant difference between the opinions of Japanese investors and overseas investors where the p-value was more than 0.01. Furthermore, some responses indicated a 99% confidence interval (significance level of 1%) based on binomial distribution, although results were the same even when approximate based on normal distribution.

Q1. What do you expect most in wake of Japan's Corporate Governance Code?

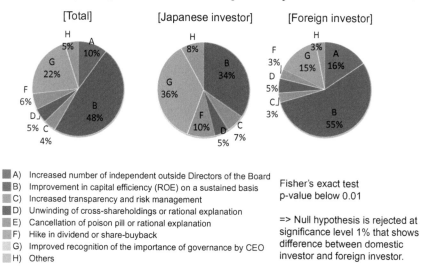

[Total]   [Japanese investor]   [Foreign investor]

A) Increased number of independent outside Directors of the Board
B) Improvement in capital efficiency (ROE) on a sustained basis
C) Increased transparency and risk management
D) Unwinding of cross-shareholdings or rational explanation
E) Cancellation of poison pill or rational explanation
F) Hike in dividend or share-buyback
G) Improved recognition of the importance of governance by CEO
H) Others

Fisher's exact test
p-value below 0.01

=> Null hypothesis is rejected at
significance level 1% that shows
difference between domestic
investor and foreign investor.

Are You Satisfied with Overall CG at Japanese Companies?

In **Question 2**, I asked about the CG at Japanese companies. Only 20% of investors indicated satisfaction. In Yanagi 2015, approximately 30% indicated their satisfaction, in part based on reform expectations; the decrease can be attributed to harsher perceptions due to superficial approaches to the Corporate Governance Code (CGC) and other factors, including a fall in stock prices in early 2016. Statistically, the CG satisfaction rate falls between 16.2% and 33.3% with a confidence interval of 99%. No difference was observed between Japanese and overseas investors, with both groups indicating dissatisfaction with CG.

Q2. Are you satisfied with Japan's corporate governance in general?

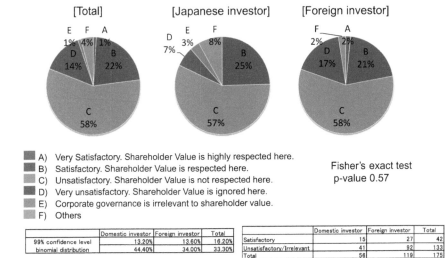

A) Very Satisfactory. Shareholder Value is highly respected here.
B) Satisfactory. Shareholder Value is respected here.
C) Unsatisfactory. Shareholder Value is not respected here.
D) Very unsatisfactory. Shareholder Value is ignored here.
E) Corporate governance is irrelevant to shareholder value.
F) Others

Fisher's exact test
p-value 0.57

	Domestic investor	Foreign investor	Total
99% confidence level	13.20%	13.60%	16.20%
binomial distribution	44.40%	34.00%	33.30%

	Domestic investor	Foreign investor	Total
Satisfactory	15	27	42
Unsatisfactory/Irrelevant	41	92	133
Total	56	119	175

⇒ 16.2% to 33.3% of the total shows satisfactory. (Confidence level 99%)

Are You Satisfied with ROE at Japanese Companies?

In **Question 3**, I asked about ROE at Japanese companies. Only 15% of investors indicated satisfaction. However, this was an improvement over the 10% satisfaction rate recorded in the previous year (Yanagi 2015) and is attributed to recent improvements in ROE performance, target-setting, and strengthened shareholder returns. The satisfaction rate among overseas investors in particular, increased from 6 to 16%. However, there remains a strong, deep-seated dissatisfaction among investors regarding ROE. No significant difference was observed between Japanese and overseas investors; statistically, the satisfaction rate falls between 9.4 and 24.2% with a confidence interval of 99%.

Q3. Are you satisfied with Japan's ROE in general?

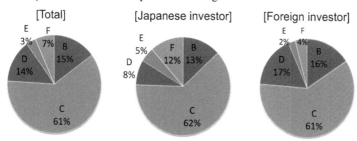

[Total]   [Japanese investor]   [Foreign investor]

A) Very satisfactory. ROE is much higher than cost of equity.
B) Satisfactory. ROE is above COE.
C) Unsatisfactory. ROE is below COE.   Fisher's exact test
D) Very unsatisfactory. ROE is much below COE.   p-value 1.00
E) ROE is irrelevant.
F) Others

	Domestic investor	Foreign investor	Total
99% confidence level binomial distribution	5.0%	8.6%	9.4%
	31.1%	26.8%	24.2%

	Domestic investor	Foreign investor	Total
Satisfactory	8	19	27
Unsatisfactory/Irrelevant	46	98	144
Total	54	117	171

=>Satisfaction rating of Japan's ROE is 9.4% to 24.2% of the total. (Confidence level 99%)

Is There Any Relationship Between CG and ROE?

In **Question 4**, I inquired about the relationship between CG and ROE. Irrespective of empirical research (or lack thereof), 44% of investors worldwide acknowledged a causal relationship and 35% believed there was a correlation. This indicated that the majority of investors recognized a relationship between CG and ROE. As qualitative evidence, this may have far-reaching implications. Incidentally, while overseas investors tended to emphasize a causal relationship, Japanese investors were more likely to emphasize a correlation.

Q4. Corporate Governance is related to capital efficiency (ROE)?

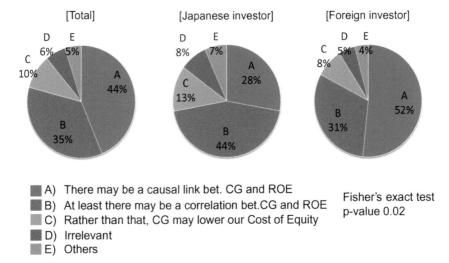

A) There may be a causal link bet. CG and ROE
B) At least there may be a correlation bet.CG and ROE
C) Rather than that, CG may lower our Cost of Equity
D) Irrelevant
E) Others

Fisher's exact test
p-value 0.02

How Much Do You Estimate Shareholders' Equity Cost to Be (Although Different for Individual Companies, Given in Average Japanese Stock Based on 1-Beta Premise)?

In **Question 5**, I asked about shareholders' equity cost (required minimum level of ROE). The responses averaged to 7.6%. The mode and median were both 8%, consistent with the trend in previous years (Yanagi 2013,[3] 2014, 2015). Furthermore, it is statistically significant that 78.8–92.6% of investors were satisfied with an 8% ROE. This is once again compelling evidence for the Ito Review 8% ROE guideline.

---

[3]Referenced in the Ito Review: "Cost of capital refers to the rate of return expected by the market. As there is no absolute definition, there are diverse views over the appropriate level of cost of capital. One particular survey shows that the cost of equity expected for Japanese shares by both domestic and overseas investors vary considerably with the average for overseas investors being 7.2% and that for domestic investors being 6.3%." "According to one survey, the expected cost of capital for Japanese companies by global institutional investors is in excess of 7%. According to this survey, an ROE of 8% or more would satisfy the expected cost of capital of over 90% of global investors." (Source: Ryohei Yanagi 2013).

Q5. In general, what is cost of equity (COE) for corporate Japan? (COE depends on each company but let assume all Japan average generally, that is beta=1 TOPIX condition)

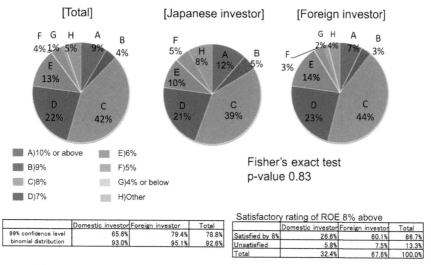

Fisher's exact test
p-value 0.83

	Domestic investor	Foreign investor	Total
99% confidence level	65.6%	79.4%	78.8%
binomial distribution	93.0%	95.1%	92.6%

Satisfactory rating of ROE 8% above

	Domestic investor	Foreign investor	Total
Satisfied by 8%	26.6%	60.1%	86.7%
Unsatisfied	5.8%	7.5%	13.3%
Total	32.4%	67.6%	100.0%

⇒ ROE 8 % satisfies 78.8% to 92.6% of the total (Confidence level 99%)

Are You in Favor of an 8% Minimum ROE as Recommended in the Ito Review?[4]

In **Question 6**, I inquired about whether investors were in agreement with the 8% ROE guideline recommended in the Ito Review. The support rate has remained high, at 85% this year compared to the previous year's 88% (Yanagi 2015). Statistically, between 77.9 and 91.7% of investors indicated their support. There was no difference between overseas and Japanese investors. The result was also consistent with the findings on shareholders' equity cost (required minimum level of ROE) in Question 5.

---

[4]Ito Review Final Report published by Japanese Ministry of Economy, Trade and Industry (METI) in August 2014. The author served as a committee member and was involved in drafting sections related to ROE and cost of capital, with the following excerpts by the author also referenced in the report: "Although the actual cost of capital differs between companies, the first step in receiving recognition from global investors is for a company to commit to achieving a minimum ROE of 8%. Companies should further strive to achieve a higher ROE appropriate to their specific business and that will contribute to sustainable growth."

Q6. Do you agree with the statement "Japanese companies should seek at least 8% or higher ROE" in "Ito Review"?

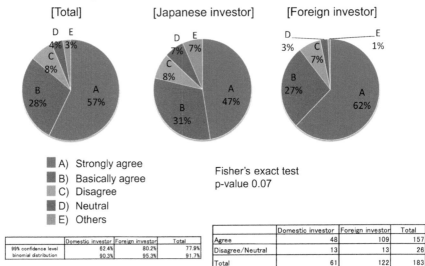

	Domestic investor	Foreign investor	Total
99% confidence level binomial distribution	62.4% 90.3%	80.2% 95.3%	77.9% 91.7%

	Domestic investor	Foreign investor	Total
Agree	48	109	157
Disagree/Neutral	13	13	26
Total	61	122	183

⇒ Approval rating of the total is 77.9% to 91.7%. (Confidence level 99%)

Do You Agree with ISS' Voting Guidelines[5] About Voting Against the CEO in Cases Where the Five-Year ROE Average Is Less Than 5%?

In **Question 7**, I asked if investors were in support of the "5% rule" recommended by ISS. With 70% of investors in agreement, there was no change in support since Yanagi 2015. However, the findings also indicated a difference in stance between Japanese and overseas investors. While overseas investors actively supported the rule, Japanese investors tended to be more conservative about their support. Incidentally and statistically, between 68.6 and 88.0% of overseas investors supported the rule.

---

[5]ISS, a leading global advisory organization specializing in the area of exercising voting rights, revised their advisory policy on exercising voting rights in Japan in fiscal 2015, recommending against proposals to elect directors by top management at "companies with a five-year ROE average of less than 5%."

Q7. Do you agree the ISS proxy guideline "vote against the reelection of CEO if 5 years average ROE is lower than 5% "?

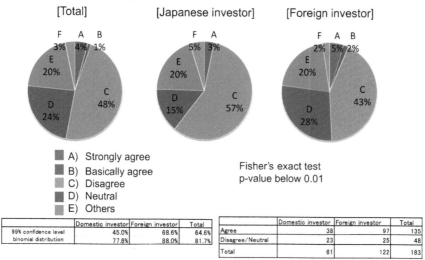

[Total]   [Japanese investor]   [Foreign investor]

A) Strongly agree
B) Basically agree
C) Disagree
D) Neutral
E) Others

Fisher's exact test
p-value below 0.01

	Domestic investor	Foreign investor	Total
99% confidence level	45.0%	68.6%	64.6%
binomial distribution	77.6%	88.0%	81.7%

	Domestic investor	Foreign investor	Total
Agree	38	97	135
Disagree/Neutral	23	25	48
Total	61	122	183

=>Domestic investor's approval rating is 45.0% to 77.5%. (Confidence level 99%)
=>Foreign investor's approval rating is 68.6% to 88.0%. (Confidence level 99%)

Equity Spread (ROE Minus Shareholders' Equity Cost, ES)[6] Was also Introduced in the Ito Review as a Proxy Variable for Value Creation. Do You Support the Proposal that ES Should Be Disclosed in Tokyo Stock Exchange Financial Statements and Discussed in Order to "Educate on Achieving ROE Above Cost of Capital"?

In **Question 8**, I inquired about support for the proposal regarding ES disclosure in the financial statements filed and ensuing dialogue (Yanagi 2013). As with Yanagi 2015, 70% of investors indicated that they were in agreement. While the support rate from Japanese investors stopped at 56% due to perceived difficulties in

---

[6]See Yanagi 2013. Also referenced in the Ito Review: "Equity spread (calculated as ROE minus cost of equity (investment returns expected by shareholders) is one of the KPIs for corporate value creation. In the eyes of investors, companies with positive equity spread are regarded as value-creating companies, and companies with minus equity spread are regarded as value-destructive companies." (Source: Ryohei Yanagi 2010).

disclosing cost of capital and other factors, 74% of overseas investors were in favor of ES disclosure and dialogue. Furthermore, the usefulness of voluntary disclosure of ES, the proxy of corporate value creation as a KPI (and raising awareness about the importance of returns being above cost of capital) was particularly strongly supported among overseas investors. Statistically, between 63.2 and 84.0% of overseas investors were in agreement.

Q8. Do you support the proposal that Equity Spread must be disclosed in fiscal filing document with TSE and be openly discussed with investors in a bid to solicit more financial literacy (ROE must be higher than COE) on the part of Japanese CEOs generally?

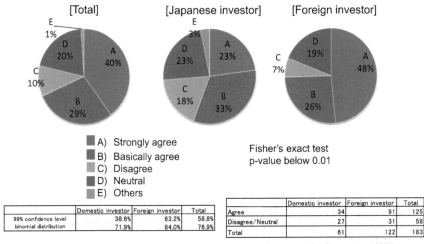

A) Strongly agree
B) Basically agree
C) Disagree
D) Neutral
E) Others

Fisher's exact test
p-value below 0.01

	Domestic investor	Foreign investor	Total
99% confidence level binomial distribution	38.6%	63.2%	58.8%
	71.9%	84.0%	76.9%

	Domestic investor	Foreign investor	Total
Agree	34	91	125
Disagree/Neutral	27	31	58
Total	61	122	183

=>Domestic investor's approval rating is 38.6% to 71.9% of the total. (Confidence level 99%)

What Is the Overall Most Important Issue Regarding Dividend Policies of Japanese Companies?

In **Question 9**, I inquired about dividend policy criteria. While 30% of Japanese investors indicated dividend payout ratio due in part to (profit and loss–based) dividend payout ratio being already heavily emphasized in Japan, two-thirds of investors overall emphasized optimal dividend policy based on (balance sheet–based) optimal capital structure. Due to the fact that many survey participants were also highly knowledgeable long-term investors, this can be interpreted as the result of the high level of financial literacy of the respondents. (Consistent with Yanagi 2014)

Q9. In general what is the most important in dividend policy in Japan?

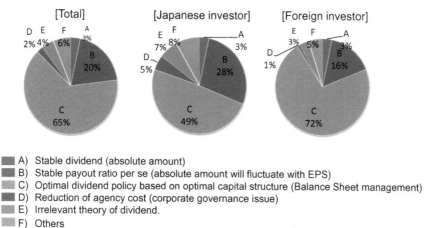

[Total]   [Japanese investor]   [Foreign investor]

A) Stable dividend (absolute amount)
B) Stable payout ratio per se (absolute amount will fluctuate with EPS)
C) Optimal dividend policy based on optimal capital structure (Balance Sheet management)
D) Reduction of agency cost (corporate governance issue)
E) Irrelevant theory of dividend.
F) Others

Fisher's exact test
p-value 0.021

Do You Agree that Good-Quality CG Reduces Cost of Capital?

In **Question 10**, I inquired about the negative correlation between CG and cost of capital. Seventy-eight percent of investors recognized a correlation. This can be interpreted to mean that what investors expect from Japanese companies in terms of

Q10. There is an assertion that quality corporate governance will lower the cost of capital to investors. Do you support such a theory in general?

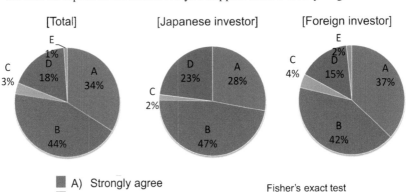

[Total]	[Japanese investor]	[Foreign investor]

A) Strongly agree
B) Basically agree
C) Disagree
D) Neutral
E) Others

Fisher's exact test
p-value 0.71

	Domestic investor	Foreign investor	Total
99% confidence level	58.8%	67.7%	68.7%
binomial distribution	88.0%	87.4%	85.0%

	Domestic investor	Foreign investor	Total
Agree	46	96	142
Disagree/Neutral	15	26	41
Total	61	122	183

⇒Approval rating is 68.7% to 85.0% of the total.(Confidence level 99%)

improving CG, is that successfully doing so will reduce cost of capital and increase corporate value (DCF value).

What Do You Think About ESG (and Integrated Report Disclosures) by Japanese Companies?

In **Question 11**, I inquired about ESG disclosure and explanations by Japanese companies. Close to half of investors overall were in favor of disclosing value-relevance between ROE and ESG. Meanwhile, with Japanese companies

Q11. What do you think about Japanese Companies' ESG and its disclosure (by integrated reports)?

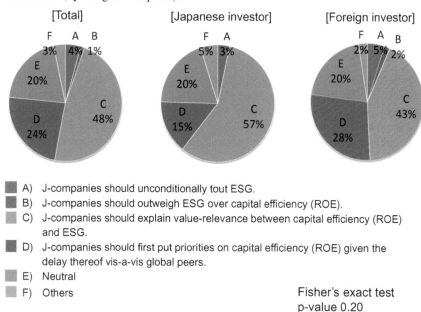

[Total] [Japanese investor] [Foreign investor]

A) J-companies should unconditionally tout ESG.
B) J-companies should outweigh ESG over capital efficiency (ROE).
C) J-companies should explain value-relevance between capital efficiency (ROE) and ESG.
D) J-companies should first put priorities on capital efficiency (ROE) given the delay thereof vis-a-vis global peers.
E) Neutral
F) Others

Fisher's exact test
p-value 0.20

behind the times, it should be pointed out that given the choice, 30% of overseas investors preferred full explanations on ROE over information on ESG.

Lastly, How Do You View the Outcomes to Date in Recent Years in the Japanese Market, Such as the Abenomics CG Reforms? (Total of Japanese Investor and Foreign Investor)

In **Question 12**, I inquired about investors' views on the series of CG reforms. The CGC and Ito Review were rated particularly highly, and there was increased support for the amended Companies Act, JPX400, and GPIF reform. Overseas investors overall tended to more actively support the Abenomics CG reforms. Incidentally, overseas investors tended to rate the Ito Review highest of all.

Major qualitative comments made by overseas investors about CG reform (Excerpts).

In this section, in order for readers to more concretely understand the opinions of overseas investors, I will introduce some of the more representative qualitative comments. All of these are candid (anonymous) comments made by major overseas investors who tend toward long-term investments. I believe that they are full of suggestions that are useful for Japanese companies (Excerpted and translated by the author.).

Q12. Last but not least, what is your overall assessment on the effect of the Abenomics' Corporate Governance reforms so far?

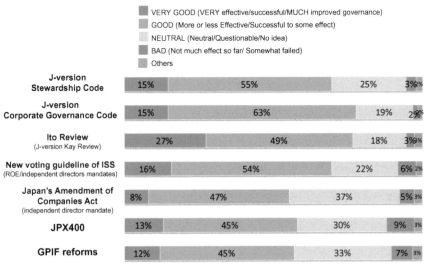

1. *Positive but conditional*

"I think that the recent reforms are a positive step in the right direction and that CG will improve in the long term. For example, improvement in the quality of engagement they have with institutional investors, and in how corporations approach shareholder value creation. But aside from these hopeful observations, I am also unable to cast off my skepticism that the current management teams at the companies and external directors will actually reform the way they do things. I hope that the next generation of directors will carry out their fiduciary responsibilities to stockholders in the true sense. And I believe that the way to fulfil those fiduciary responsibilities is through corporate decision-making that considers how to benefit long-term investors."

"I rate the initiatives mentioned in Question 12 (SC and CGC, Ito Review, etc.) very highly. Furthermore, I believe that the necessity of having such measures will only continue to increase in the future. This is because these arguably address the issues and practices in Japan related to ROE and corporate value that have been obstructing the establishment of CG in that country. I can see signs of reform starting to take place now at many of the companies. And I hope that even more companies will begin to catch on."

"I feel that CG in Japan has been improving, as evident from the many proposals for active measures and promotion of rapid reforms. On the other hand, Toyota's issuing of class shares last year is a cause for concern."

"I feel that the recent CG reforms have raised the standard of Japanese companies but there is still a big difference between them and those in Europe and the Americas. Companies should be obligated to disclose their target equity ratio as optimal capital structure. There is also need for a more thorough Stewardship Code (SC) for Japanese investors."

2. *Critical of the present situation*

"The CG reforms so far have been obstacles to placing proper focus on the core issues and are not worth the attention. There are two cores to CG. The first is the existence of completely independent, external directors. The second is the power for shareholders to sue in cases where management is deemed to have not carried out its fiduciary responsibilities. Shareholders elect an independent board of directors and that board is able to dismiss the management from their post for poor management. The management is then sued for breaching their fiduciary responsibilities to the shareholders, and only then does CG come into the issue. After all, ROE, dividends—everything—is only there in the first place because management put there all into making it happen."

"In other countries, completely independent boards are a condition for being listed on the stock market. The Tokyo Stock Exchange is unable to take on the role of establishing CG and in Japan that awareness has yet to take root. There are several reasons for why it feels like awareness of CG initiatives is still low in Japan. For one, companies like Hitachi assign directors from their headquarters to their subsidiaries, which leads to classic cases where they might claim that there is an independent external director, or where an M&A agreement is made with the board of directors having no idea what constitutes a fair price."

"The case of Mr. Yoshiaki Murakami being subjected to a criminal investigation is a representative example of this, but there is no transparency regarding just how well understood dialogue between regulatory agencies and corporations or investors really is. The same also applies to activist-like activities. When investors promoting engagement activities are accused of being "activists" with bad intentions, the SC arguably becomes a fiasco. That it has become easier to engage in dialogue with companies about shareholder returns is a positive change, but that does not yet extend to essential discussions on issues such as policy on layoffs and restructuring due to unprofitable businesses."

"Japanese companies have been slow in implementing the reforms and this time I think will be no different. Although they are making progress, they are unable to act as fast as possible and many companies are just formally responding to the requirements proposed by the government or adjusting the accounts for their mid-term plans. While it is an improvement over the past when minority share-holders were ignored, the policies recently proposed are rather than companies referring to balance sheets and implementing reforms in the true sense, I feel that they are merely doing what the government wants the companies to do. I'm just concerned about the future, but it seems like the result is that with stocks prices now companies are overly swayed, and I think we shouldn't repeat the same mistakes (i.e., stocking cash to unnecessary levels)."

3. *Would like to see more improvements*

"We are in ongoing, direct dialogue with management, working to address our company's concerns. For example, balancing investment for future growth with returning cash to shareholders, policies on capital productivity, including returning cash to shareholders, and how external communications are currently handled. Continuing ongoing dialogue is necessary to promote a change in corporate stance."

"It is not necessary for all employees to be aware of shareholder value, but when it comes to management, I expect them to fully understand the implications of being listed on the stock market, having corporate ownership by shareholders, the responsibilities of management and board members, principal agent relations, and similar. For board members these things go without saying and they do not want to tolerate having such matters being brought up from the investors' side. I understand that management is already too busy with their responsibilities, but that does not justify a refusal to communicate with investors and shareholders seeking dialogue on mid- and long-term strategies and value creation. On the other hand, there are a significant number of investors whose dialogue and questions are lacking. For example, they might repeat questions about information that has already been disclosed to the public, conduct interviews without first researching into the com-pany's past strategies, performance, and even changes, in some cases only inquiring about quarterly figures without attempting to know the strategies and business models behind them. I think that this is something that would be good to publicly criticize from the company's side, and that doing so would be for the benefit of all involved."

"Management should reconfirm that corporate owners in their company are in fact shareholders and that it is their responsibility to strive to increase sustainable benefits for shareholders over the long term. Furthermore, not all stakeholders are equal. Compared to bondholders, employees, and external stakeholders, equity investors take on considerable risk and should obtain returns proportionate to that risk."

"With the CG policy being promoted in Japan, my point of concern is that company growth is considered foremost. In Japan, there is a declining population and many companies conduct business in mature markets; there are also few Japanese companies that have successfully expanded overseas. As a result, in most cases the optimal, value creation–based solution is how to go about managing the company in a situation where there is negative growth. This emphasized approach is arguably extreme and likely difficult to accept. Consequently, I think that while I am not surprised that dialogue proposing negative growth as a foremost concern is not being raised, I do think it a little unfortunate."

4. *Financial theory proponents*

"Compared to the Anglo-Saxon market, CG at Japanese companies is behind the times. Society's capital rationing is still far from optimal, and when comparing the wealth created by companies on both sides in the economic activities over the past two decades, the opportunity cost is enormous. In other words, the mechanism associated with the value creation spread (that is Equity Spread: ES) emphasized by Mr. Yanagi is not working and because of that, after misusing the already existing capital and spending it on running the company and cost of capital, there have been many value-destructive companies that were unable to add any value at all. These companies, after feeding their own feet (provided by the shareholders) to their suppliers, clients, and employees, have nothing left and so have had no societal raison d'être as a public company."

"I feel that the CG reforms have lost some of their momentum compared to April of last year (2015). While stock buy-back and dividends are receiving attention, I think that a lot of management has come to underestimate discussion on cash management, which is at the core of the issue. Is it not necessary for management to refuse the concept of CG overall? It is still too early to say that all companies are now participating in the wave of CG reforms. Even now, many SMEs are unable to hide their anger when discussing cash flow and improving corporate value. Even in large companies who have the extra capacity for making improvements, they are behind in their level of progress in making such improvements and tend not to take in changes readily (i.e., banks, real estate, and conglomerates)."

"Overall, I have the impression that the stance of prioritizing employees over stockholders is unchanged. While ROE is now a point of emphasis, leverage is not something that should be focused on as the most important issue of all. Further, things like recap CB (share buyback via issuance of convertible bonds that is tautology) are foolish. I think that it is precisely returns on excessively accumulated equity base that is the fundamental cause of low ROE. There are some companies with excessively overcapitalized balance sheet, but many companies' returns are far too low."

"I am strongly opposed to dividend payout ratios as KPI. If it's DOE (Dividend on Equity), it can increase stably the dividends without influencing initial PL. Furthermore, DOE indicates dividend policy in the form that is compared to the values that ROE should be. For example, regarding the target ROE of 8%, if it is 4% DOE, it becomes a message that half of mid-term benefits will be returned to shareholders. DOE is a superior index compared to dividend payout ratios."

"Estimating shareholders' equity cost at 8% might be a little high, but this reflects the result of the value destruction of Japanese companies extended over a long period. Through improving CG, I believe we can reduce cost of capital."

2017 Survey Results

The latest investor survey was conducted January 10th through February 22, 2017 obtaining the qualified answers below;

Japanese Investors: 77 respondents

Overseas Investors: 62 respondents

Total: 139 respondents

For readers' reference, total equity investment amount in Japanese market held by all the survey participants is estimated to be circa 100 trillion yen,[7] covering a significant portion of institutional shareholders' holdings of listed companies in Japan.

The trend of global investor perception basically remains intact vis-à-vis 2016 survey despite certain improvement compared with 2012 results.

The outcome of 2017 survey is summarized as below;

Are You Satisfied with Japan's Corporate Governance in General?

---

[7]Estimated by UBS Securities Japan.

Q1.

a. 2017 result

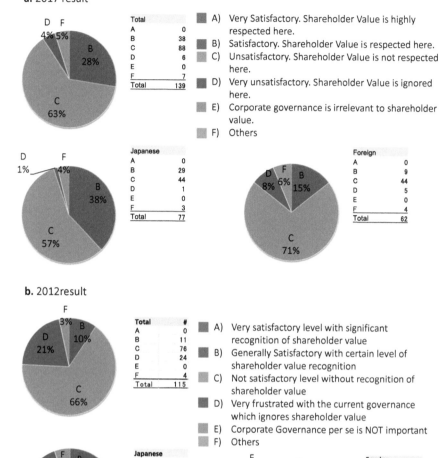

Total
A	0
B	38
C	88
D	6
E	0
F	7
Total	139

A) Very Satisfactory. Shareholder Value is highly respected here.

B) Satisfactory. Shareholder Value is respected here.

C) Unsatisfactory. Shareholder Value is not respected here.

D) Very unsatisfactory. Shareholder Value is ignored here.

E) Corporate governance is irrelevant to shareholder value.

F) Others

Japanese
A	0
B	29
C	44
D	1
E	0
F	3
Total	77

Foreign
A	0
B	9
C	44
D	5
E	0
F	4
Total	62

b. 2012result

Total
	#
A	0
B	11
C	76
D	24
E	0
F	4
Total	115

A) Very satisfactory level with significant recognition of shareholder value

B) Generally Satisfactory with certain level of shareholder value recognition

C) Not satisfactory level without recognition of shareholder value

D) Very frustrated with the current governance which ignores shareholder value

E) Corporate Governance per se is NOT important

F) Others

Japanese
A	0
B	7
C	39
D	8
E	0
F	3
Total	57

Foreign
A	0
B	4
C	37
D	16
E	0
F	1
Total	58

Are You Satisfied with Japan's ROE in General?

Q2.

a. 2017 result

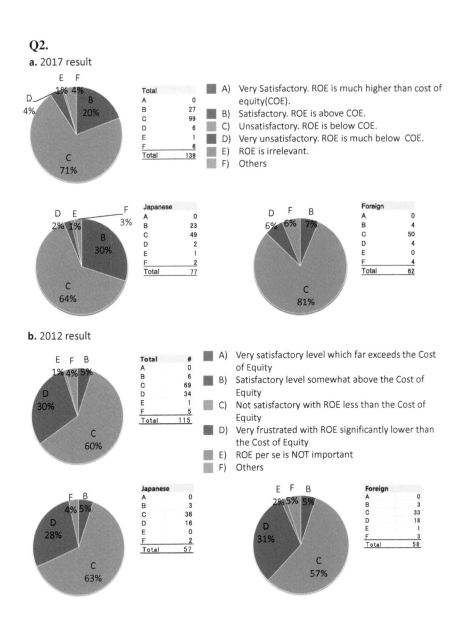

Total	
A	0
B	27
C	99
D	6
E	1
F	6
Total	139

A) Very Satisfactory. ROE is much higher than cost of equity(COE).

B) Satisfactory. ROE is above COE.

C) Unsatisfactory. ROE is below COE.

D) Very unsatisfactory. ROE is much below COE.

E) ROE is irrelevant.

F) Others

Japanese	
A	0
B	23
C	49
D	2
E	1
F	2
Total	77

Foreign	
A	0
B	4
C	50
D	4
E	0
F	4
Total	62

b. 2012 result

Total	#
A	0
B	6
C	69
D	34
E	1
F	5
Total	115

A) Very satisfactory level which far exceeds the Cost of Equity

B) Satisfactory level somewhat above the Cost of Equity

C) Not satisfactory with ROE less than the Cost of Equity

D) Very frustrated with ROE significantly lower than the Cost of Equity

E) ROE per se is NOT important

F) Others

Japanese	
A	0
B	3
C	36
D	16
E	0
F	2
Total	57

Foreign	
A	0
B	3
C	33
D	18
E	1
F	3
Total	58

How About "Financial Literacy" of Japanese Corporate Executives?

Q3.

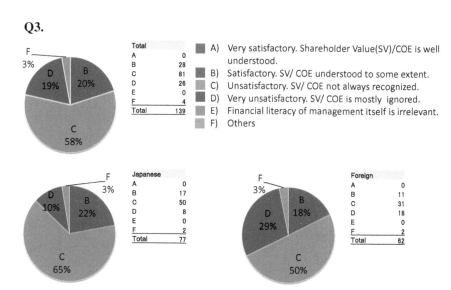

Total	
A	0
B	28
C	81
D	26
E	0
F	4
Total	139

A) Very satisfactory. Shareholder Value(SV)/COE is well understood.
B) Satisfactory. SV/ COE understood to some extent.
C) Unsatisfactory. SV/ COE not always recognized.
D) Very unsatisfactory. SV/ COE is mostly ignored.
E) Financial literacy of management itself is irrelevant.
F) Others

Japanese	
A	0
B	17
C	50
D	8
E	0
F	2
Total	77

Foreign	
A	0
B	11
C	31
D	18
E	0
F	2
Total	62

In General, What Is Cost of Equity (CoE) for Corporate Japan? (COE Depends on Each Company but Let Assume All Japan Average Generally, that Is Beta = 1 TOPIX Condition)

Q4.

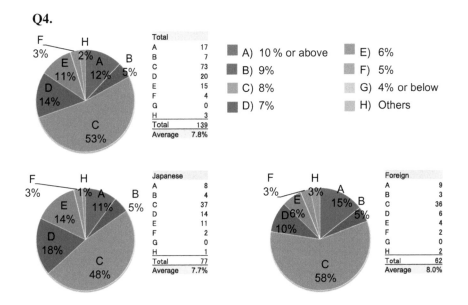

Do You Agree with the Statement "Japanese Companies Should Seek at Least 8% ROE" as Stated in "The Ito Review"?

Q5.

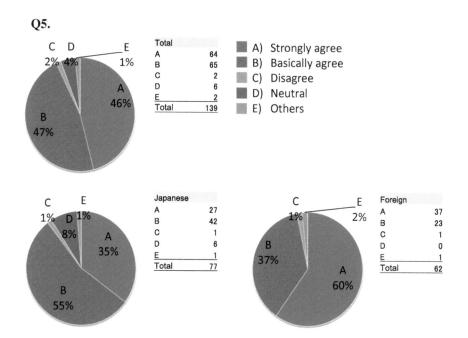

Total

A	64
B	65
C	2
D	6
E	2
Total	139

- A) Strongly agree
- B) Basically agree
- C) Disagree
- D) Neutral
- E) Others

Japanese

A	27
B	42
C	1
D	6
E	1
Total	77

Foreign

A	37
B	23
C	1
D	0
E	1
Total	62

Do You Agree with the Proposal "Equity Spread (= ROE Minus Cost of Equity) Should Be Discussed to Enhance the Literacy of ROE Above COE"?

Q6.

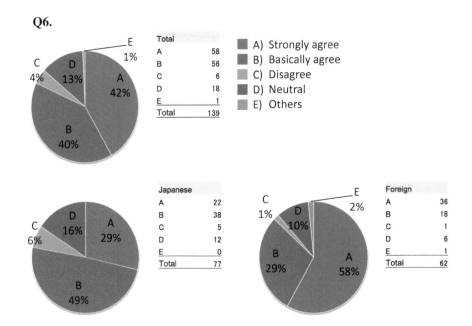

Total

A	58
B	56
C	6
D	18
E	1
Total	139

- A) Strongly agree
- B) Basically agree
- C) Disagree
- D) Neutral
- E) Others

Japanese

A	22
B	38
C	5
D	12
E	0
Total	77

Foreign

A	36
B	18
C	1
D	6
E	1
Total	62

What Do You Think About Japanese Companies' ESG (Environment, Social, Governance) and Its Disclosure (by Integrated Reports)?

Q7.

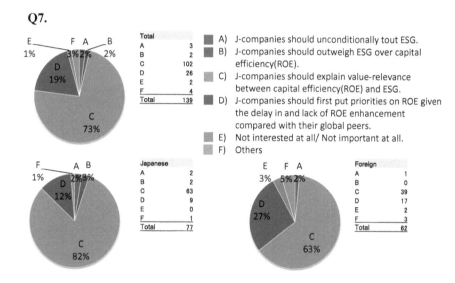

Total	
A	3
B	2
C	102
D	26
E	2
F	4
Total	139

A) J-companies should unconditionally tout ESG.

B) J-companies should outweigh ESG over capital efficiency(ROE).

C) J-companies should explain value-relevance between capital efficiency(ROE) and ESG.

D) J-companies should first put priorities on ROE given the delay in and lack of ROE enhancement compared with their global peers.

E) Not interested at all/ Not important at all.

F) Others

Japanese	
A	2
B	2
C	63
D	9
E	0
F	1
Total	77

Foreign	
A	1
B	0
C	39
D	17
E	2
F	3
Total	62

How Do You Factor ESG of Japanese Companies in Your Valuation/Investment Decisions?

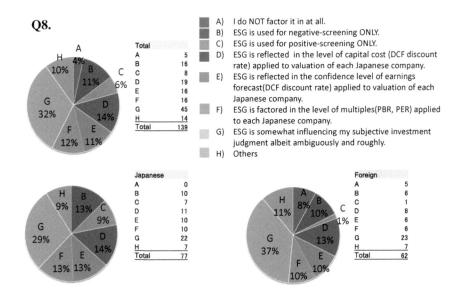

Q8.

	Total
A	5
B	16
C	8
D	19
E	16
F	16
G	45
H	14
Total	139

A) I do NOT factor it in at all.
B) ESG is used for negative-screening ONLY.
C) ESG is used for positive-screening ONLY.
D) ESG is reflected in the level of capital cost (DCF discount rate) applied to valuation of each Japanese company.
E) ESG is reflected in the confidence level of earnings forecast(DCF discount rate) applied to valuation of each Japanese company.
F) ESG is factored in the level of multiples(PBR, PER) applied to each Japanese company.
G) ESG is somewhat influencing my subjective investment judgment albeit ambiguously and roughly.
H) Others

Japanese	
A	0
B	10
C	7
D	11
E	10
F	10
G	22
H	7
Total	77

Foreign	
A	5
B	6
C	1
D	8
E	6
F	6
G	23
H	7
Total	62

Implications

Although CG reforms in Japan have seen rapid progress in recent years and are not lacking from an institutional standpoint, when considering the harsh assessments provided by overseas investors and clarified in this report it is evident that there is still considerable work left to be done. Companies and investors are in the same figurative boat and as such should forge long-term, mutually beneficial relations. This calls for long-term, concrete efforts toward the improvement of capital efficiency as represented to an extent by CG and ROE, and with the aim of increasing sustainable corporate value. With compelling business model aligned with corporate philosophy, empirical evidence of value-relevence, proactive engagement with global markets and sufficient disclosure, Japan should materialize and convert its touted latent value of ESG, non-financials, social contribution into actual corporate value concretely on a long-term basis. To that end, the conclusive value proposition of this book, "Non-Financial Capitals and Equity Spread Synchronization Model" could create win-win situation. Ultimately, in taking the route of enhancing corporate value, increasing global capital acquisition, improving pension fund investment yield and other similar approaches, I believe that we are attempting to revitalize the Japanese economy via CG reform and in doing so, maximizing our national wealth.

Index

© Springer Nature Singapore Pte Ltd. 2018
R. Yanagi, *Corporate Governance and Value Creation in Japan*,
https://doi.org/10.1007/978-981-10-8503-1